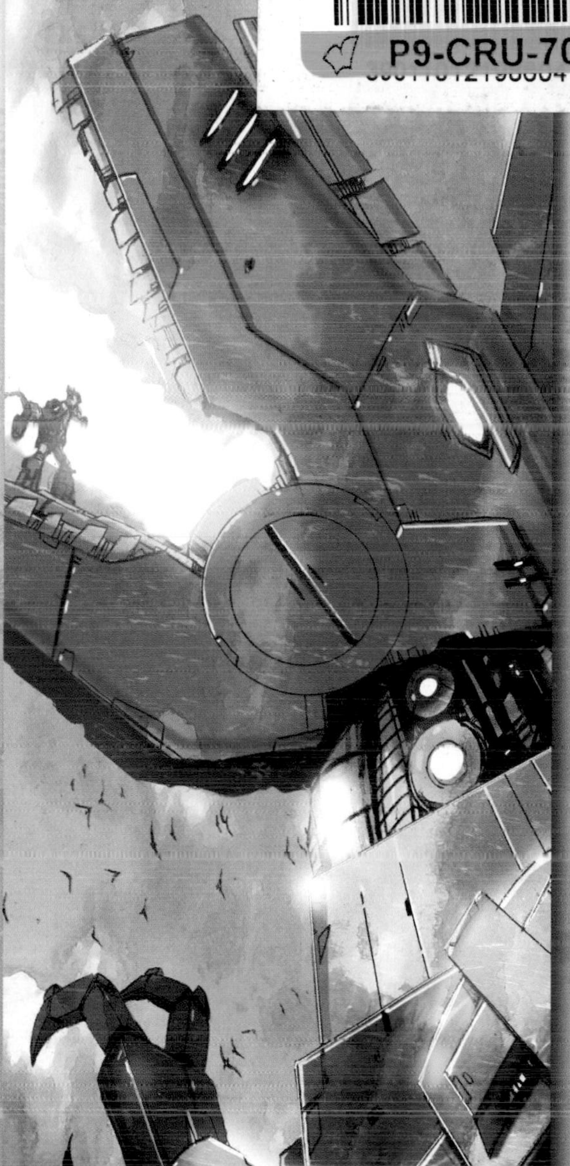

# TRANSFORMERS
## REDEMPTION OF THE DINOBOTS

Become our fan on Facebook **facebook.com/idwpublishing**
Follow us on Twitter **@idwpublishing**
Subscribe to us on YouTube **youtube.com/idwpublishing**
See what's new on Tumblr **tumblr.idwpublishing.com**
Check us out on Instagram **instagram.com/idwpublishing**

www.IDWPUBLISHING.com

Licensed By:

Greg Goldstein, President & Publisher
Robbie Robbins, EVP & Sr. Art Director
Chris Ryall, Chief Creative Officer & Editor-in-Chief
Matthew Ruzicka, CPA, Chief Financial Officer
David Hedgecock, Associate Publisher
Laurie Windrow, Senior Vice President of Sales & Marketing
Lorelei Bunjes, VP of Digital Services
Eric Moss, Sr. Director, Licensing & Business Development

COVER ART BY
**LIVIO RAMONDELLI**

Ted Adams, Founder & CEO of IDW Media Holdings

ISBN: 978-1-68405-183-0      21 20 19 18      1 2 3 4

COLLECTION EDITS BY
**JUSTIN EISINGER**
AND **ALONZO SIMON**

COLLECTION DESIGN BY
**CLAUDIA CHONG**

PUBLISHER
**GREG GOLDSTEIN**

Originally published as THE TRANSFORMERS: PUNISHMENT, THE TRANSFORMERS: REDEMPTION, and THE TRANSFORMERS: SALVATION.

Special thanks to Ben Montano, Josh Feldman, Ed Lane, Beth Artale, and Michael Kelly for their invaluable assistance.

For international rights, contact licensing@idwpublishing.com

# TRANSFORMERS
## REDEMPTION
### OF THE DINOBOTS

WRITTEN BY
**JOHN BARBER**

ART BY
**LIVIO RAMONDELLI**

LETTERS BY
**TOM B. LONG**

SERIES EDITS BY
**CARLOS GUZMAN**

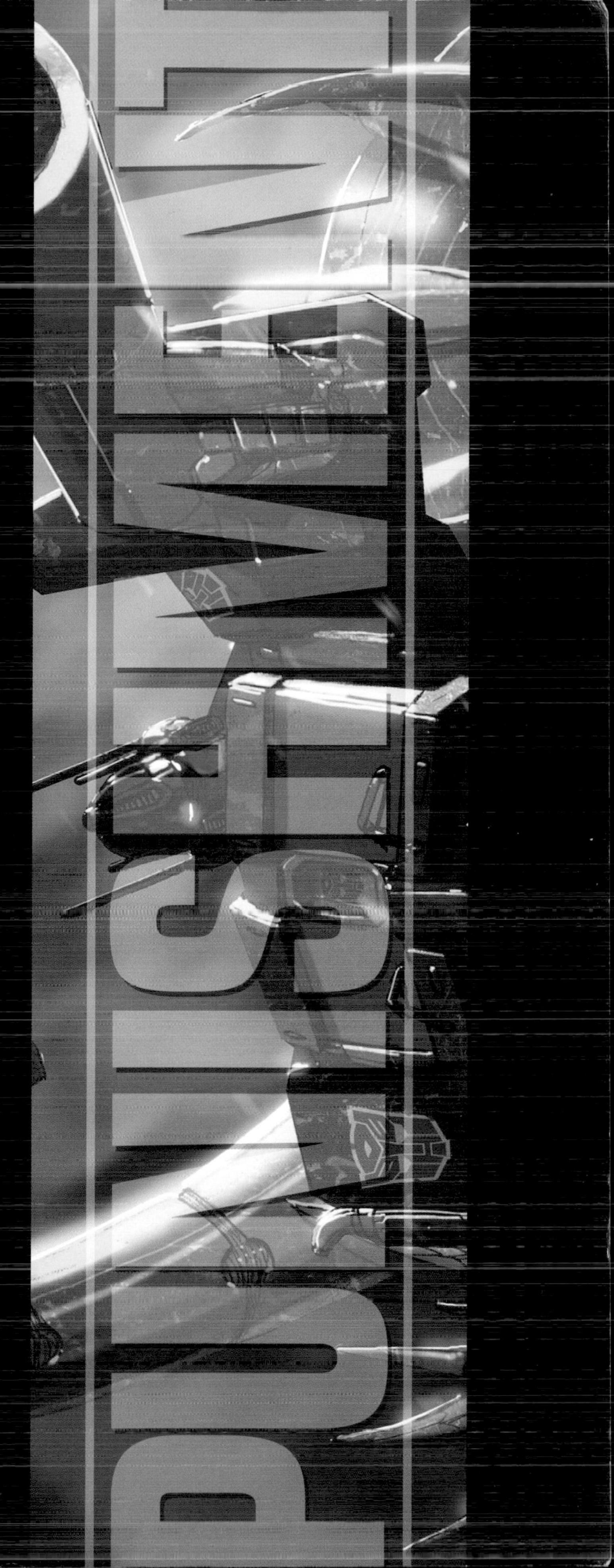
PUNISHMENT

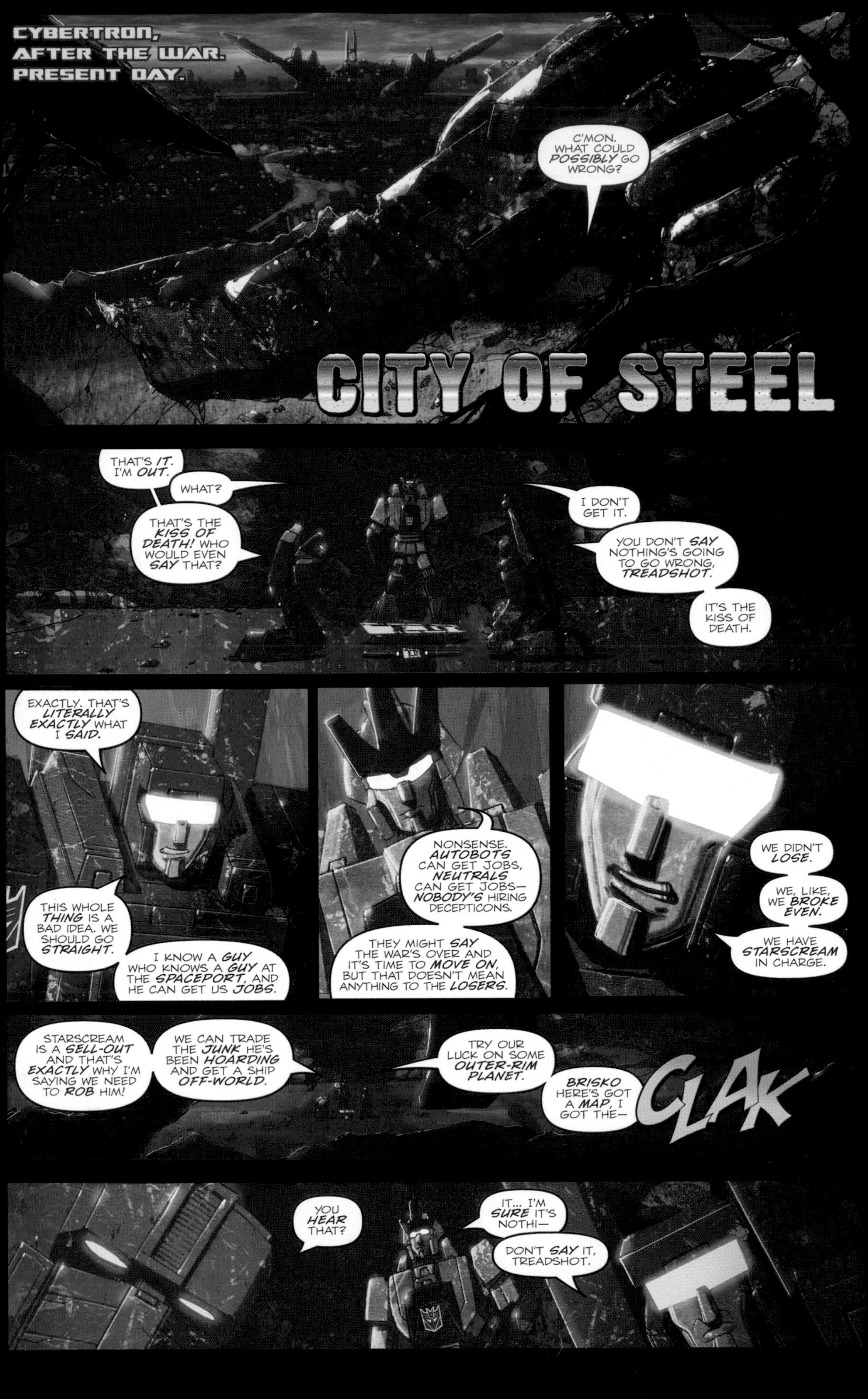
CYBERTRON, AFTER THE WAR. PRESENT DAY.
C'MON. WHAT COULD POSSIBLY GO WRONG?
CITY OF STEEL
THAT'S IT. I'M OUT.
WHAT?
THAT'S THE KISS OF DEATH! WHO WOULD EVEN SAY THAT?
I DON'T GET IT.
YOU DON'T SAY NOTHING'S GOING TO GO WRONG, TREADSHOT.
IT'S THE KISS OF DEATH.
EXACTLY. THAT'S LITERALLY EXACTLY WHAT I SAID.
THIS WHOLE THING IS A BAD IDEA. WE SHOULD GO STRAIGHT.
I KNOW A GUY WHO KNOWS A GUY AT THE SPACEPORT, AND HE CAN GET US JOBS.
NONSENSE. AUTOBOTS CAN GET JOBS, NEUTRALS CAN GET JOBS— NOBODY'S HIRING DECEPTICONS.
THEY MIGHT SAY THE WAR'S OVER AND IT'S TIME TO MOVE ON, BUT THAT DOESN'T MEAN ANYTHING TO THE LOSERS.
WE DIDN'T LOSE.
WE, LIKE, WE BROKE EVEN.
WE HAVE STARSCREAM IN CHARGE.
STARSCREAM IS A SELL-OUT AND THAT'S EXACTLY WHY I'M SAYING WE NEED TO ROB HIM!
WE CAN TRADE THE JUNK HE'S BEEN HOARDING AND GET A SHIP OFF-WORLD.
TRY OUR LUCK ON SOME OUTER-RIM PLANET.
BRISKO HERE'S GOT A MAP, I GOT THE—
CLAK
YOU HEAR THAT?
IT... I'M SURE IT'S NOTHI—
DON'T SAY IT, TREADSHOT.

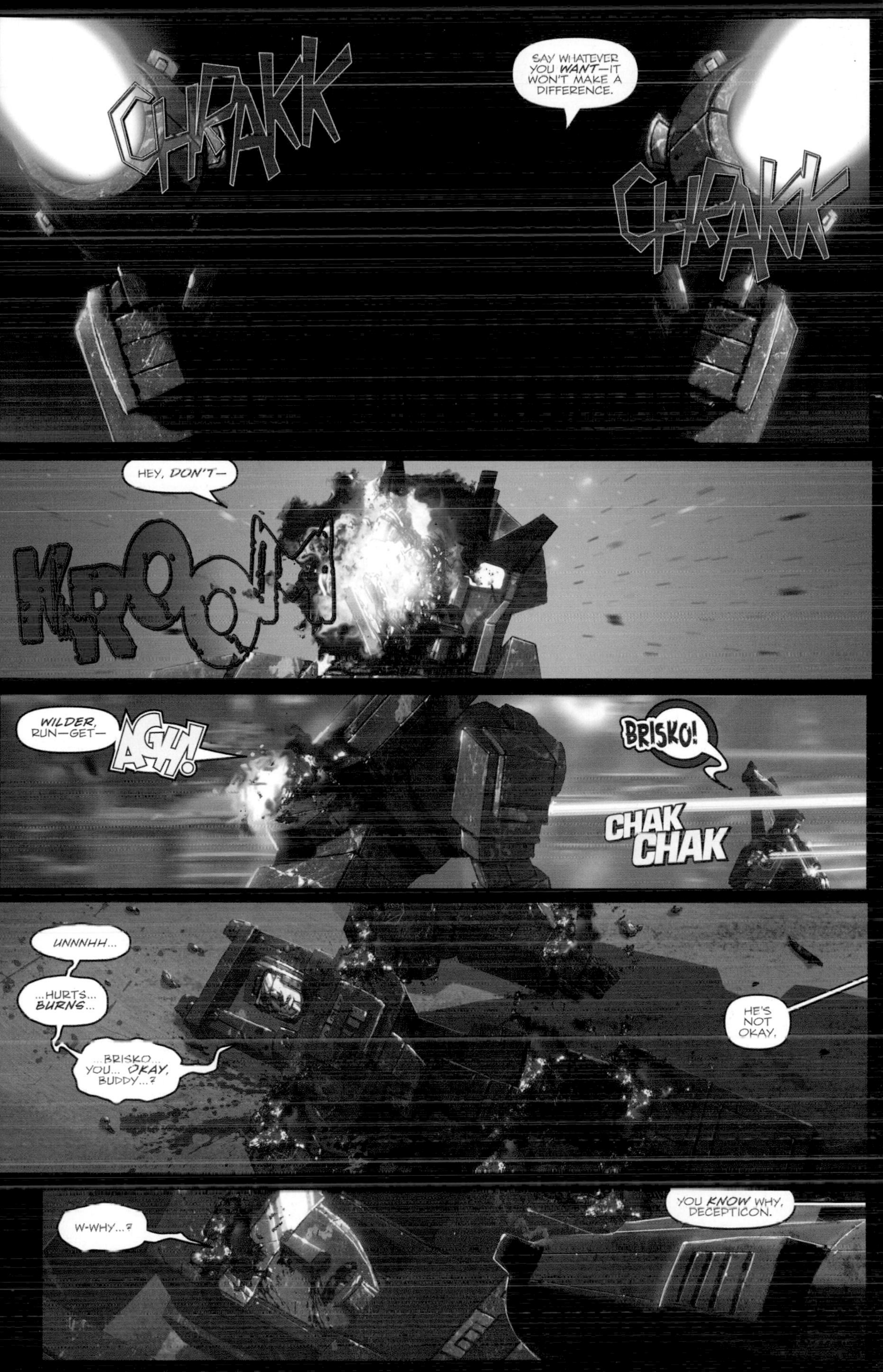
CHRAKK
SAY WHATEVER YOU WANT—IT WON'T MAKE A DIFFERENCE.
CHRAKK
HEY, DON'T—
KRROOM
WILDER, RUN—GET—
AGH!
BRISKO!
CHAK CHAK
UNNNHH...
...HURTS... BURNS...
...BRISKO... YOU... OKAY, BUDDY...?
HE'S NOT OKAY.
W-WHY...?
YOU KNOW WHY, DECEPTICON.

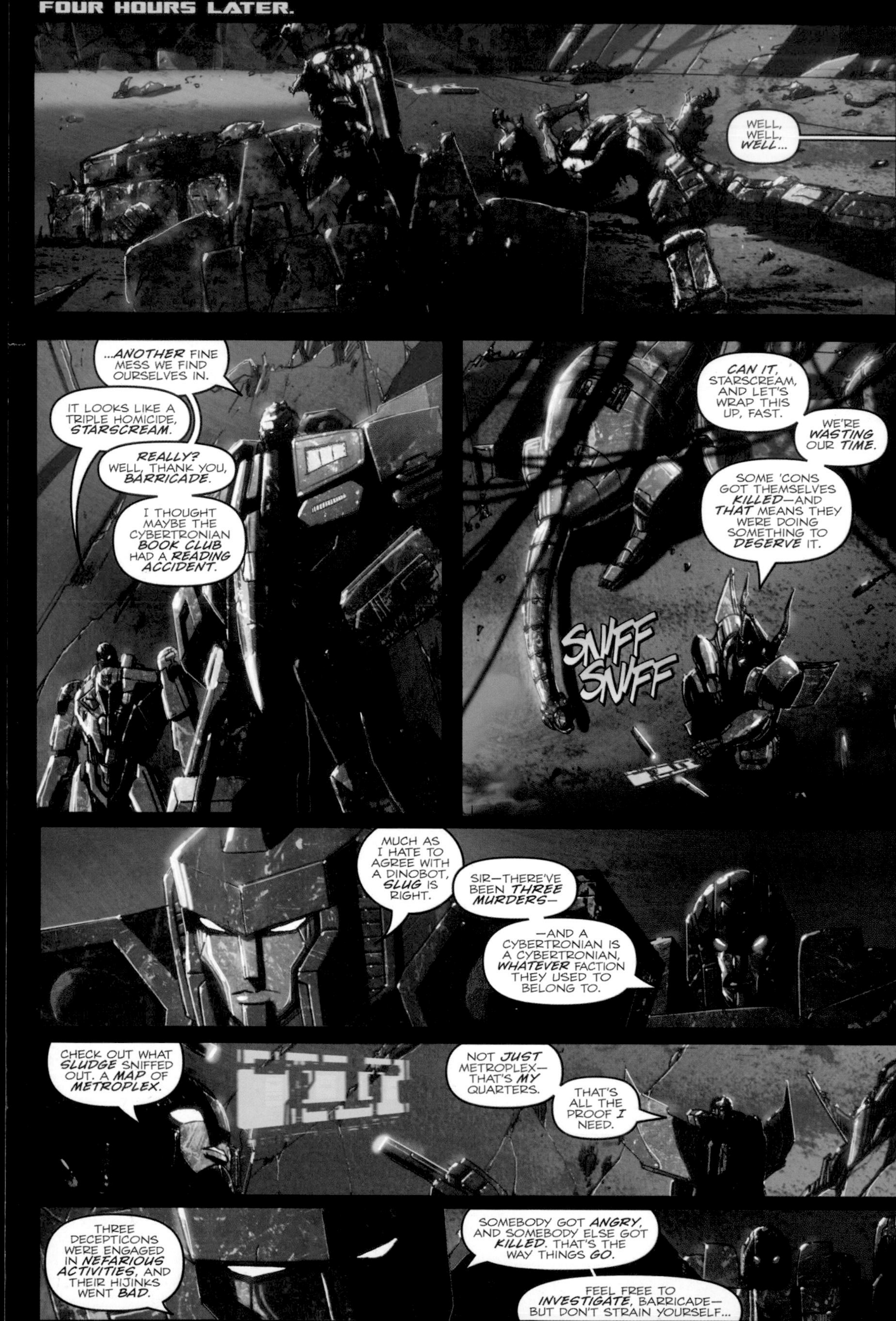
FOUR HOURS LATER.
WELL, WELL, WELL...
...ANOTHER FINE MESS WE FIND OURSELVES IN.
IT LOOKS LIKE A TRIPLE HOMICIDE, STARSCREAM.
REALLY? WELL, THANK YOU, BARRICADE.
I THOUGHT MAYBE THE CYBERTRONIAN BOOK CLUB HAD A READING ACCIDENT.
CAN IT, STARSCREAM, AND LET'S WRAP THIS UP, FAST.
WE'RE WASTING OUR TIME.
SOME 'CONS GOT THEMSELVES KILLED—AND THAT MEANS THEY WERE DOING SOMETHING TO DESERVE IT.
SNIFF SNIFF
MUCH AS I HATE TO AGREE WITH A DINOBOT, SLUG IS RIGHT.
SIR—THERE'VE BEEN THREE MURDERS—
—AND A CYBERTRONIAN IS A CYBERTRONIAN, WHATEVER FACTION THEY USED TO BELONG TO.
CHECK OUT WHAT SLUDGE SNIFFED OUT. A MAP OF METROPLEX.
NOT JUST METROPLEX—THAT'S MY QUARTERS.
THAT'S ALL THE PROOF I NEED.
THREE DECEPTICONS WERE ENGAGED IN NEFARIOUS ACTIVITIES, AND THEIR HIJINKS WENT BAD.
SOMEBODY GOT ANGRY, AND SOMEBODY ELSE GOT KILLED. THAT'S THE WAY THINGS GO.
FEEL FREE TO INVESTIGATE, BARRICADE—BUT DON'T STRAIN YOURSELF...

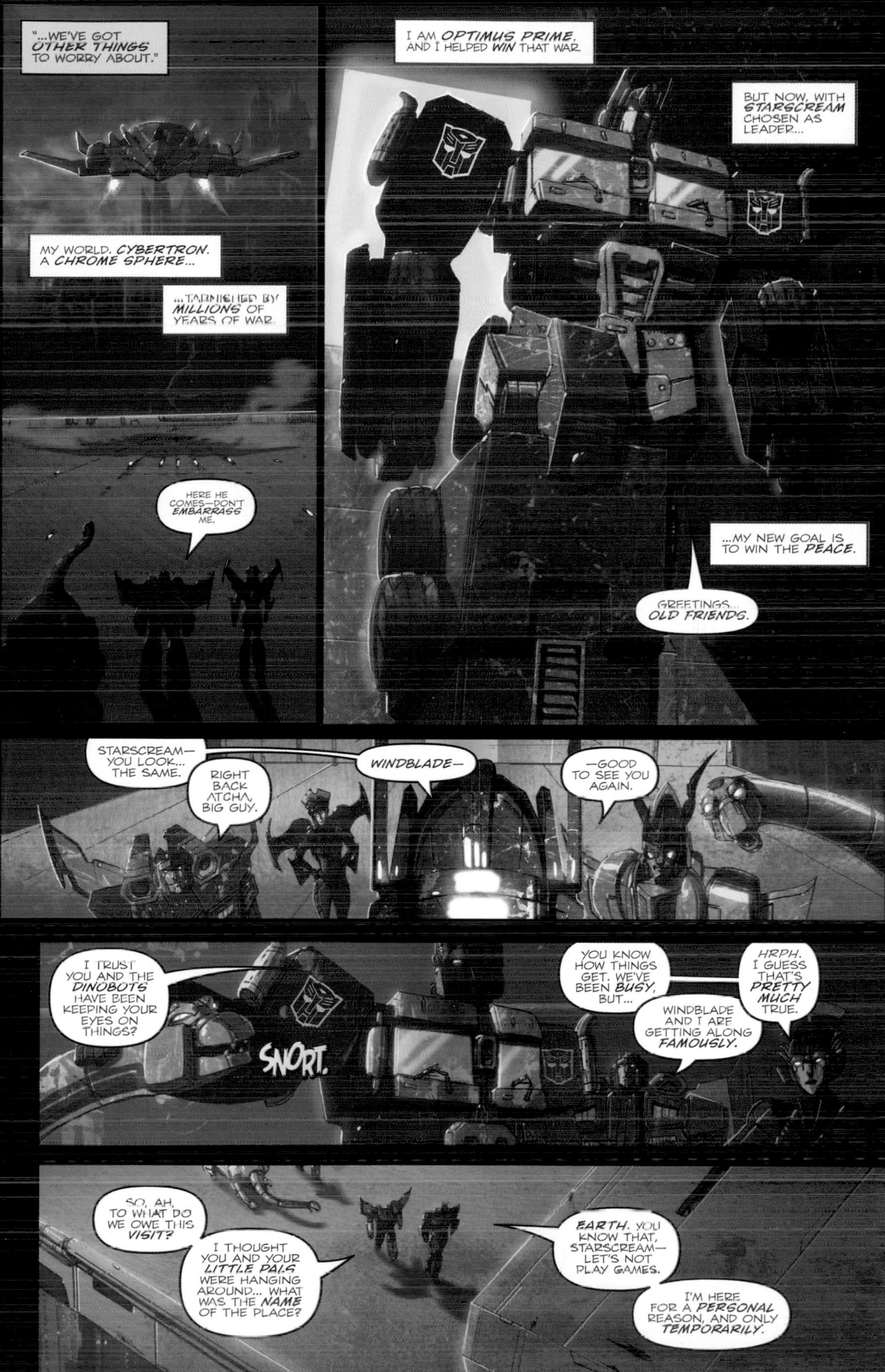
"...WE'VE GOT OTHER THINGS TO WORRY ABOUT."
MY WORLD. CYBERTRON. A CHROME SPHERE...
...TARNISHED BY MILLIONS OF YEARS OF WAR.
HERE HE COMES—DON'T EMBARRASS ME.
I AM OPTIMUS PRIME, AND I HELPED WIN THAT WAR.
BUT NOW, WITH STARSCREAM CHOSEN AS LEADER...
...MY NEW GOAL IS TO WIN THE PEACE.
GREETINGS... OLD FRIENDS.
STARSCREAM—YOU LOOK... THE SAME.
RIGHT BACK ATCHA, BIG GUY.
WINDBLADE—
—GOOD TO SEE YOU AGAIN.
I TRUST YOU AND THE DINOBOTS HAVE BEEN KEEPING YOUR EYES ON THINGS?
SNORT.
YOU KNOW HOW THINGS GET. WE'VE BEEN BUSY, BUT...
WINDBLADE AND I ARE GETTING ALONG FAMOUSLY.
HRPH. I GUESS THAT'S PRETTY MUCH TRUE.
SO, AH, TO WHAT DO WE OWE THIS VISIT?
I THOUGHT YOU AND YOUR LITTLE PALS WERE HANGING AROUND... WHAT WAS THE NAME OF THE PLACE?
EARTH. YOU KNOW THAT, STARSCREAM—LET'S NOT PLAY GAMES.
I'M HERE FOR A PERSONAL REASON, AND ONLY TEMPORARILY.

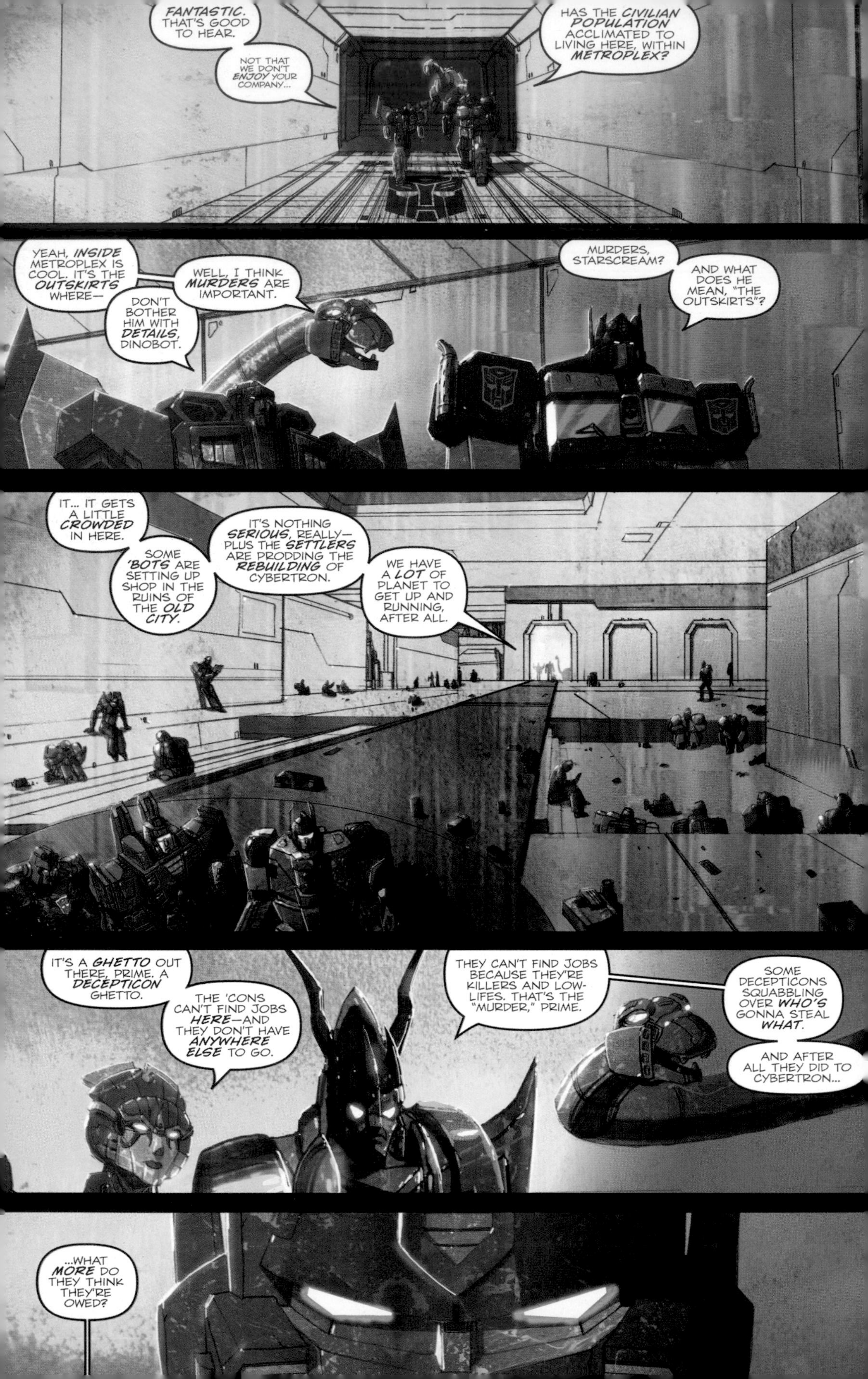
FANTASTIC. THAT'S GOOD TO HEAR.
NOT THAT WE DON'T ENJOY YOUR COMPANY...
HAS THE CIVILIAN POPULATION ACCLIMATED TO LIVING HERE, WITHIN METROPLEX?
YEAH, INSIDE METROPLEX IS COOL. IT'S THE OUTSKIRTS WHERE—
WELL, I THINK MURDERS ARE IMPORTANT.
DON'T BOTHER HIM WITH DETAILS, DINOBOT.
MURDERS, STARSCREAM?
AND WHAT DOES HE MEAN, "THE OUTSKIRTS"?
IT... IT GETS A LITTLE CROWDED IN HERE.
SOME 'BOTS ARE SETTING UP SHOP IN THE RUINS OF THE OLD CITY.
IT'S NOTHING SERIOUS, REALLY— PLUS THE SETTLERS ARE PRODDING THE REBUILDING OF CYBERTRON.
WE HAVE A LOT OF PLANET TO GET UP AND RUNNING, AFTER ALL.
IT'S A GHETTO OUT THERE, PRIME. A DECEPTICON GHETTO.
THE 'CONS CAN'T FIND JOBS HERE—AND THEY DON'T HAVE ANYWHERE ELSE TO GO.
THEY CAN'T FIND JOBS BECAUSE THEY'RE KILLERS AND LOW-LIFES. THAT'S THE "MURDER," PRIME.
SOME DECEPTICONS SQUABBLING OVER WHO'S GONNA STEAL WHAT.
AND AFTER ALL THEY DID TO CYBERTRON...
...WHAT MORE DO THEY THINK THEY'RE OWED?

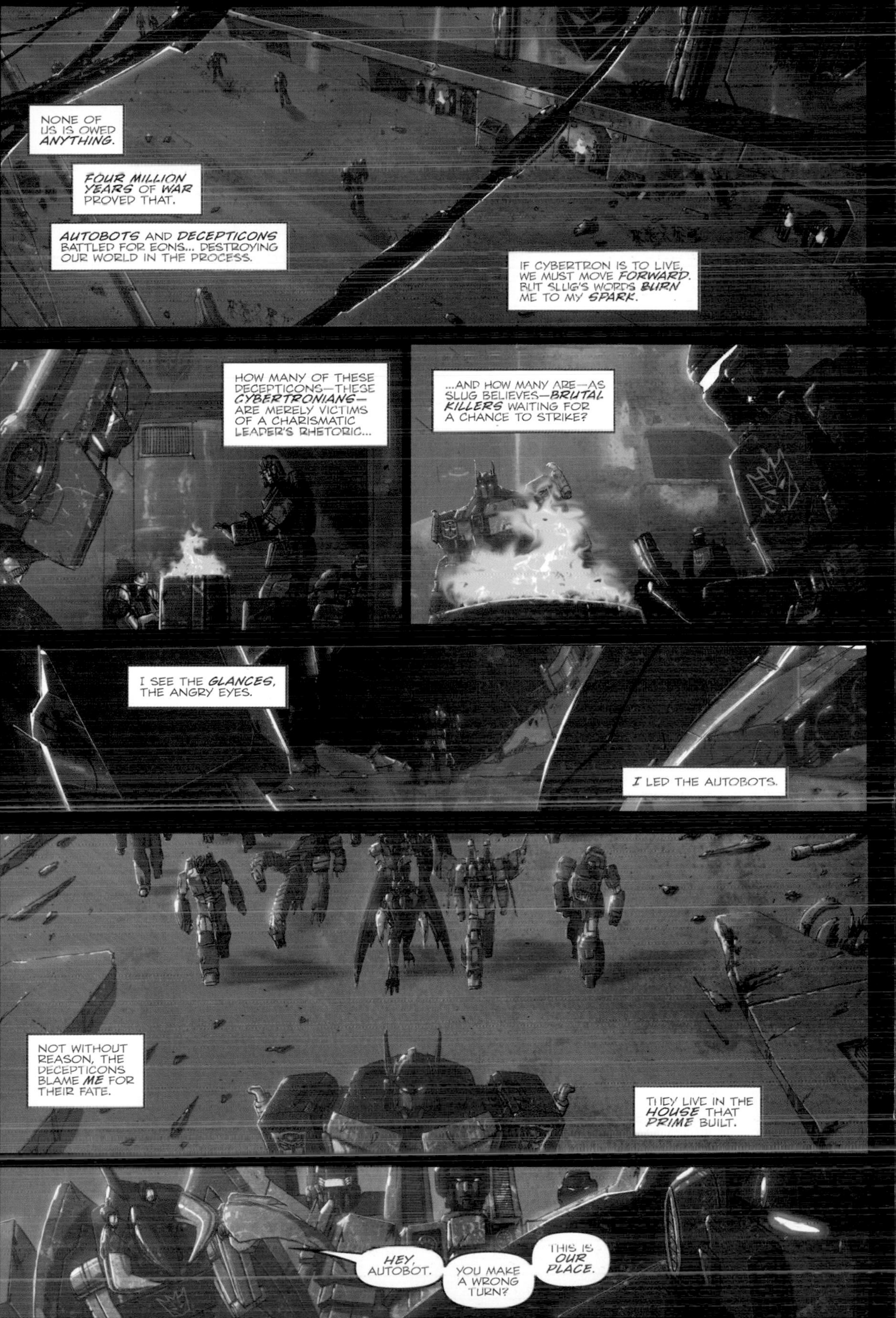
NONE OF US IS OWED ANYTHING.
FOUR MILLION YEARS OF WAR PROVED THAT.
AUTOBOTS AND DECEPTICONS BATTLED FOR EONS... DESTROYING OUR WORLD IN THE PROCESS.
IF CYBERTRON IS TO LIVE, WE MUST MOVE FORWARD. BUT SLUG'S WORDS BURN ME TO MY SPARK.
HOW MANY OF THESE DECEPTICONS—THESE CYBERTRONIANS—ARE MERELY VICTIMS OF A CHARISMATIC LEADER'S RHETORIC...
...AND HOW MANY ARE—AS SLUG BELIEVES—BRUTAL KILLERS WAITING FOR A CHANCE TO STRIKE?
I SEE THE GLANCES, THE ANGRY EYES.
I LED THE AUTOBOTS.
NOT WITHOUT REASON, THE DECEPTICONS BLAME ME FOR THEIR FATE.
THEY LIVE IN THE HOUSE THAT PRIME BUILT.
HEY, AUTOBOT.
YOU MAKE A WRONG TURN?
THIS IS OUR PLACE.

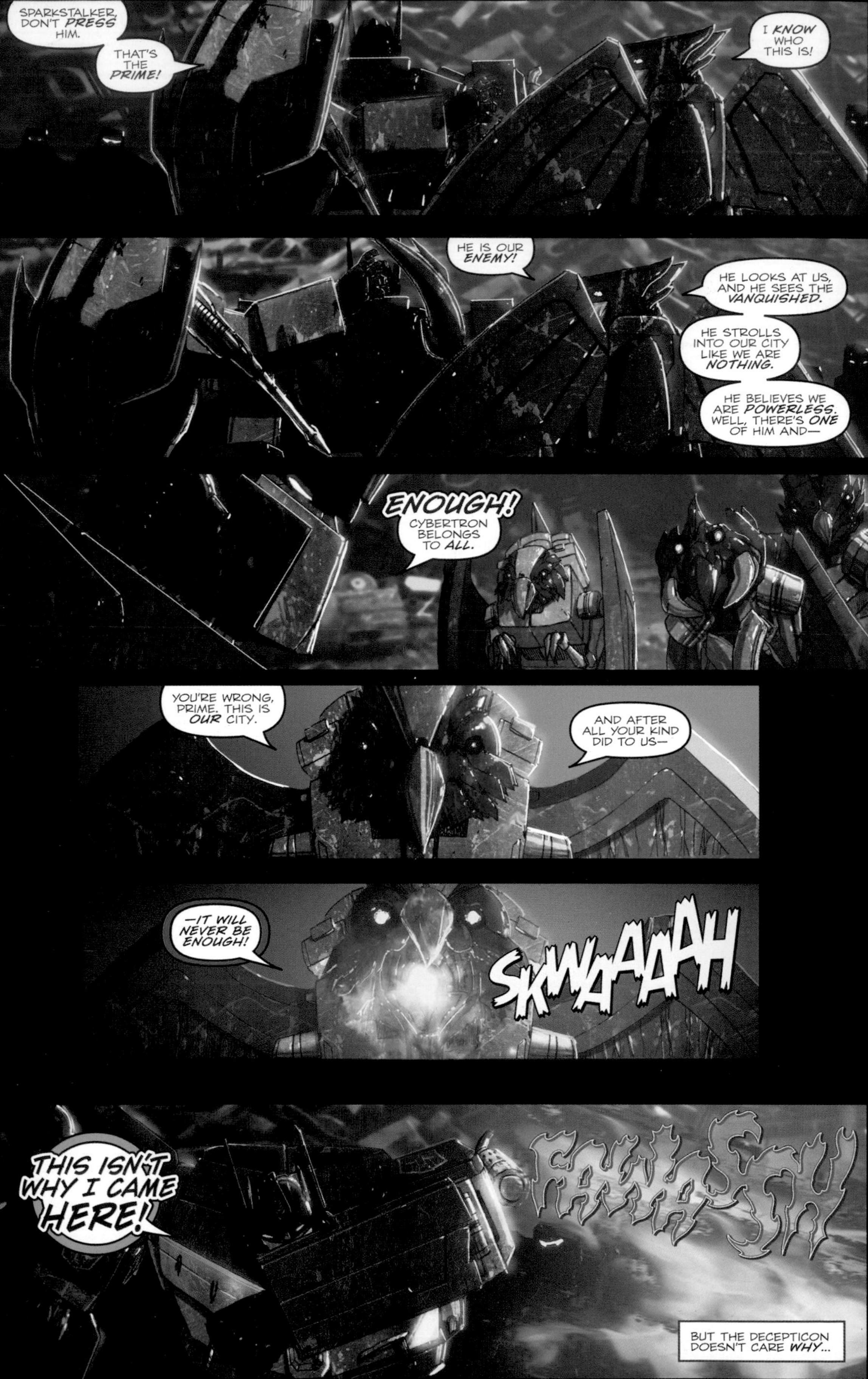
SPARKSTALKER, DON'T PRESS HIM.
THAT'S THE PRIME!
I KNOW WHO THIS IS!
HE IS OUR ENEMY!
HE LOOKS AT US, AND HE SEES THE VANQUISHED.
HE STROLLS INTO OUR CITY LIKE WE ARE NOTHING.
HE BELIEVES WE ARE POWERLESS. WELL, THERE'S ONE OF HIM AND—
ENOUGH! CYBERTRON BELONGS TO ALL.
YOU'RE WRONG, PRIME. THIS IS OUR CITY.
AND AFTER ALL YOUR KIND DID TO US—
—IT WILL NEVER BE ENOUGH!
SKWAAAAH
THIS ISN'T WHY I CAME HERE!
BUT THE DECEPTICON DOESN'T CARE WHY...

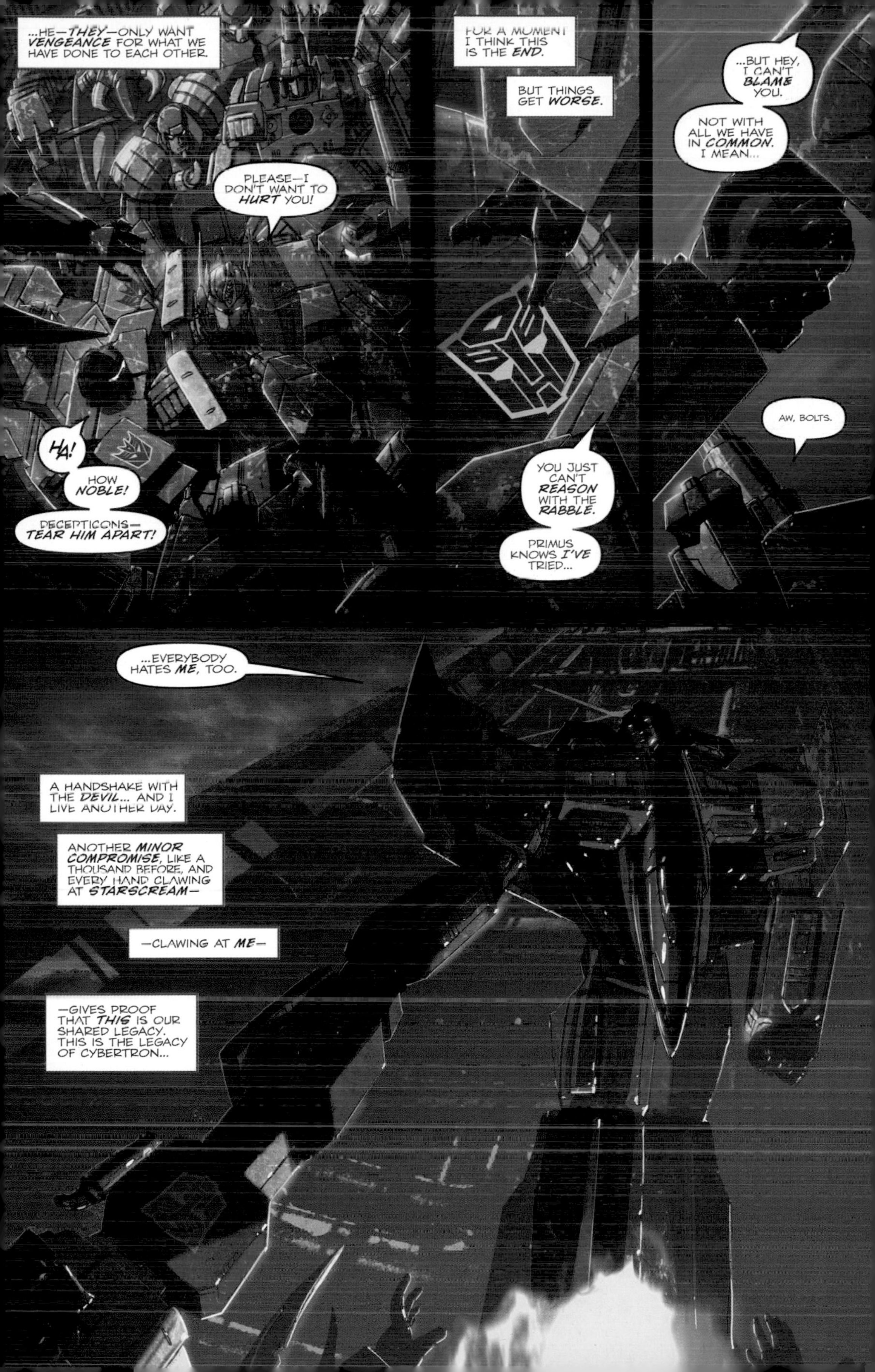
...HE—THEY—ONLY WANT VENGEANCE FOR WHAT WE HAVE DONE TO EACH OTHER.
PLEASE—I DON'T WANT TO HURT YOU!
HA!
HOW NOBLE!
DECEPTICONS— TEAR HIM APART!
FOR A MOMENT I THINK THIS IS THE END.
BUT THINGS GET WORSE.
YOU JUST CAN'T REASON WITH THE RABBLE.
PRIMUS KNOWS I'VE TRIED...
...BUT HEY, I CAN'T BLAME YOU.
NOT WITH ALL WE HAVE IN COMMON. I MEAN...
AW, BOLTS.
...EVERYBODY HATES ME, TOO.
A HANDSHAKE WITH THE DEVIL... AND I LIVE ANOTHER DAY.
ANOTHER MINOR COMPROMISE, LIKE A THOUSAND BEFORE, AND EVERY HAND CLAWING AT STARSCREAM—
—CLAWING AT ME—
—GIVES PROOF THAT THIS IS OUR SHARED LEGACY. THIS IS THE LEGACY OF CYBERTRON...

...OF MY WORLD.
YOU'VE BEEN AROUND A WHILE—YOU'RE A GUY THAT MAKES THINGS HAPPEN.
WHY'D YOU NEVER PICK UP A FLYING MODE FOR YOURSELF, PRIME?
SEEMS LIKE IT'D COME IN HANDY—LIKE, YOU KNOW, WHEN EVERYBODY'S SHOOTING AT YOU.
IT'S NOT EVERYONE.
STARSCREAM—THE FORMER DECEPTICON WHO'S MANIPULATED THE POST-WAR WORLD FOR PERSONAL GLORY...
...FOR THE BRIEFEST OF MOMENTS—HE'S THE ONLY THING KEEPING ME ALIVE...
FIGHT OR FLEE

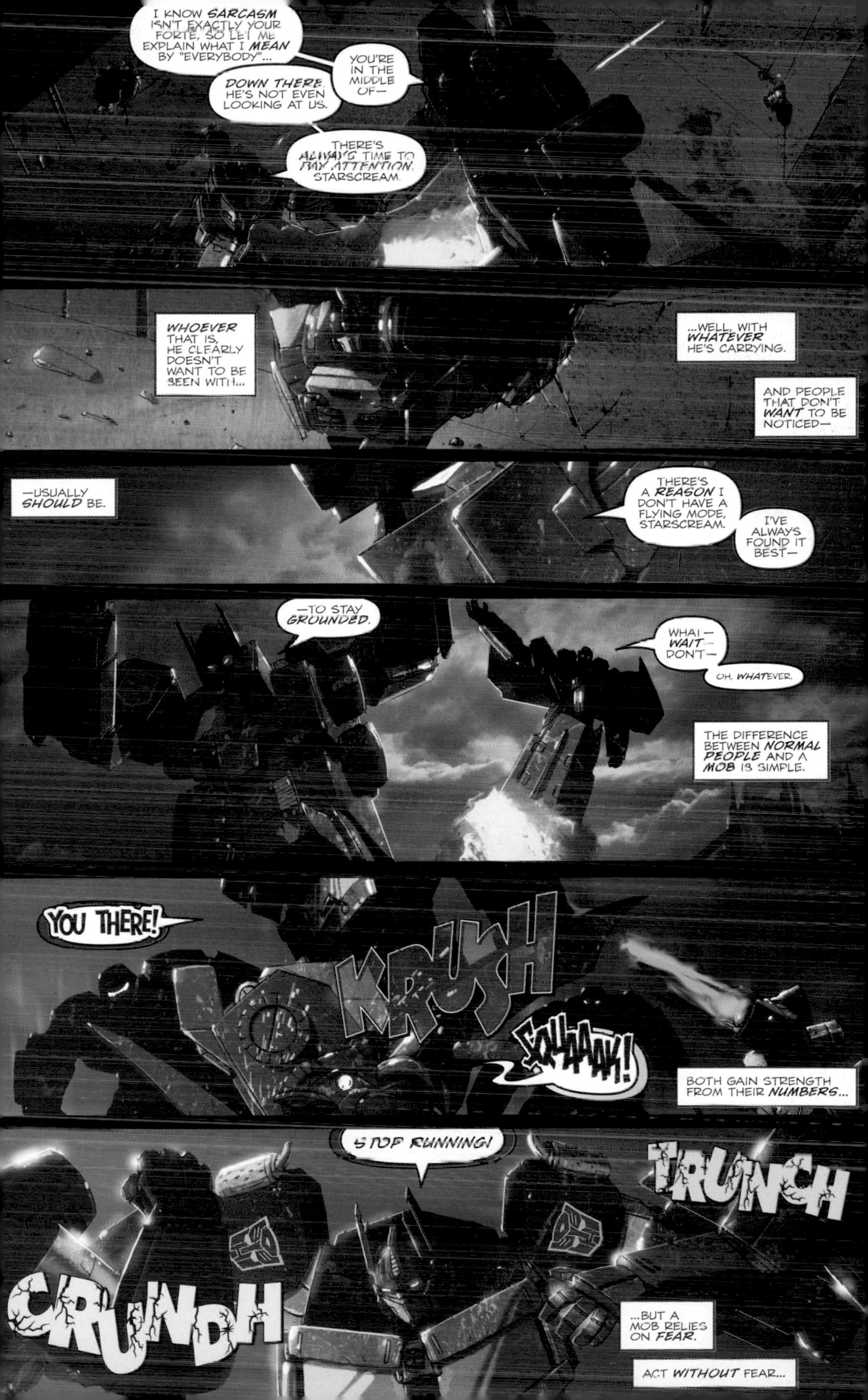
I KNOW SARCASM ISN'T EXACTLY YOUR FORTE, SO LET ME EXPLAIN WHAT I MEAN BY "EVERYBODY"...
YOU'RE IN THE MIDDLE OF—
DOWN THERE. HE'S NOT EVEN LOOKING AT US.
THERE'S ALWAYS TIME TO PAY ATTENTION, STARSCREAM.
WHOEVER THAT IS, HE CLEARLY DOESN'T WANT TO BE SEEN WITH...
...WELL, WITH WHATEVER HE'S CARRYING.
AND PEOPLE THAT DON'T WANT TO BE NOTICED—
—USUALLY SHOULD BE.
THERE'S A REASON I DON'T HAVE A FLYING MODE, STARSCREAM.
I'VE ALWAYS FOUND IT BEST—
—TO STAY GROUNDED.
WHAT—WAIT—DON'T—
OH, WHATEVER.
THE DIFFERENCE BETWEEN NORMAL PEOPLE AND A MOB IS SIMPLE.
YOU THERE!
KRUSH
SQUAAAK!
BOTH GAIN STRENGTH FROM THEIR NUMBERS...
STOP RUNNING!
TRUNCH
CRUNCH
...BUT A MOB RELIES ON FEAR.
ACT WITHOUT FEAR...

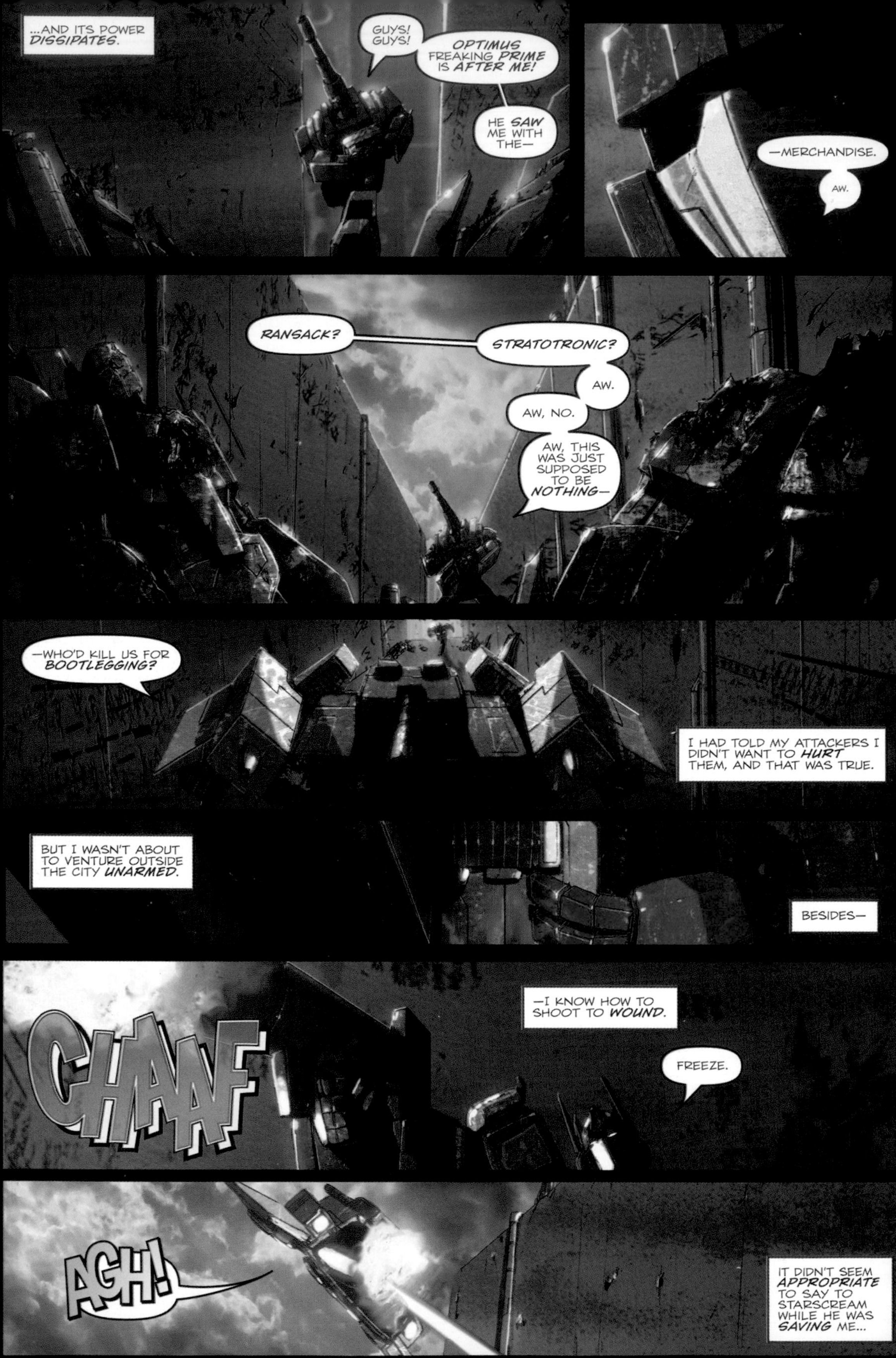
...AND ITS POWER DISSIPATES.
GUYS! GUYS!
OPTIMUS FREAKING PRIME IS AFTER ME!
HE SAW ME WITH THE—
—MERCHANDISE.
AW.
RANSACK?
STRATOTRONIC?
AW.
AW, NO.
AW, THIS WAS JUST SUPPOSED TO BE NOTHING—
—WHO'D KILL US FOR BOOTLEGGING?
I HAD TOLD MY ATTACKERS I DIDN'T WANT TO HURT THEM, AND THAT WAS TRUE.
BUT I WASN'T ABOUT TO VENTURE OUTSIDE THE CITY UNARMED.
BESIDES—
CHAAF
—I KNOW HOW TO SHOOT TO WOUND.
FREEZE.
AGH!
IT DIDN'T SEEM APPROPRIATE TO SAY TO STARSCREAM WHILE HE WAS SAVING ME...

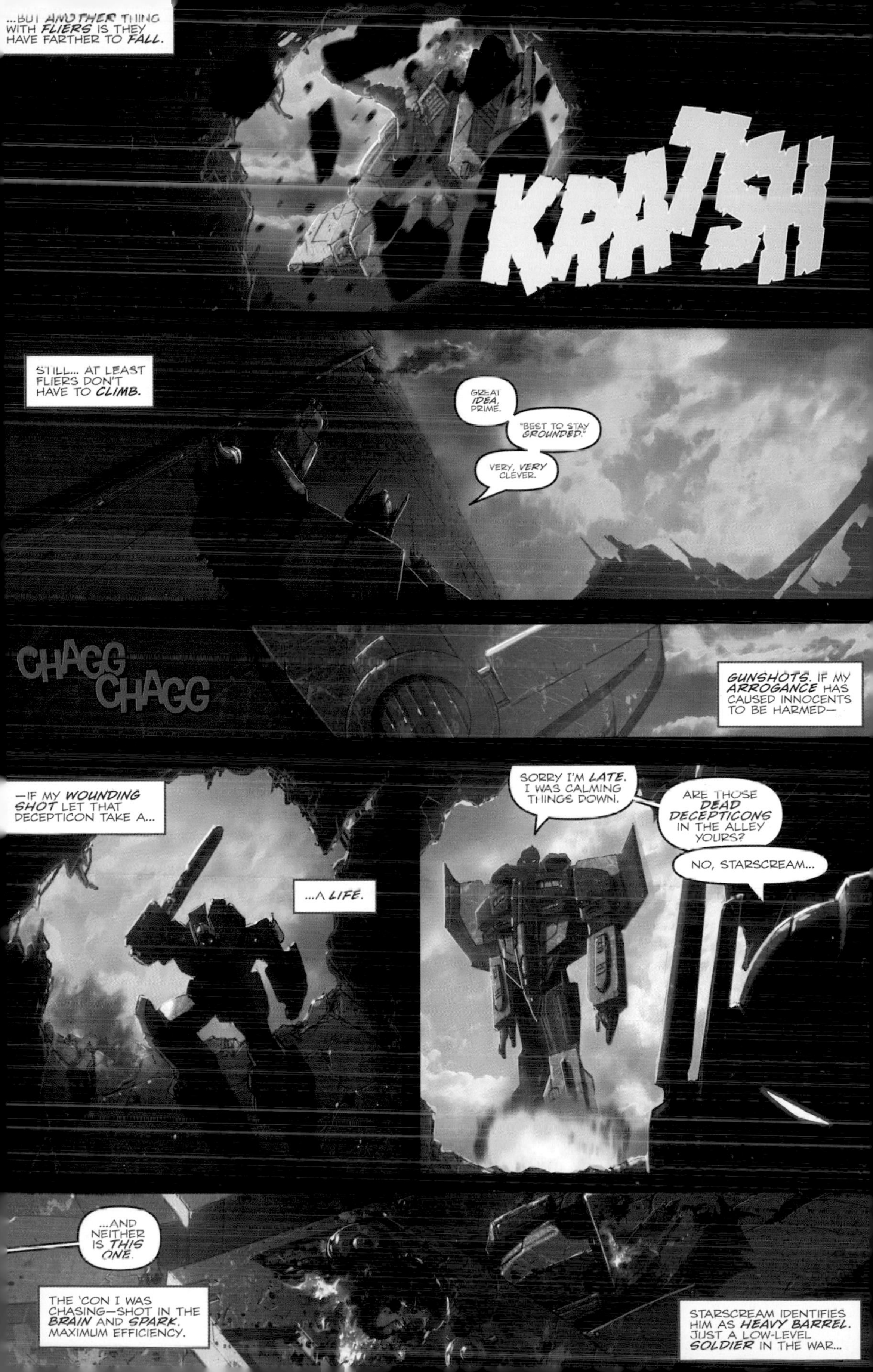
...BUT ANOTHER THING WITH FLIERS IS THEY HAVE FARTHER TO FALL.
KRATSH
STILL... AT LEAST FLIERS DON'T HAVE TO CLIMB.
GREAT IDEA, PRIME.
"BEST TO STAY GROUNDED."
VERY, VERY CLEVER.
CHAGG CHAGG
GUNSHOTS. IF MY ARROGANCE HAS CAUSED INNOCENTS TO BE HARMED—
—IF MY WOUNDING SHOT LET THAT DECEPTICON TAKE A...
...A LIFE.
SORRY I'M LATE. I WAS CALMING THINGS DOWN.
ARE THOSE DEAD DECEPTICONS IN THE ALLEY YOURS?
NO, STARSCREAM...
...AND NEITHER IS THIS ONE.
THE 'CON I WAS CHASING—SHOT IN THE BRAIN AND SPARK. MAXIMUM EFFICIENCY.
STARSCREAM IDENTIFIES HIM AS HEAVY BARREL. JUST A LOW-LEVEL SOLDIER IN THE WAR...

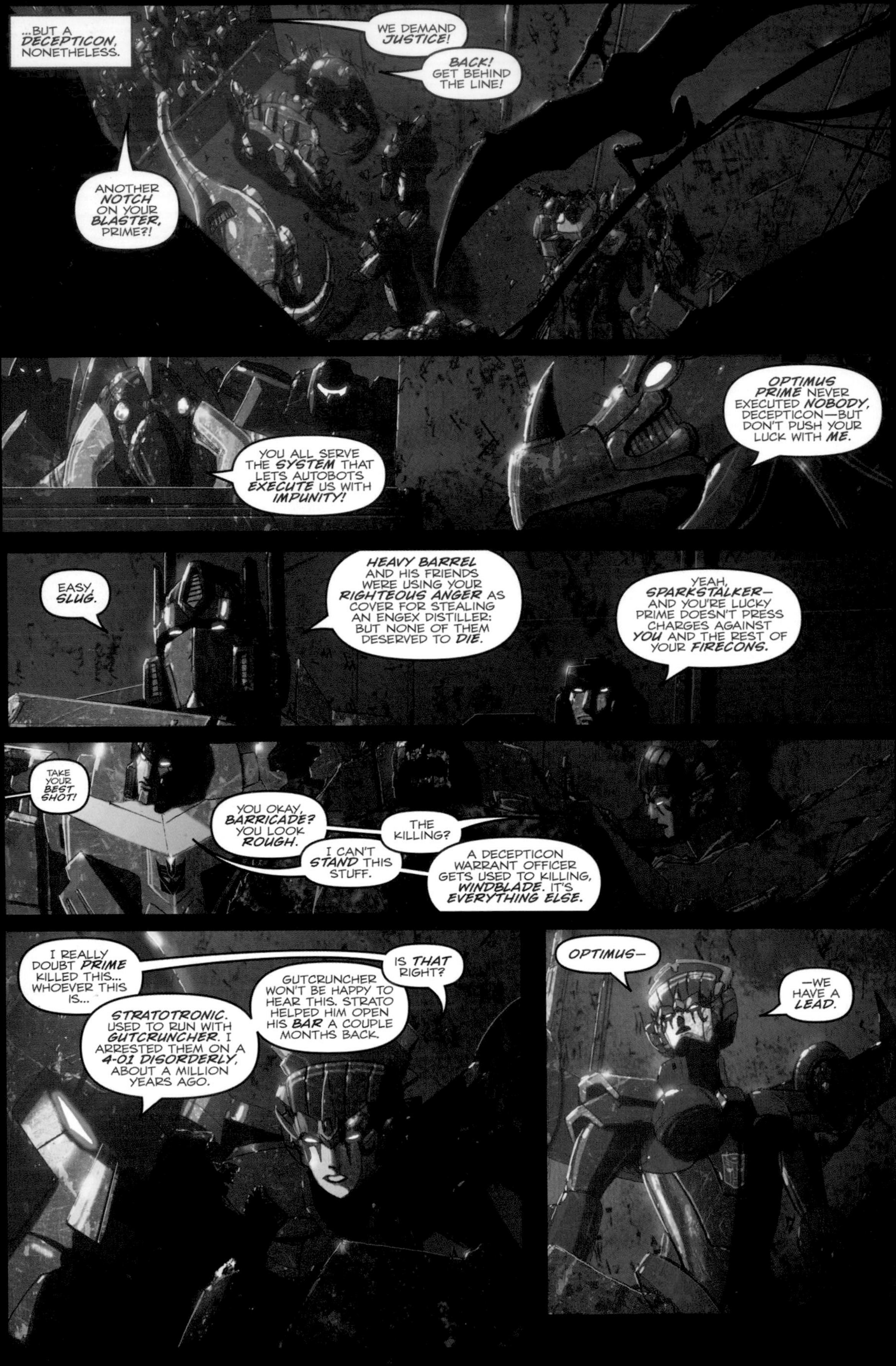

...BUT A DECEPTICON, NONETHELESS.
WE DEMAND JUSTICE!
BACK! GET BEHIND THE LINE!
ANOTHER NOTCH ON YOUR BLASTER, PRIME?!
YOU ALL SERVE THE SYSTEM THAT LETS AUTOBOTS EXECUTE US WITH IMPUNITY!
OPTIMUS PRIME NEVER EXECUTED NOBODY, DECEPTICON—BUT DON'T PUSH YOUR LUCK WITH ME.
EASY, SLUG.
HEAVY BARREL AND HIS FRIENDS WERE USING YOUR RIGHTEOUS ANGER AS COVER FOR STEALING AN ENGEX DISTILLER: BUT NONE OF THEM DESERVED TO DIE.
YEAH, SPARKSTALKER— AND YOU'RE LUCKY PRIME DOESN'T PRESS CHARGES AGAINST YOU AND THE REST OF YOUR FIRECONS.
TAKE YOUR BEST SHOT!
YOU OKAY, BARRICADE? YOU LOOK ROUGH.
I CAN'T STAND THIS STUFF.
THE KILLING?
A DECEPTICON WARRANT OFFICER GETS USED TO KILLING, WINDBLADE. IT'S EVERYTHING ELSE.
I REALLY DOUBT PRIME KILLED THIS... WHOEVER THIS IS...
STRATOTRONIC. USED TO RUN WITH GUTCRUNCHER. I ARRESTED THEM ON A 4-01 DISORDERLY, ABOUT A MILLION YEARS AGO.
IS THAT RIGHT?
GUTCRUNCHER WON'T BE HAPPY TO HEAR THIS. STRATO HELPED HIM OPEN HIS BAR A COUPLE MONTHS BACK.
OPTIMUS—
—WE HAVE A LEAD.

THE BAR IS ONLY A FEW BLOCKS AWAY.
STRATOTRONIC AND HEAVY BARREL WERE RUNNING AN ENGEX BOOTLEGGING OPERATION. THE CONNECTION IS CLEAR.
WHAT WE NEED NEXT IS MOTIVE.
WINDBLADE COMES ALONG TO LEARN ABOUT CYBERTRONIAN MOTIVATIONS— AND TO KEEP ME OUT OF TROUBLE.
I TAKE YOU TO THE NICEST PLACES, PRIME.
YOU—
—YOUR KIND ISN'T WANTED HERE.
AND WHAT KIND WOULD THAT BE?
GIMME A BREAK. I MEAN AUTOBOTS.
WELL, I'M NOT AN AUTOBOT. AT LEAST I WASN'T A PART OF YOUR WAR.
YOU WEAR THE SIGIL. AND ANYWAY...
...YOUR BUDDY IS AUTOBOT ENOUGH FOR THE BOTH OF YOU.
YOU SHOULD BE HONORED TO HAVE HIM IN YOUR BAR, GUTCRUNCHER.
THIS IS THE TRUE PRIME— THE 'BOT THAT TURNED MEGATRON GOOD.
ISN'T THAT RIGHT?
SANDSTORM. IT'S BEEN A WHILE, OLD—
DON'T "OLD FRIEND" ME, PRIME.

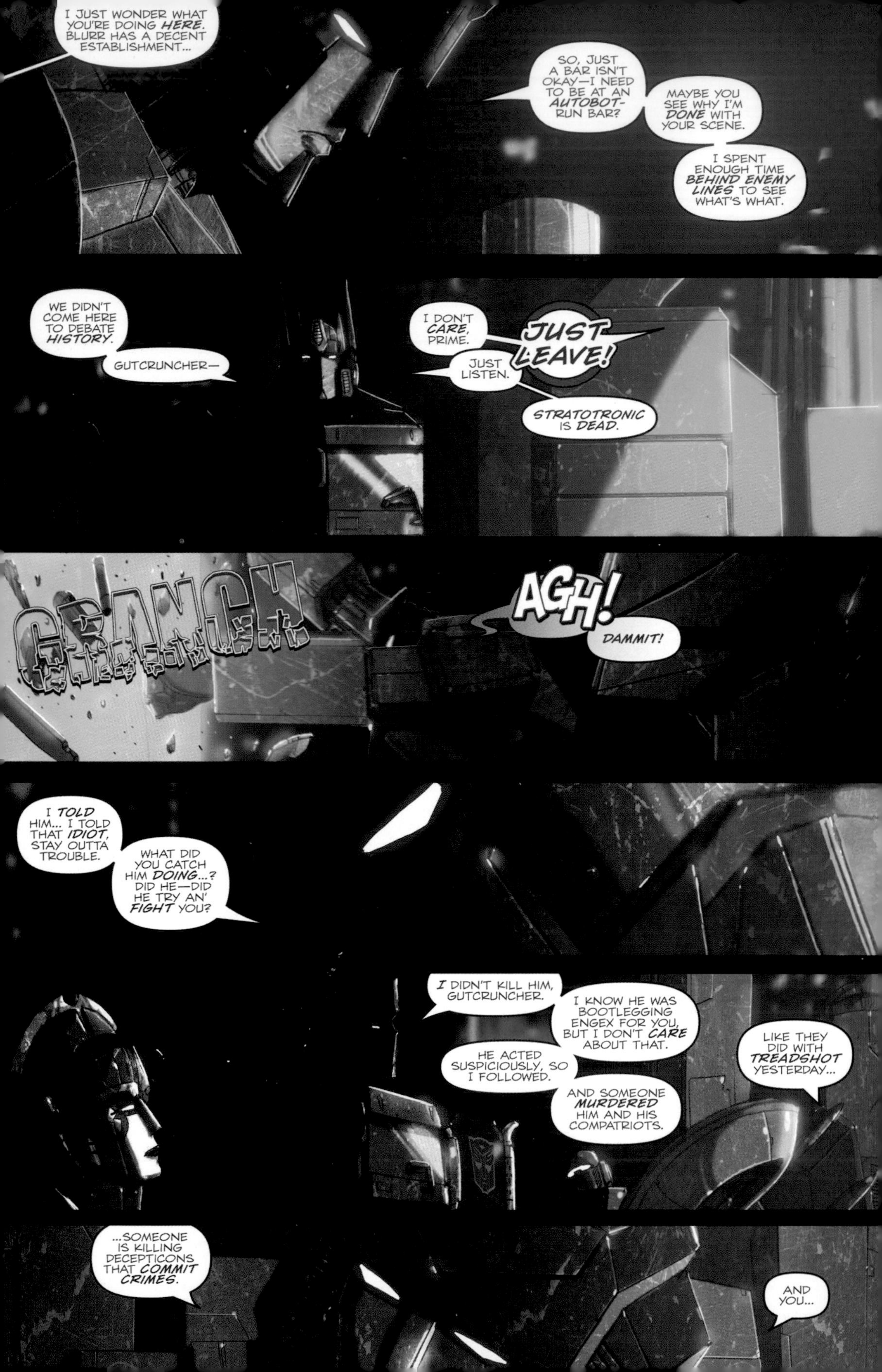

I JUST WONDER WHAT YOU'RE DOING HERE. BLURR HAS A DECENT ESTABLISHMENT...
SO, JUST A BAR ISN'T OKAY—I NEED TO BE AT AN AUTOBOT-RUN BAR?
MAYBE YOU SEE WHY I'M DONE WITH YOUR SCENE.
I SPENT ENOUGH TIME BEHIND ENEMY LINES TO SEE WHAT'S WHAT.
WE DIDN'T COME HERE TO DEBATE HISTORY.
GUTCRUNCHER—
I DON'T CARE, PRIME.
JUST LEAVE!
JUST LISTEN.
STRATOTRONIC IS DEAD.
GRANCH
AGH!
DAMMIT!
I TOLD HIM... I TOLD THAT IDIOT, STAY OUTTA TROUBLE.
WHAT DID YOU CATCH HIM DOING...? DID HE—DID HE TRY AN' FIGHT YOU?
I DIDN'T KILL HIM, GUTCRUNCHER.
I KNOW HE WAS BOOTLEGGING ENGEX FOR YOU, BUT I DON'T CARE ABOUT THAT.
HE ACTED SUSPICIOUSLY, SO I FOLLOWED.
AND SOMEONE MURDERED HIM AND HIS COMPATRIOTS.
LIKE THEY DID WITH TREADSHOT YESTERDAY...
...SOMEONE IS KILLING DECEPTICONS THAT COMMIT CRIMES.
AND YOU...

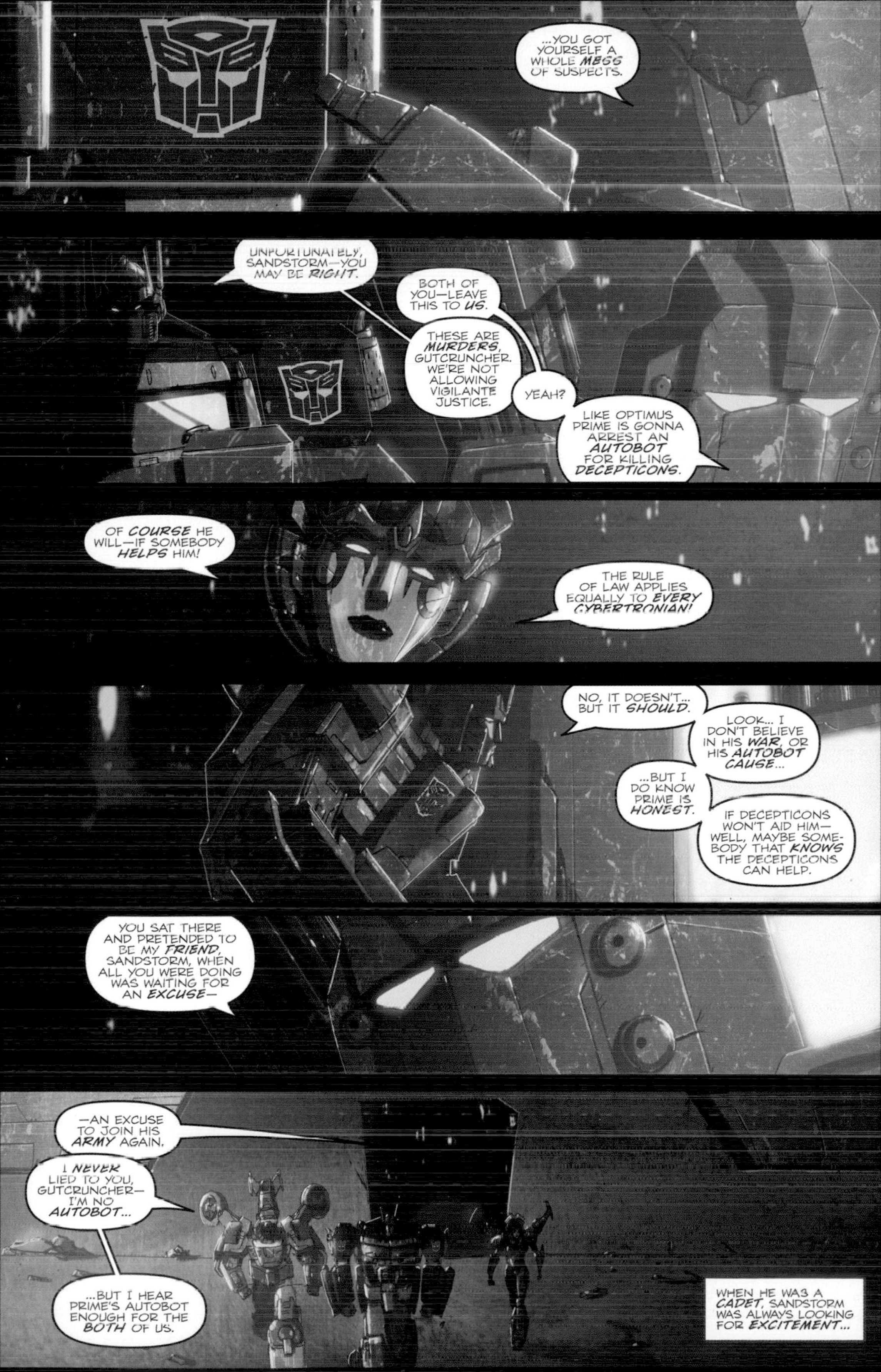

...YOU GOT YOURSELF A WHOLE MESS OF SUSPECTS.
UNFORTUNATELY, SANDSTORM—YOU MAY BE RIGHT.
BOTH OF YOU—LEAVE THIS TO US.
THESE ARE MURDERS, GUTCRUNCHER. WE'RE NOT ALLOWING VIGILANTE JUSTICE.
YEAH?
LIKE OPTIMUS PRIME IS GONNA ARREST AN AUTOBOT FOR KILLING DECEPTICONS.
OF COURSE HE WILL—IF SOMEBODY HELPS HIM!
THE RULE OF LAW APPLIES EQUALLY TO EVERY CYBERTRONIAN!
NO, IT DOESN'T... BUT IT SHOULD.
LOOK... I DON'T BELIEVE IN HIS WAR, OR HIS AUTOBOT CAUSE...
...BUT I DO KNOW PRIME IS HONEST.
IF DECEPTICONS WON'T AID HIM—WELL, MAYBE SOMEBODY THAT KNOWS THE DECEPTICONS CAN HELP.
YOU SAT THERE AND PRETENDED TO BE MY FRIEND, SANDSTORM, WHEN ALL YOU WERE DOING WAS WAITING FOR AN EXCUSE—
—AN EXCUSE TO JOIN HIS ARMY AGAIN.
I NEVER LIED TO YOU, GUTCRUNCHER—I'M NO AUTOBOT...
...BUT I HEAR PRIME'S AUTOBOT ENOUGH FOR THE BOTH OF US.
WHEN HE WAS A CADET, SANDSTORM WAS ALWAYS LOOKING FOR EXCITEMENT...

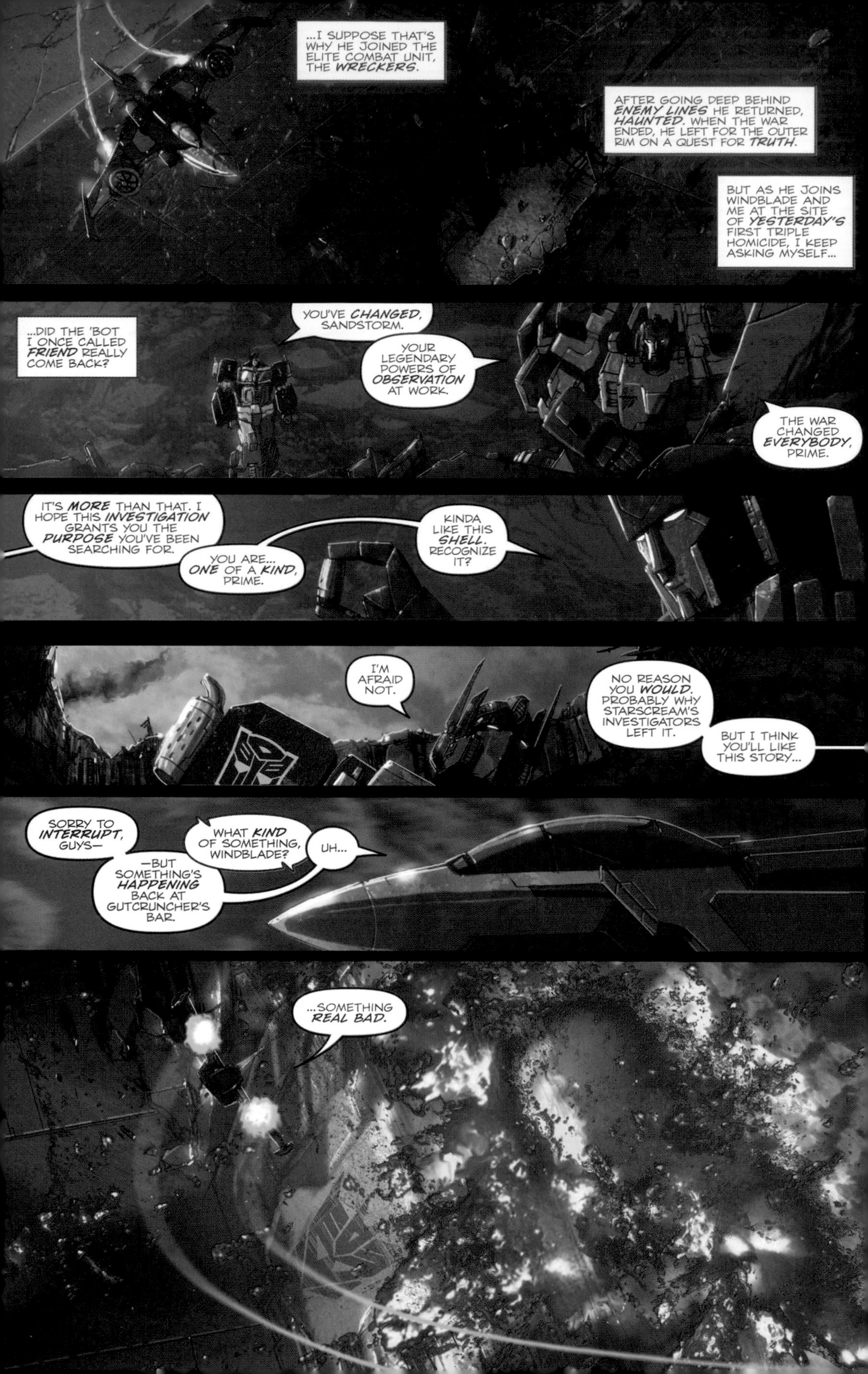
...I SUPPOSE THAT'S WHY HE JOINED THE ELITE COMBAT UNIT, THE WRECKERS.
AFTER GOING DEEP BEHIND ENEMY LINES HE RETURNED, HAUNTED. WHEN THE WAR ENDED, HE LEFT FOR THE OUTER RIM ON A QUEST FOR TRUTH.
BUT AS HE JOINS WINDBLADE AND ME AT THE SITE OF YESTERDAY'S FIRST TRIPLE HOMICIDE, I KEEP ASKING MYSELF...
...DID THE 'BOT I ONCE CALLED FRIEND REALLY COME BACK?
YOU'VE CHANGED, SANDSTORM.
YOUR LEGENDARY POWERS OF OBSERVATION AT WORK.
THE WAR CHANGED EVERYBODY, PRIME.
IT'S MORE THAN THAT. I HOPE THIS INVESTIGATION GRANTS YOU THE PURPOSE YOU'VE BEEN SEARCHING FOR.
YOU ARE... ONE OF A KIND, PRIME.
KINDA LIKE THIS SHELL. RECOGNIZE IT?
I'M AFRAID NOT.
NO REASON YOU WOULD. PROBABLY WHY STARSCREAM'S INVESTIGATORS LEFT IT.
BUT I THINK YOU'LL LIKE THIS STORY...
SORRY TO INTERRUPT, GUYS—
—BUT SOMETHING'S HAPPENING BACK AT GUTCRUNCHER'S BAR.
WHAT KIND OF SOMETHING, WINDBLADE?
UH...
...SOMETHING REAL BAD.

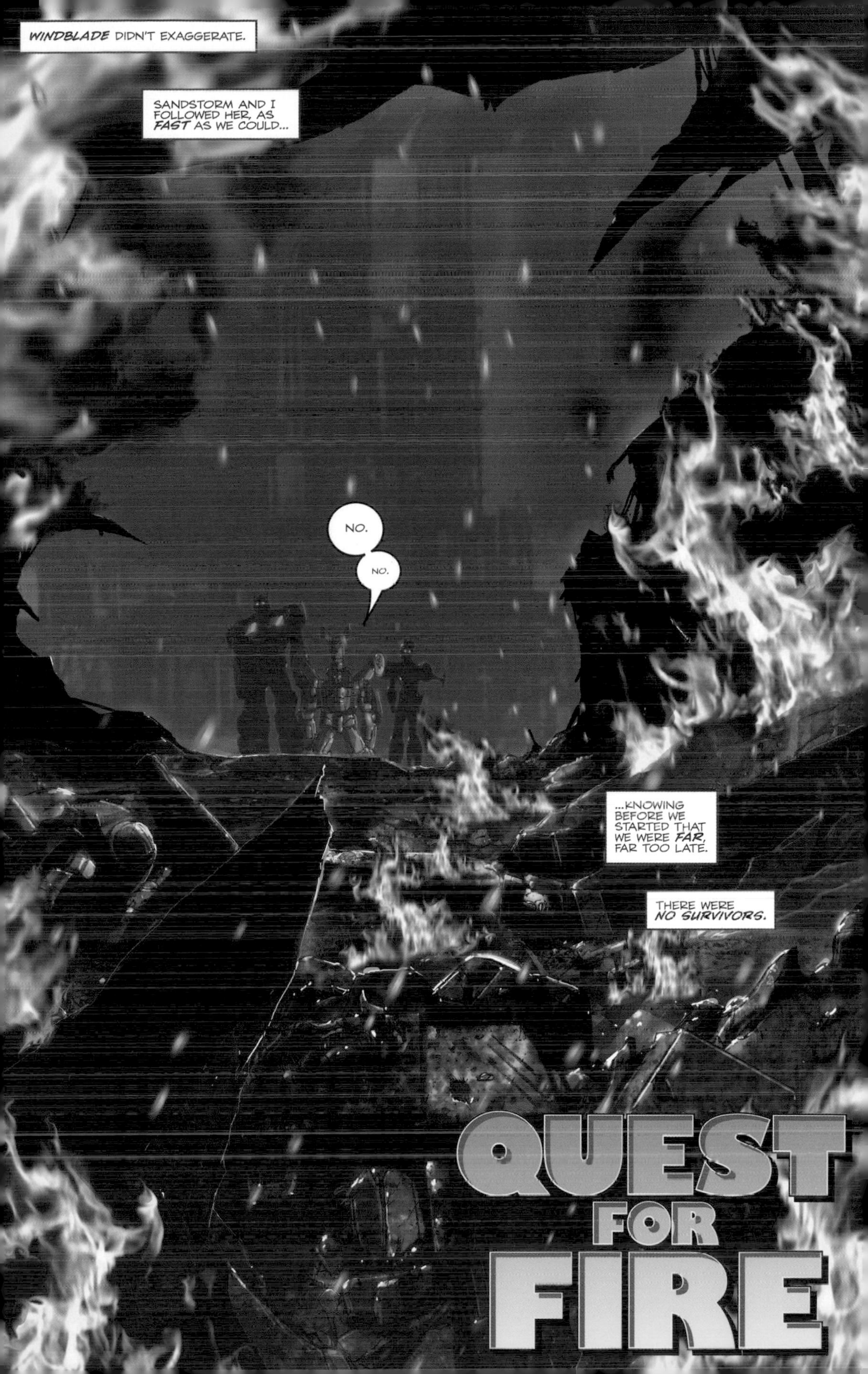
WINDBLADE DIDN'T EXAGGERATE.
SANDSTORM AND I FOLLOWED HER, AS FAST AS WE COULD...
NO.
NO.
...KNOWING BEFORE WE STARTED THAT WE WERE FAR, FAR TOO LATE.
THERE WERE NO SURVIVORS.
QUEST FOR FIRE

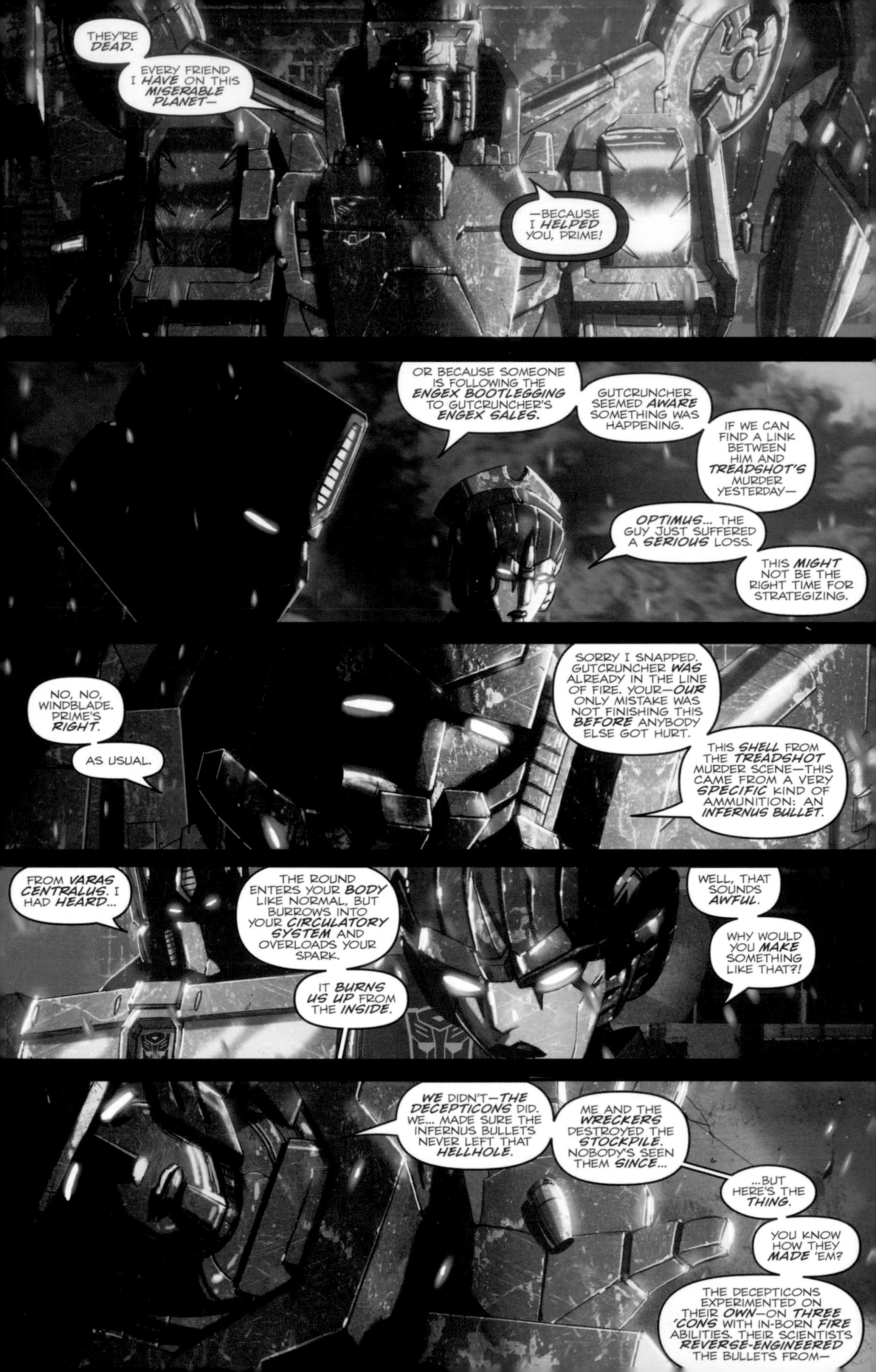

THEY'RE DEAD.
EVERY FRIEND I HAVE ON THIS MISERABLE PLANET—
—BECAUSE I HELPED YOU, PRIME!
OR BECAUSE SOMEONE IS FOLLOWING THE ENGEX BOOTLEGGING TO GUTCRUNCHER'S ENGEX SALES.
GUTCRUNCHER SEEMED AWARE SOMETHING WAS HAPPENING.
IF WE CAN FIND A LINK BETWEEN HIM AND TREADSHOT'S MURDER YESTERDAY—
OPTIMUS... THE GUY JUST SUFFERED A SERIOUS LOSS.
THIS MIGHT NOT BE THE RIGHT TIME FOR STRATEGIZING.
NO, NO, WINDBLADE. PRIME'S RIGHT.
AS USUAL.
SORRY I SNAPPED. GUTCRUNCHER WAS ALREADY IN THE LINE OF FIRE. YOUR—OUR ONLY MISTAKE WAS NOT FINISHING THIS BEFORE ANYBODY ELSE GOT HURT.
THIS SHELL FROM THE TREADSHOT MURDER SCENE—THIS CAME FROM A VERY SPECIFIC KIND OF AMMUNITION: AN INFERNUS BULLET.
FROM VARAS CENTRALUS. I HAD HEARD...
THE ROUND ENTERS YOUR BODY LIKE NORMAL, BUT BURROWS INTO YOUR CIRCULATORY SYSTEM AND OVERLOADS YOUR SPARK.
IT BURNS US UP FROM THE INSIDE.
WELL, THAT SOUNDS AWFUL.
WHY WOULD YOU MAKE SOMETHING LIKE THAT?!
WE DIDN'T—THE DECEPTICONS DID. WE... MADE SURE THE INFERNUS BULLETS NEVER LEFT THAT HELLHOLE.
ME AND THE WRECKERS DESTROYED THE STOCKPILE. NOBODY'S SEEN THEM SINCE...
...BUT HERE'S THE THING.
YOU KNOW HOW THEY MADE 'EM?
THE DECEPTICONS EXPERIMENTED ON THEIR OWN—ON THREE 'CONS WITH IN-BORN FIRE ABILITIES. THEIR SCIENTISTS REVERSE-ENGINEERED THE BULLETS FROM—

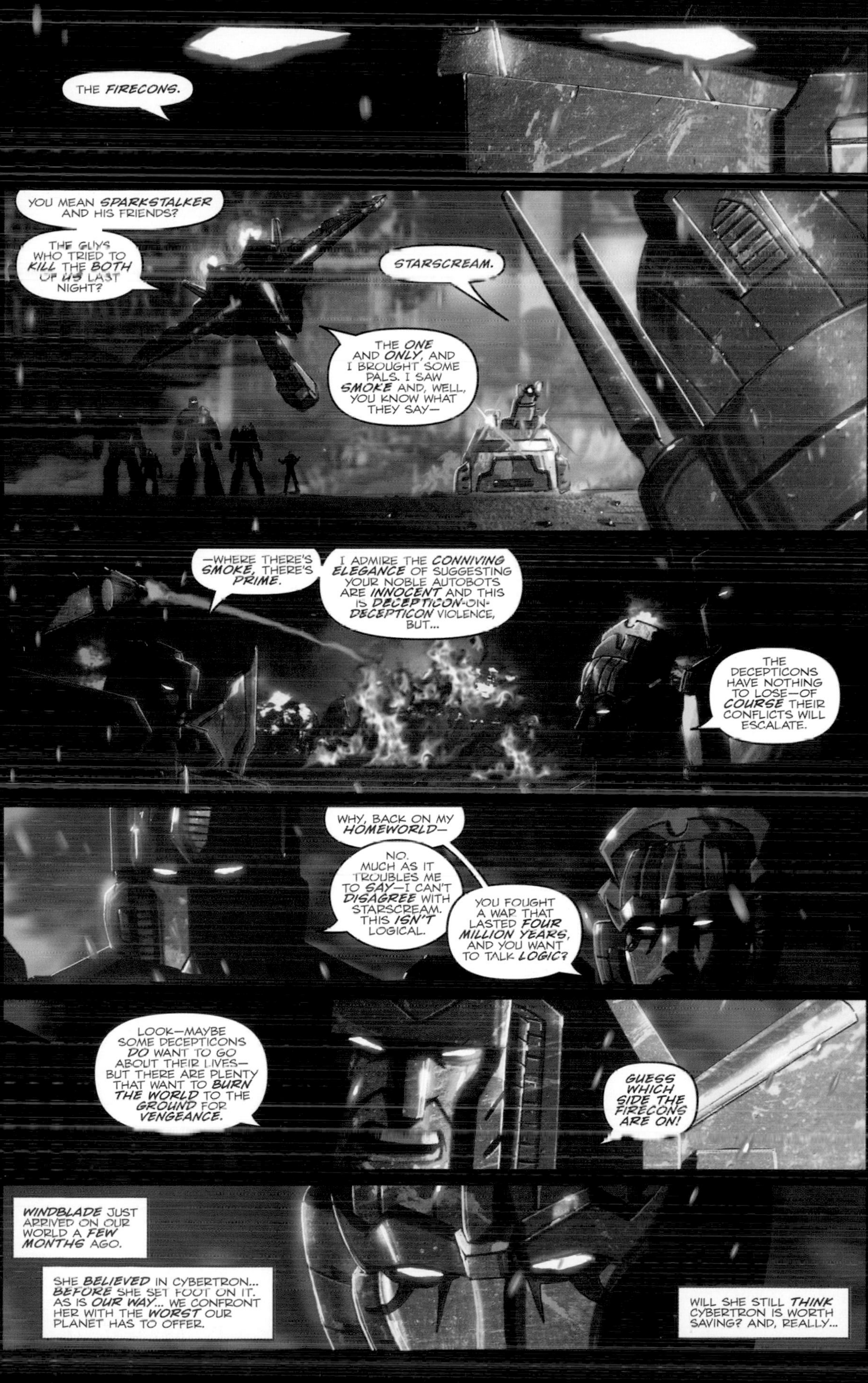
THE FIRECONS.
YOU MEAN SPARKSTALKER AND HIS FRIENDS?
THE GUYS WHO TRIED TO KILL THE BOTH OF US LAST NIGHT?
STARSCREAM.
THE ONE AND ONLY, AND I BROUGHT SOME PALS. I SAW SMOKE AND, WELL, YOU KNOW WHAT THEY SAY—
—WHERE THERE'S SMOKE, THERE'S PRIME.
I ADMIRE THE CONNIVING ELEGANCE OF SUGGESTING YOUR NOBLE AUTOBOTS ARE INNOCENT AND THIS IS DECEPTICON-ON-DECEPTICON VIOLENCE, BUT...
THE DECEPTICONS HAVE NOTHING TO LOSE—OF COURSE THEIR CONFLICTS WILL ESCALATE.
WHY, BACK ON MY HOMEWORLD—
NO. MUCH AS IT TROUBLES ME TO SAY—I CAN'T DISAGREE WITH STARSCREAM. THIS ISN'T LOGICAL.
YOU FOUGHT A WAR THAT LASTED FOUR MILLION YEARS, AND YOU WANT TO TALK LOGIC?
LOOK—MAYBE SOME DECEPTICONS DO WANT TO GO ABOUT THEIR LIVES—BUT THERE ARE PLENTY THAT WANT TO BURN THE WORLD TO THE GROUND FOR VENGEANCE.
GUESS WHICH SIDE THE FIRECONS ARE ON!
WINDBLADE JUST ARRIVED ON OUR WORLD A FEW MONTHS AGO.
SHE BELIEVED IN CYBERTRON... BEFORE SHE SET FOOT ON IT. AS IS OUR WAY... WE CONFRONT HER WITH THE WORST OUR PLANET HAS TO OFFER.
WILL SHE STILL THINK CYBERTRON IS WORTH SAVING? AND, REALLY...

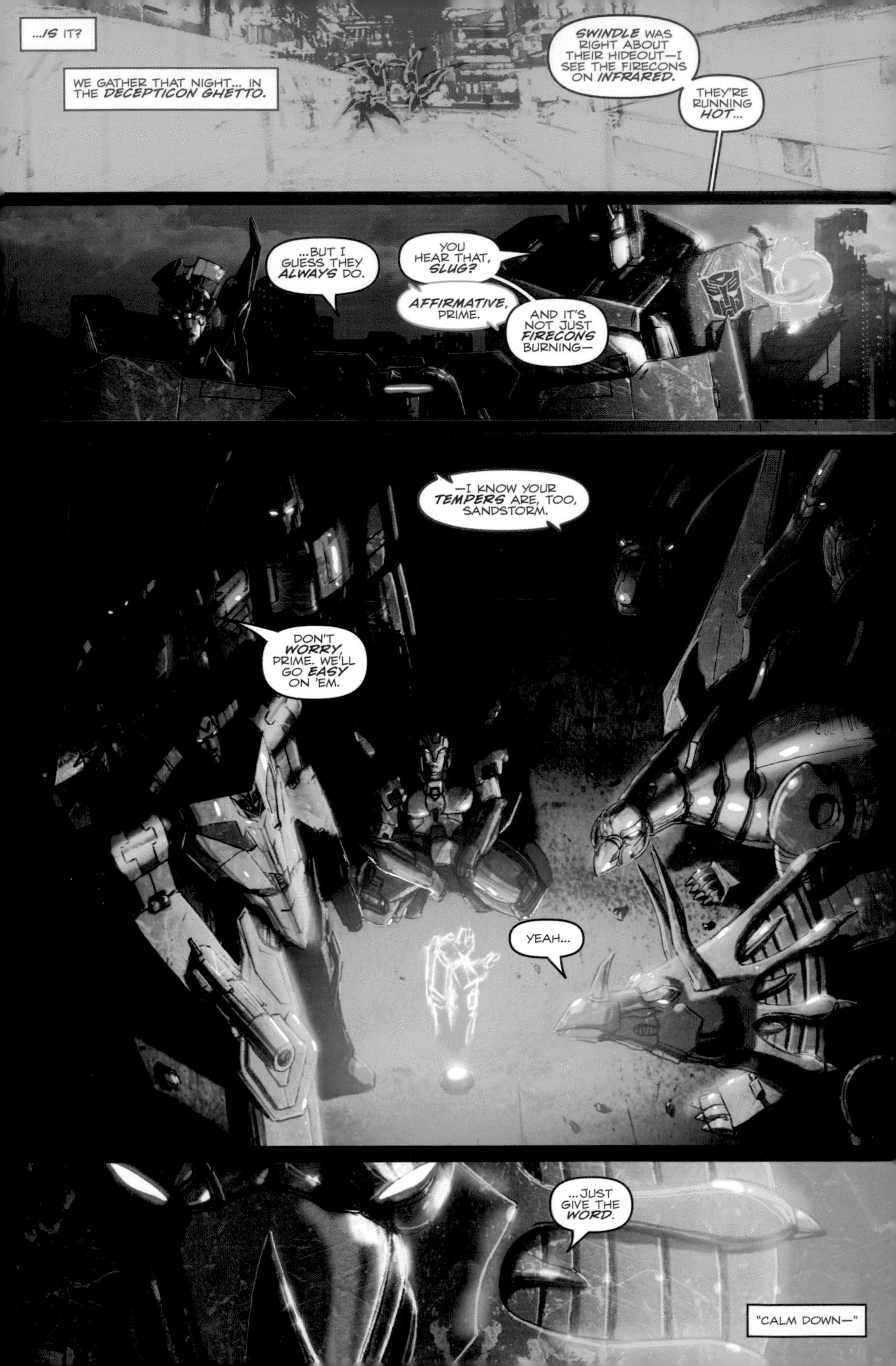
...IS IT?
WE GATHER THAT NIGHT... IN THE DECEPTICON GHETTO.
SWINDLE WAS RIGHT ABOUT THEIR HIDEOUT—I SEE THE FIRECONS ON INFRARED.
THEY'RE RUNNING HOT...
...BUT I GUESS THEY ALWAYS DO.
YOU HEAR THAT, SLUG?
AFFIRMATIVE, PRIME.
AND IT'S NOT JUST FIRECONS BURNING—
—I KNOW YOUR TEMPERS ARE, TOO, SANDSTORM.
DON'T WORRY, PRIME. WE'LL GO EASY ON 'EM.
YEAH...
...JUST GIVE THE WORD.
"CALM DOWN—"

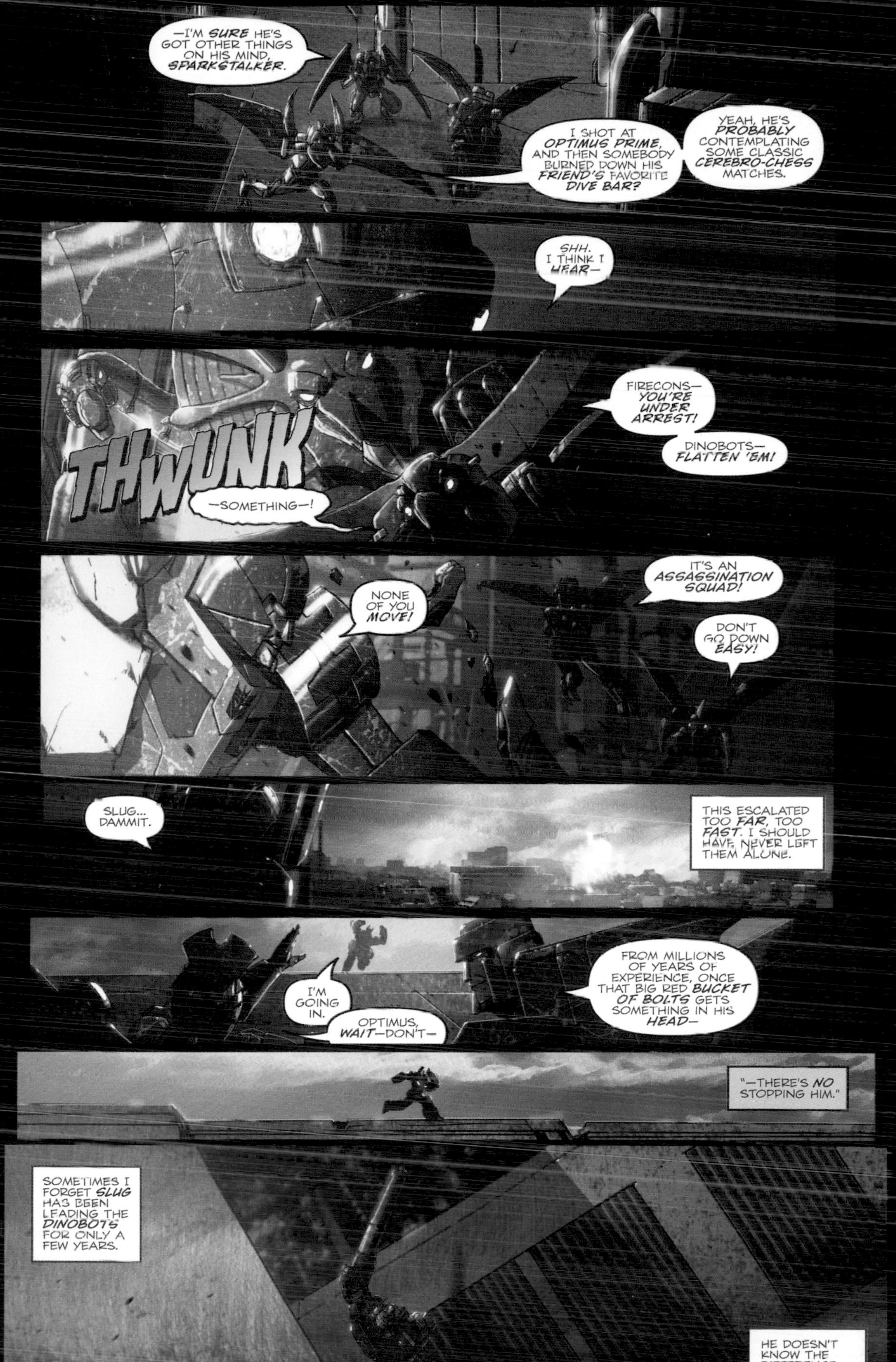
—I'M SURE HE'S GOT OTHER THINGS ON HIS MIND, SPARKSTALKER.
I SHOT AT OPTIMUS PRIME, AND THEN SOMEBODY BURNED DOWN HIS FRIEND'S FAVORITE DIVE BAR?
YEAH, HE'S PROBABLY CONTEMPLATING SOME CLASSIC CEREBRO-CHESS MATCHES.
SHH. I THINK I HEAR—
THWUNK
—SOMETHING—!
FIRECONS— YOU'RE UNDER ARREST!
DINOBOTS— FLATTEN 'EM!
IT'S AN ASSASSINATION SQUAD!
NONE OF YOU MOVE!
DON'T GO DOWN EASY!
SLUG... DAMMIT.
THIS ESCALATED TOO FAR, TOO FAST. I SHOULD HAVE NEVER LEFT THEM ALONE.
I'M GOING IN.
OPTIMUS, WAIT—DON'T—
FROM MILLIONS OF YEARS OF EXPERIENCE, ONCE THAT BIG RED BUCKET OF BOLTS GETS SOMETHING IN HIS HEAD—
"—THERE'S NO STOPPING HIM."
SOMETIMES I FORGET SLUG HAS BEEN LEADING THE DINOBOTS FOR ONLY A FEW YEARS.
HE DOESN'T KNOW THE DIFFERENCE BETWEEN BEING A WARRIOR—

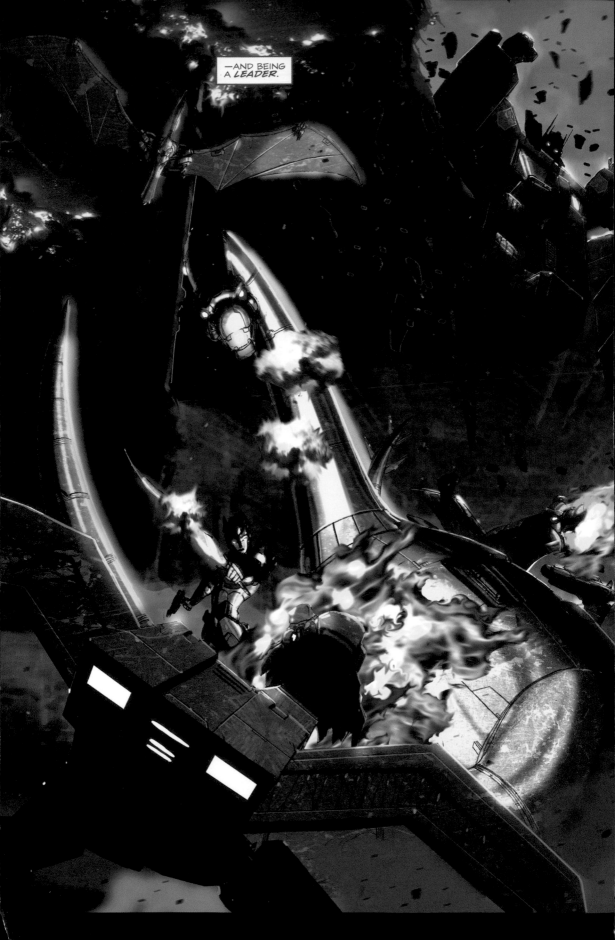

—AND BEING A *LEADER*.

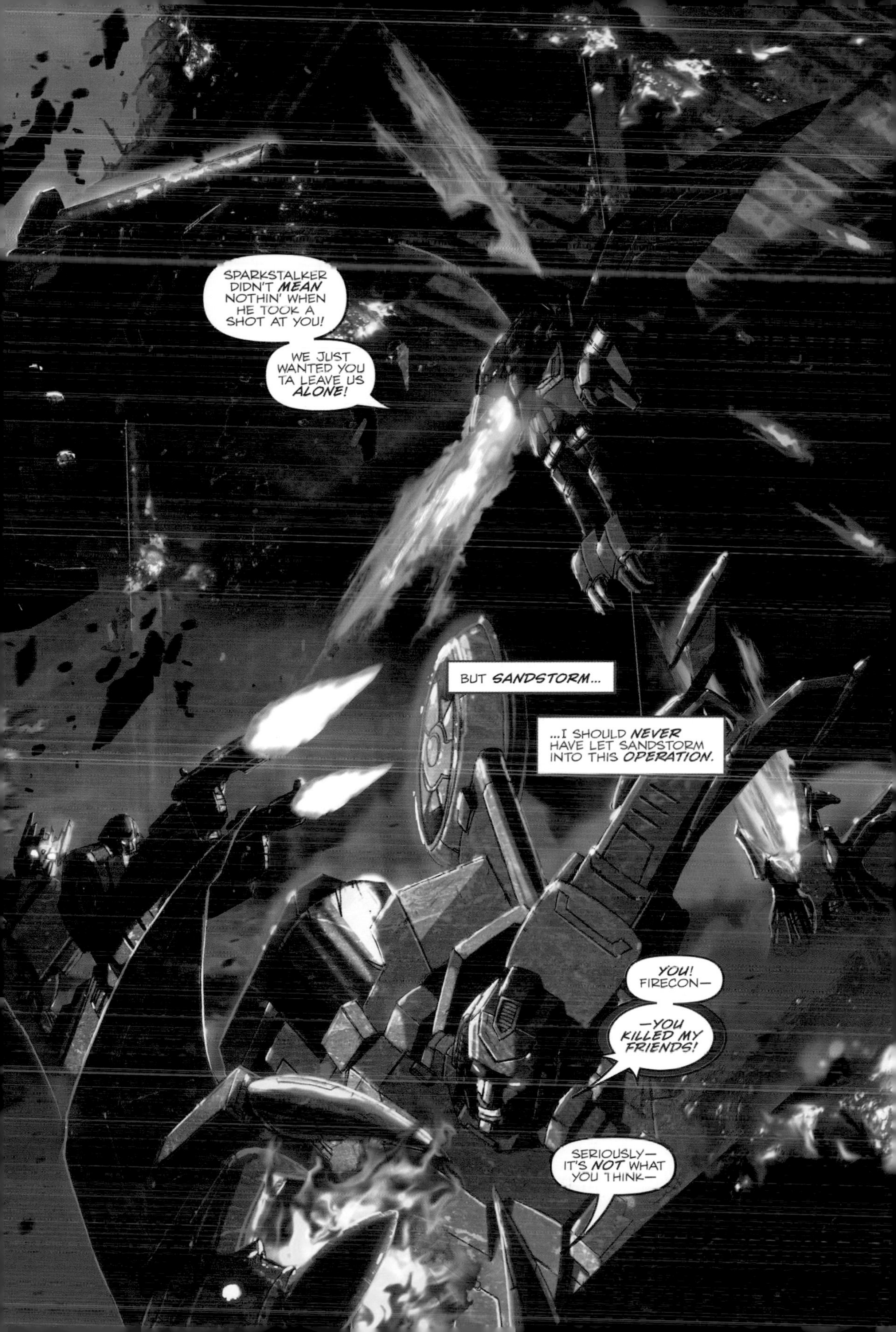
SPARKSTALKER DIDN'T MEAN NOTHIN' WHEN HE TOOK A SHOT AT YOU!
WE JUST WANTED YOU TA LEAVE US ALONE!
BUT SANDSTORM...
...I SHOULD NEVER HAVE LET SANDSTORM INTO THIS OPERATION.
YOU! FIRECON—
—YOU KILLED MY FRIENDS!
SERIOUSLY— IT'S NOT WHAT YOU THINK—

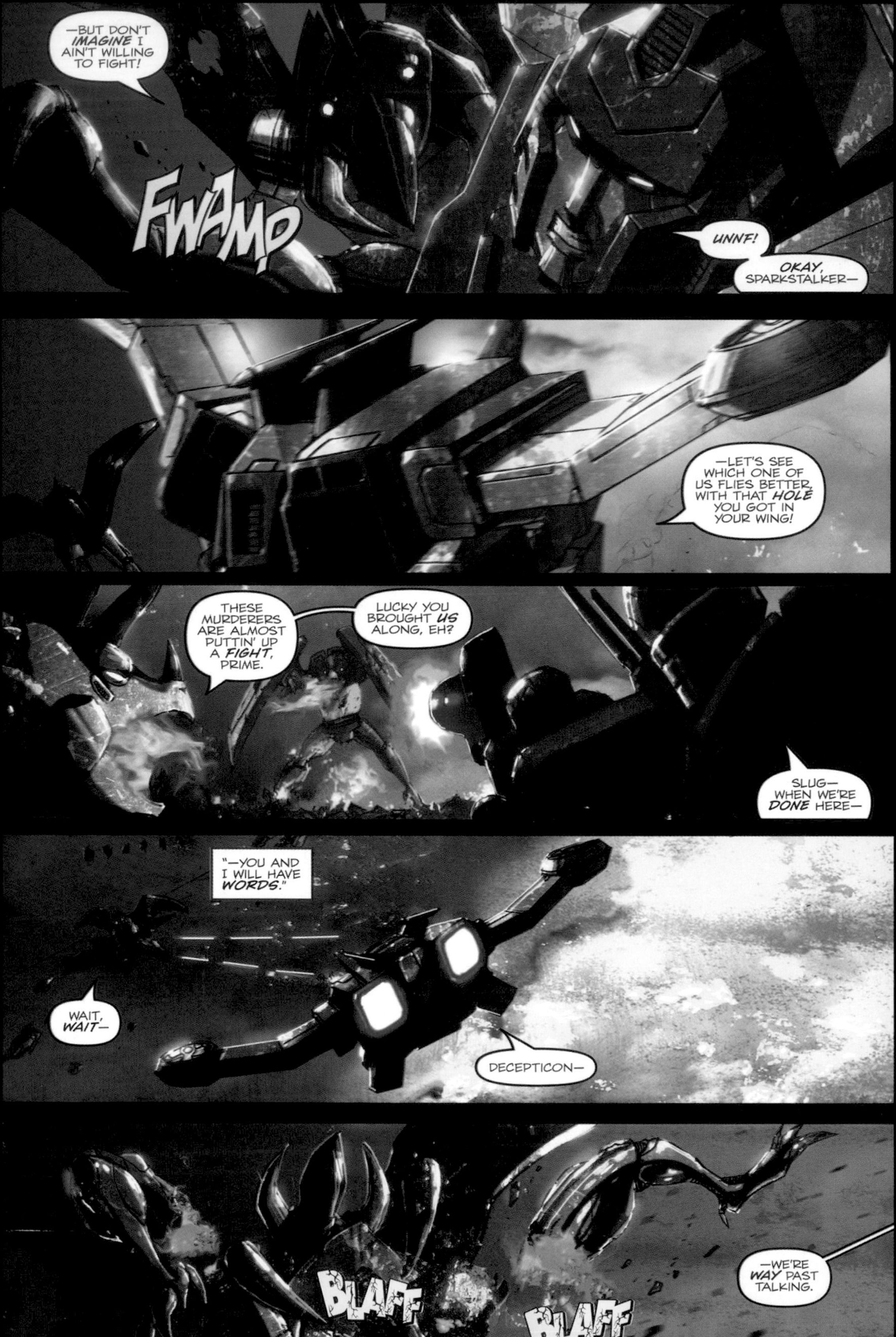
—BUT DON'T IMAGINE I AIN'T WILLING TO FIGHT!
FWAMP
UNNF!
OKAY, SPARKSTALKER—
—LET'S SEE WHICH ONE OF US FLIES BETTER, WITH THAT HOLE YOU GOT IN YOUR WING!
THESE MURDERERS ARE ALMOST PUTTIN' UP A FIGHT, PRIME.
LUCKY YOU BROUGHT US ALONG, EH?
SLUG— WHEN WE'RE DONE HERE—
"—YOU AND I WILL HAVE WORDS."
WAIT, WAIT—
DECEPTICON—
BLAFF
BLAFF
—WE'RE WAY PAST TALKING.

HANG ON! I SUR—

SHYUNK

SURRENDER ACCEPTED.

THE DINOBOTS *DO* WHAT THEY *DO*.

SNORT GOT NUMBER *TWO*.

NO—

SCHLAPP

SQUAAK!

THEY END THE BATTLE, *EFFICIENTLY* AND *RUTHLESSLY*.

NICE WORK, GUYS.

NOW IT'S *MY* TURN...

JUST LIKE *SANDSTORM* AND THE *WRECKERS* USED TO.

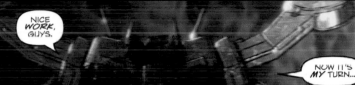

AH! AH!

...LET'S MAKE IT *THREE* FOR THREE.

LIKE WE *ALL* DID, ONCE UPON A TIME. I THINK OF WINDBLADE. OF WHAT SHE MUST THINK OF US...

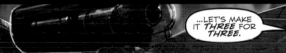

...AND I *ACT*.

STOP!

I CAN'T *ALLOW* THIS!

ONCE WE WERE *WARRIORS*.

NOW WE ARE *PEOPLE*, AND MUST *BEHAVE* AS SUCH.

AND A *LEADER*... A LEADER MUST KNOW THE *DIFFERENCE*.

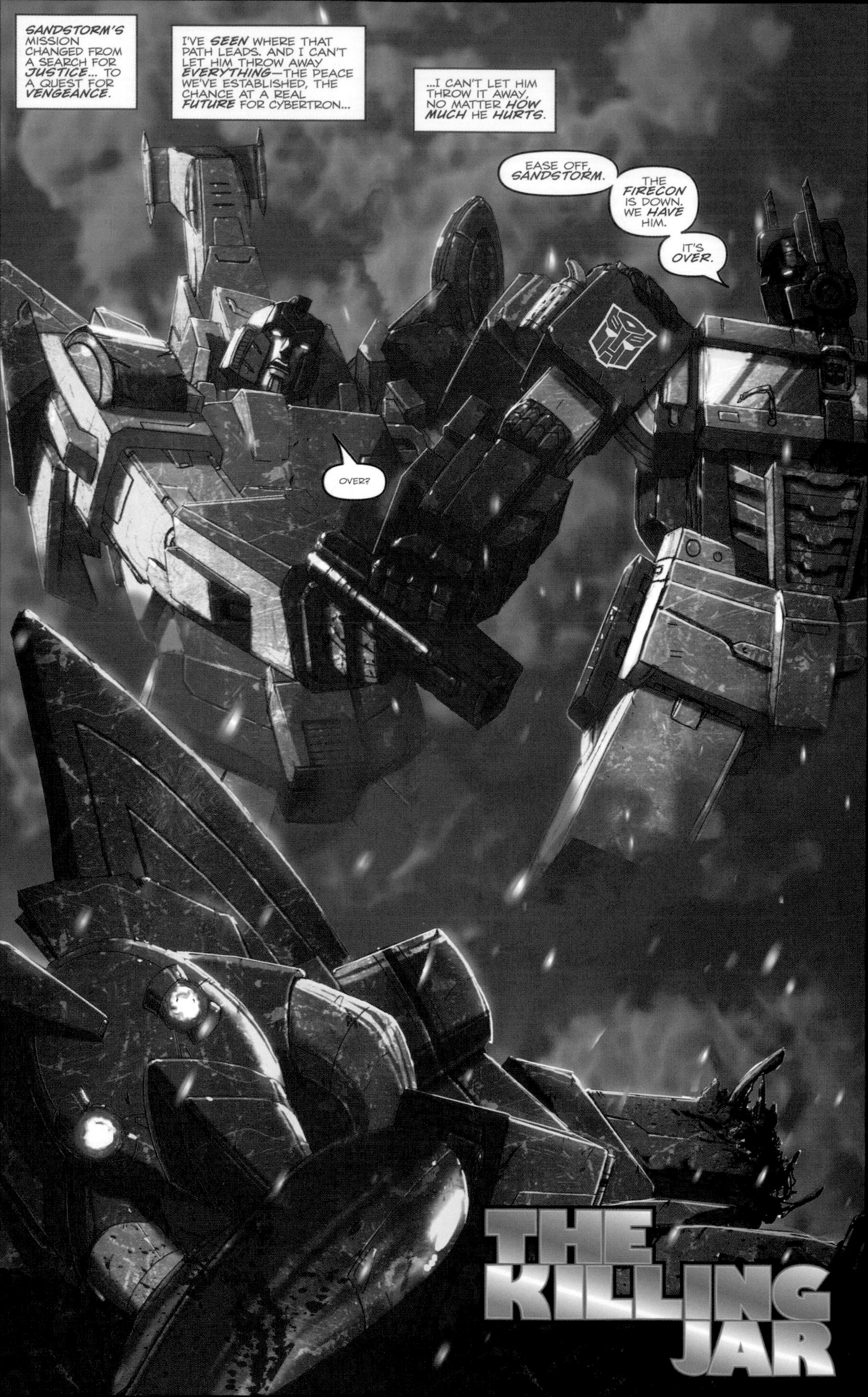
SANDSTORM'S MISSION CHANGED FROM A SEARCH FOR JUSTICE... TO A QUEST FOR VENGEANCE.
I'VE SEEN WHERE THAT PATH LEADS. AND I CAN'T LET HIM THROW AWAY EVERYTHING—THE PEACE WE'VE ESTABLISHED, THE CHANCE AT A REAL FUTURE FOR CYBERTRON...
...I CAN'T LET HIM THROW IT AWAY, NO MATTER HOW MUCH HE HURTS.
EASE OFF, SANDSTORM.
THE FIRECON IS DOWN. WE HAVE HIM.
IT'S OVER.
OVER?
THE KILLING JAR

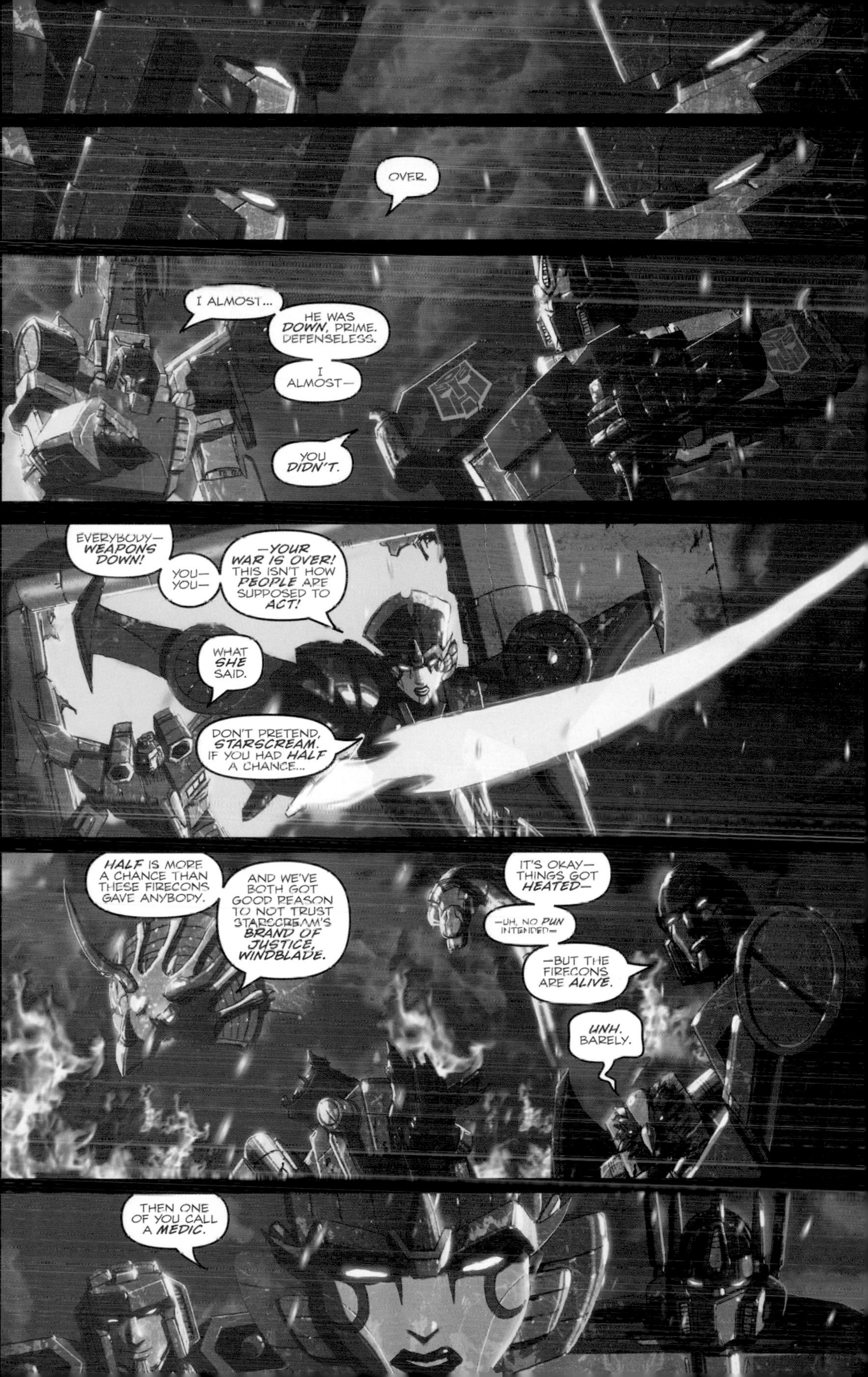
OVER.
I ALMOST...
HE WAS DOWN, PRIME. DEFENSELESS.
I ALMOST—
YOU DIDN'T.
EVERYBODY— WEAPONS DOWN!
YOU— YOU—
—YOUR WAR IS OVER! THIS ISN'T HOW PEOPLE ARE SUPPOSED TO ACT!
WHAT SHE SAID.
DON'T PRETEND, STARSCREAM. IF YOU HAD HALF A CHANCE...
HALF IS MORE A CHANCE THAN THESE FIRECONS GAVE ANYBODY.
AND WE'VE BOTH GOT GOOD REASON TO NOT TRUST STARSCREAM'S BRAND OF JUSTICE, WINDBLADE.
IT'S OKAY— THINGS GOT HEATED—
—UH, NO PUN INTENDED—
—BUT THE FIRECONS ARE ALIVE.
UNH. BARELY.
THEN ONE OF YOU CALL A MEDIC.

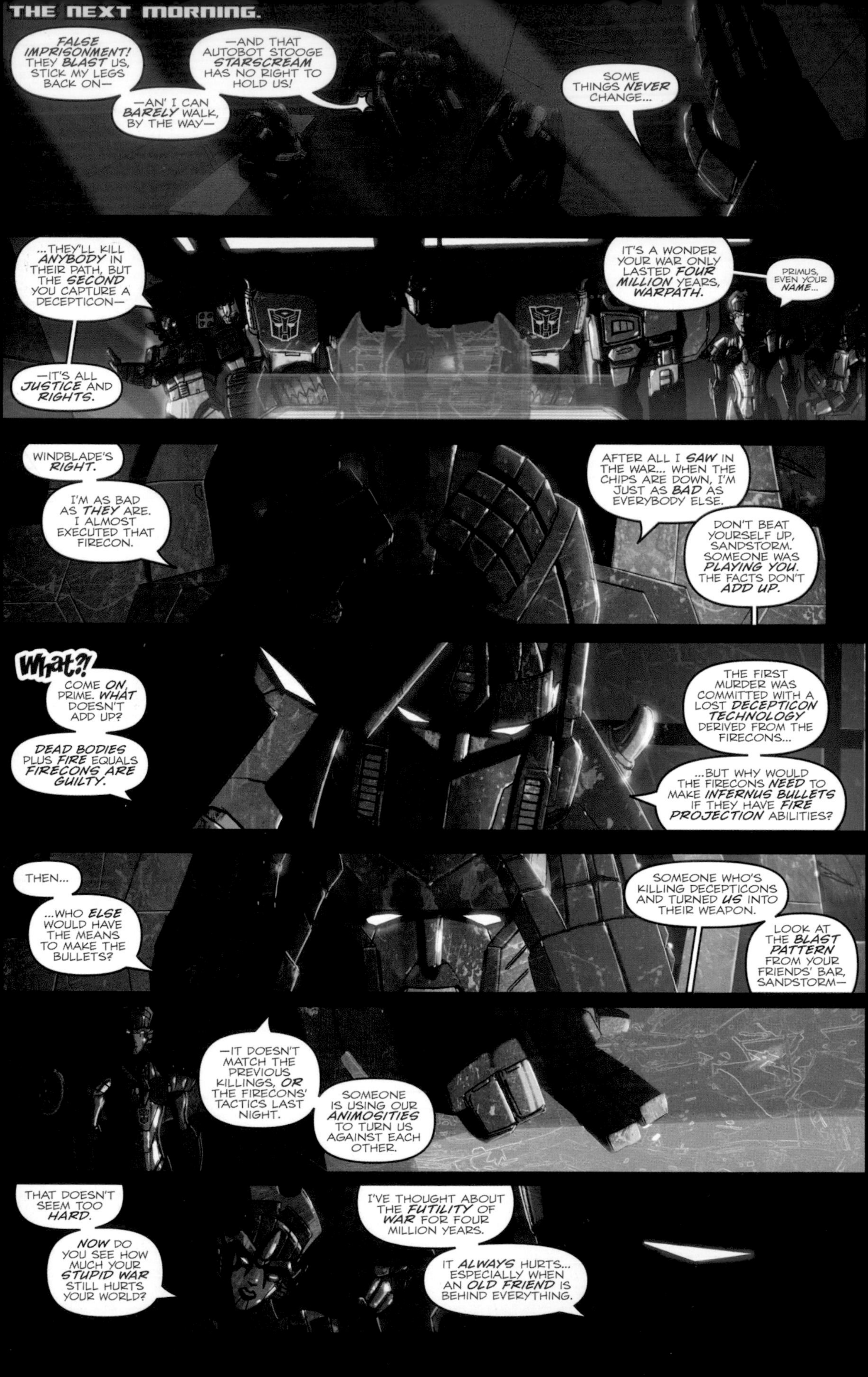
THE NEXT MORNING.
FALSE IMPRISONMENT! THEY BLAST US, STICK MY LEGS BACK ON—
—AN' I CAN BARELY WALK, BY THE WAY—
—AND THAT AUTOBOT STOOGE STARSCREAM HAS NO RIGHT TO HOLD US!
SOME THINGS NEVER CHANGE...
...THEY'LL KILL ANYBODY IN THEIR PATH, BUT THE SECOND YOU CAPTURE A DECEPTICON—
—IT'S ALL JUSTICE AND RIGHTS.
IT'S A WONDER YOUR WAR ONLY LASTED FOUR MILLION YEARS, WARPATH.
PRIMUS, EVEN YOUR NAME...
WINDBLADE'S RIGHT.
I'M AS BAD AS THEY ARE. I ALMOST EXECUTED THAT FIRECON.
AFTER ALL I SAW IN THE WAR... WHEN THE CHIPS ARE DOWN, I'M JUST AS BAD AS EVERYBODY ELSE.
DON'T BEAT YOURSELF UP, SANDSTORM. SOMEONE WAS PLAYING YOU. THE FACTS DON'T ADD UP.
What?!
COME ON, PRIME. WHAT DOESN'T ADD UP?
DEAD BODIES PLUS FIRE EQUALS FIRECONS ARE GUILTY.
THE FIRST MURDER WAS COMMITTED WITH A LOST DECEPTICON TECHNOLOGY DERIVED FROM THE FIRECONS...
...BUT WHY WOULD THE FIRECONS NEED TO MAKE INFERNUS BULLETS IF THEY HAVE FIRE PROJECTION ABILITIES?
THEN...
...WHO ELSE WOULD HAVE THE MEANS TO MAKE THE BULLETS?
SOMEONE WHO'S KILLING DECEPTICONS AND TURNED US INTO THEIR WEAPON.
LOOK AT THE BLAST PATTERN FROM YOUR FRIENDS' BAR, SANDSTORM—
—IT DOESN'T MATCH THE PREVIOUS KILLINGS, OR THE FIRECONS' TACTICS LAST NIGHT.
SOMEONE IS USING OUR ANIMOSITIES TO TURN US AGAINST EACH OTHER.
THAT DOESN'T SEEM TOO HARD.
NOW DO YOU SEE HOW MUCH YOUR STUPID WAR STILL HURTS YOUR WORLD?
I'VE THOUGHT ABOUT THE FUTILITY OF WAR FOR FOUR MILLION YEARS.
IT ALWAYS HURTS... ESPECIALLY WHEN AN OLD FRIEND IS BEHIND EVERYTHING.

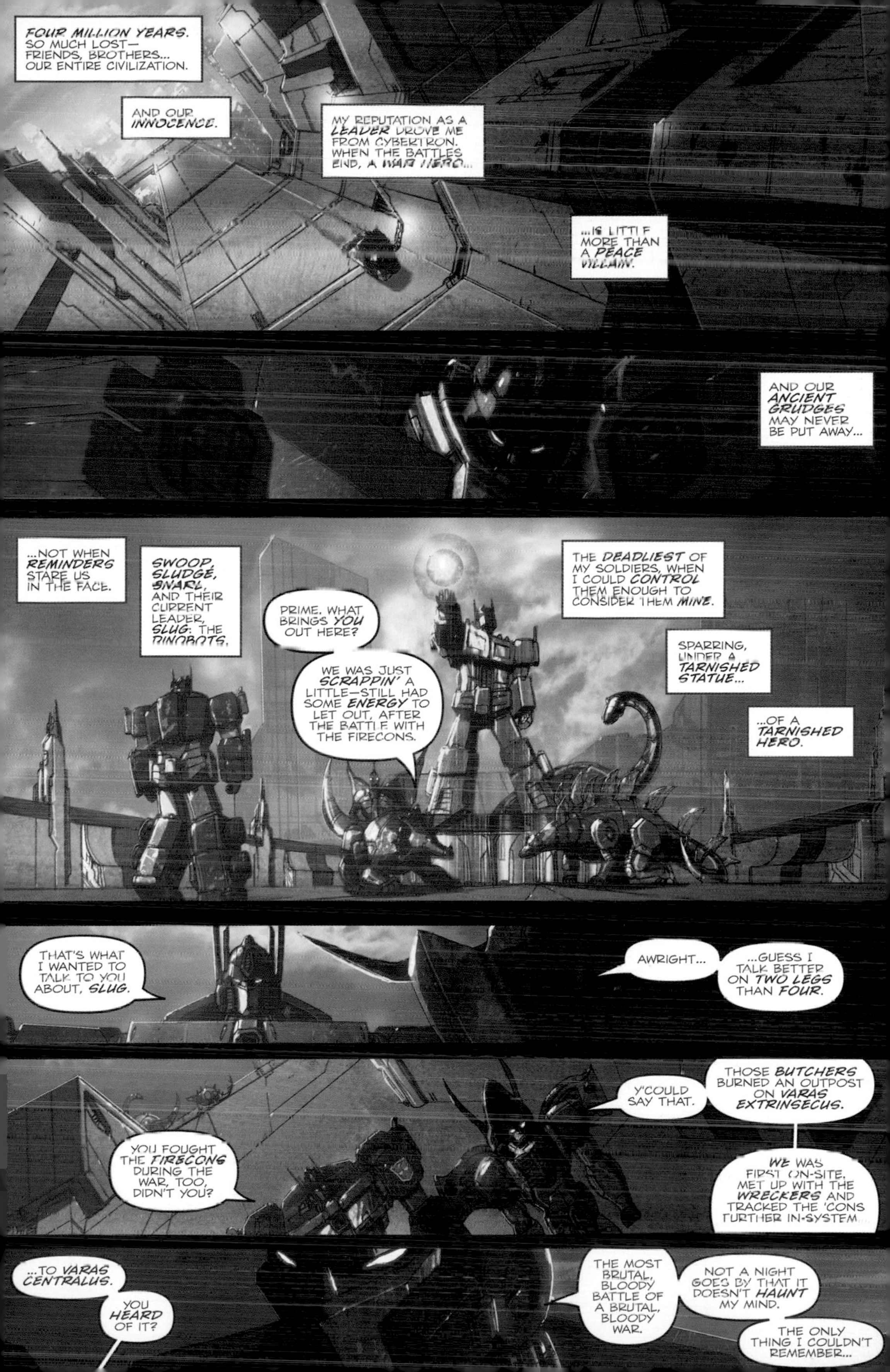
FOUR MILLION YEARS. SO MUCH LOST— FRIENDS, BROTHERS... OUR ENTIRE CIVILIZATION.
AND OUR INNOCENCE.
MY REPUTATION AS A LEADER DROVE ME FROM CYBERTRON. WHEN THE BATTLES END, A WAR HERO...
...IS LITTLE MORE THAN A PEACE VILLAIN.
AND OUR ANCIENT GRUDGES MAY NEVER BE PUT AWAY...
...NOT WHEN REMINDERS STARE US IN THE FACE.
SWOOP, SLUDGE, SNARL, AND THEIR CURRENT LEADER, SLUG: THE DINOBOTS.
PRIME. WHAT BRINGS YOU OUT HERE?
WE WAS JUST SCRAPPIN' A LITTLE—STILL HAD SOME ENERGY TO LET OUT, AFTER THE BATTLE WITH THE FIRECONS.
THE DEADLIEST OF MY SOLDIERS, WHEN I COULD CONTROL THEM ENOUGH TO CONSIDER THEM MINE.
SPARRING, UNDER A TARNISHED STATUE...
...OF A TARNISHED HERO.
THAT'S WHAT I WANTED TO TALK TO YOU ABOUT, SLUG.
AWRIGHT...
...GUESS I TALK BETTER ON TWO LEGS THAN FOUR.
YOU FOUGHT THE FIRECONS DURING THE WAR, TOO, DIDN'T YOU?
Y'COULD SAY THAT.
THOSE BUTCHERS BURNED AN OUTPOST ON VARAS EXTRINSECUS.
WE WAS FIRST ON-SITE, MET UP WITH THE WRECKERS AND TRACKED THE 'CONS FURTHER IN-SYSTEM...
...TO VARAS CENTRALUS.
YOU HEARD OF IT?
THE MOST BRUTAL, BLOODY BATTLE OF A BRUTAL, BLOODY WAR.
NOT A NIGHT GOES BY THAT IT DOESN'T HAUNT MY MIND.
THE ONLY THING I COULDN'T REMEMBER...

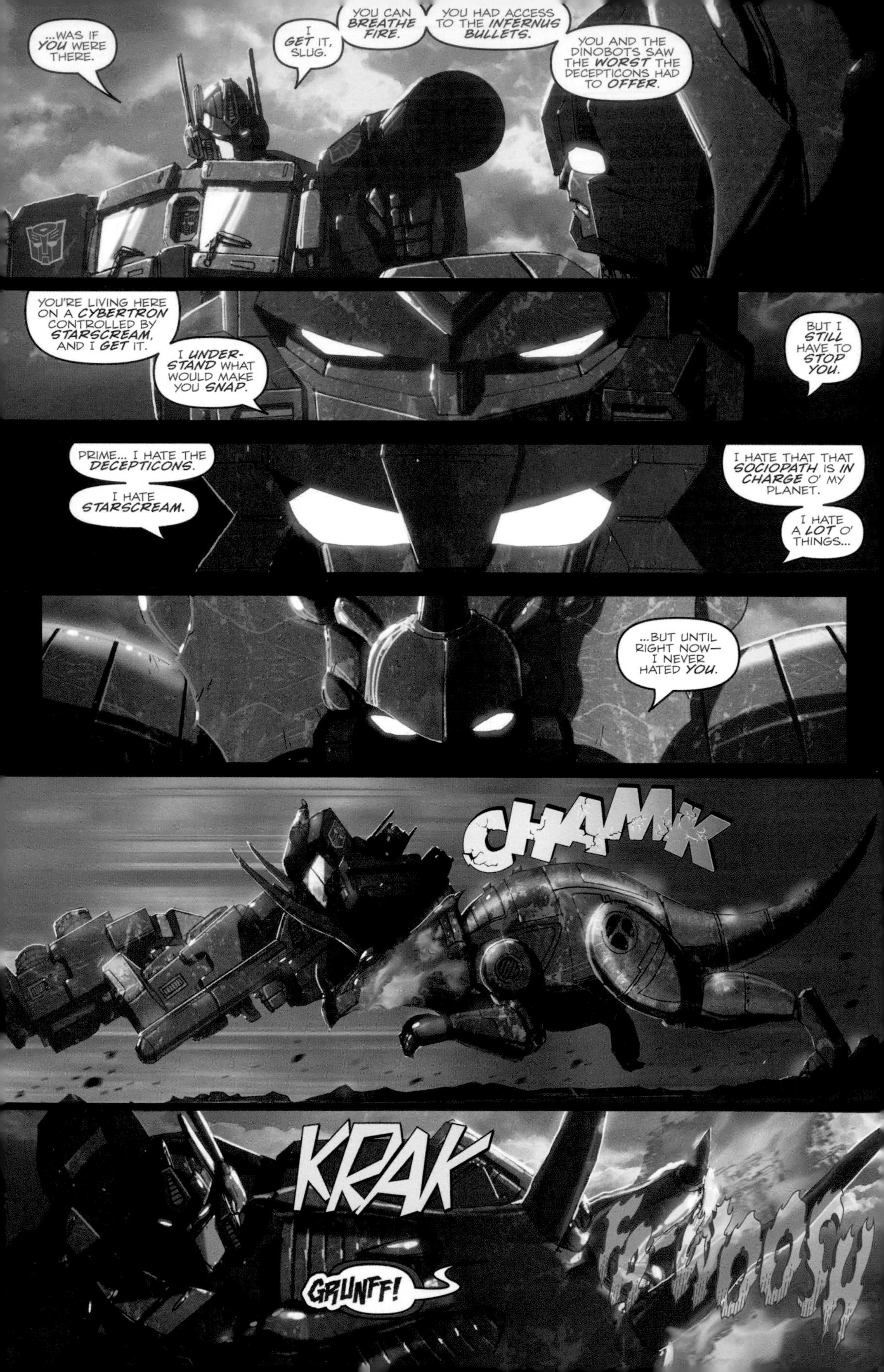
...WAS IF YOU WERE THERE.
I GET IT, SLUG.
YOU CAN BREATHE FIRE.
YOU HAD ACCESS TO THE INFERNUS BULLETS.
YOU AND THE DINOBOTS SAW THE WORST THE DECEPTICONS HAD TO OFFER.
YOU'RE LIVING HERE ON A CYBERTRON CONTROLLED BY STARSCREAM, AND I GET IT.
I UNDERSTAND WHAT WOULD MAKE YOU SNAP.
BUT I STILL HAVE TO STOP YOU.
PRIME... I HATE THE DECEPTICONS.
I HATE STARSCREAM.
I HATE THAT THAT SOCIOPATH IS IN CHARGE O' MY PLANET.
I HATE A LOT O' THINGS...
...BUT UNTIL RIGHT NOW— I NEVER HATED YOU.
CHAMK
KRAK
GRUNFF!

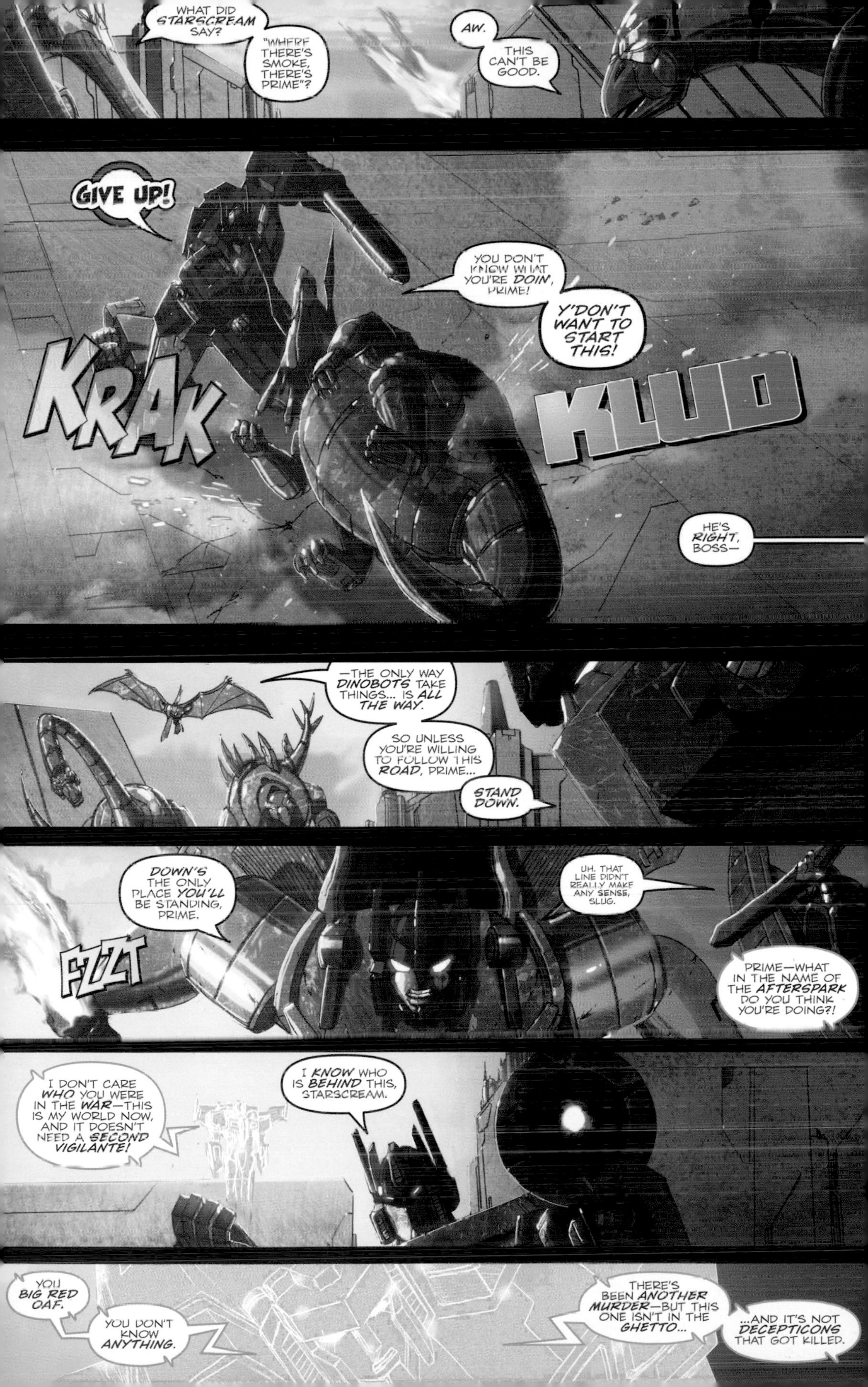
WHAT DID STARSCREAM SAY?
"WHERE THERE'S SMOKE, THERE'S PRIME"?
AW.
THIS CAN'T BE GOOD.
GIVE UP!
YOU DON'T KNOW WHAT YOU'RE DOIN', PRIME!
Y'DON'T WANT TO START THIS!
KRAK
KLUD
HE'S RIGHT, BOSS—
—THE ONLY WAY DINOBOTS TAKE THINGS... IS ALL THE WAY.
SO UNLESS YOU'RE WILLING TO FOLLOW THIS ROAD, PRIME...
STAND DOWN.
DOWN'S THE ONLY PLACE YOU'LL BE STANDING, PRIME.
FZZT
UH. THAT LINE DIDN'T REALLY MAKE ANY SENSE, SLUG.
PRIME—WHAT IN THE NAME OF THE AFTERSPARK DO YOU THINK YOU'RE DOING?!
I DON'T CARE WHO YOU WERE IN THE WAR—THIS IS MY WORLD NOW, AND IT DOESN'T NEED A SECOND VIGILANTE!
I KNOW WHO IS BEHIND THIS, STARSCREAM.
YOU BIG RED OAF.
YOU DON'T KNOW ANYTHING.
THERE'S BEEN ANOTHER MURDER—BUT THIS ONE ISN'T IN THE GHETTO...
...AND IT'S NOT DECEPTICONS THAT GOT KILLED.

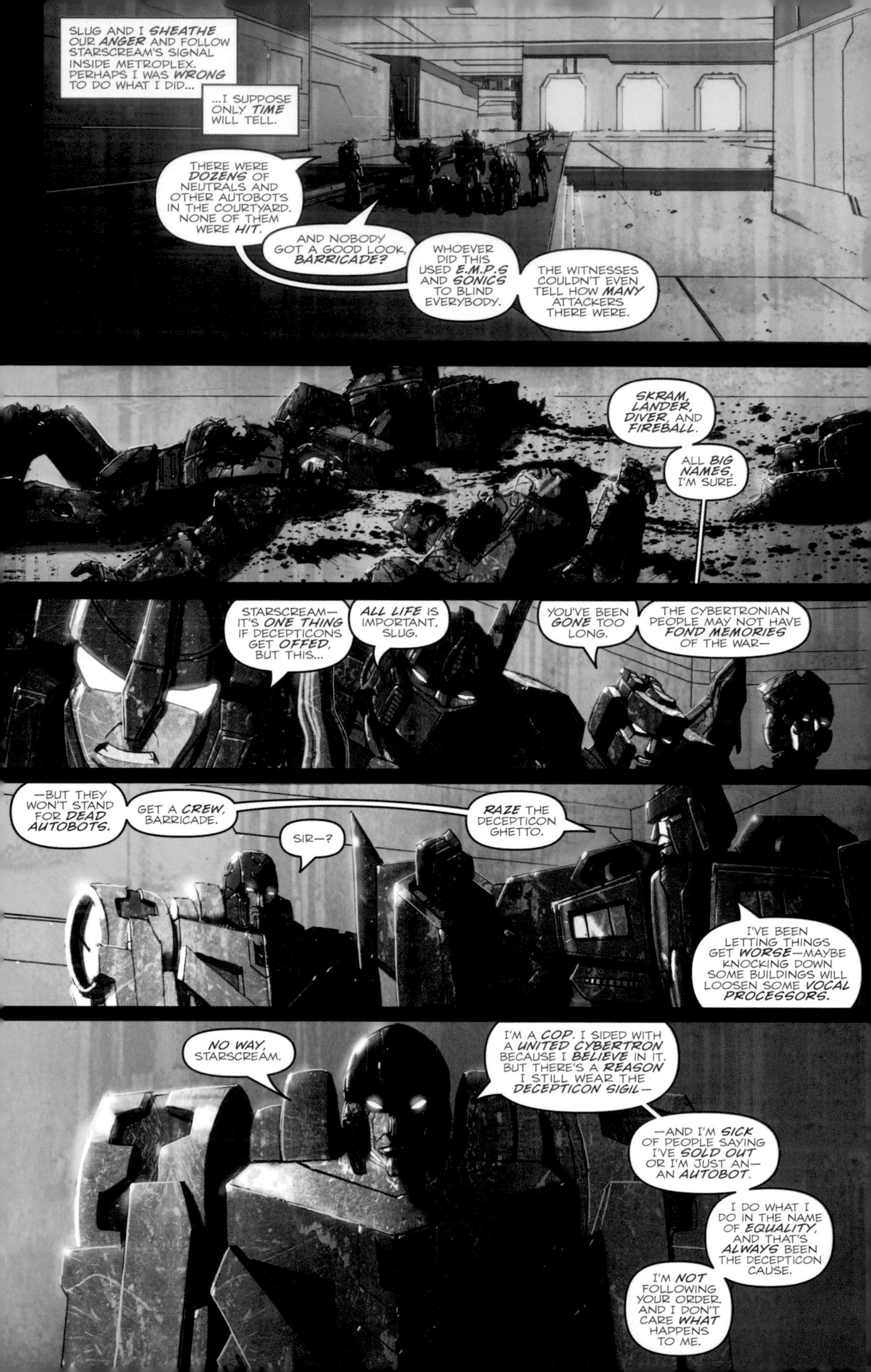
SLUG AND I SHEATHE OUR ANGER AND FOLLOW STARSCREAM'S SIGNAL INSIDE METROPLEX. PERHAPS I WAS WRONG TO DO WHAT I DID...
...I SUPPOSE ONLY TIME WILL TELL.
THERE WERE DOZENS OF NEUTRALS AND OTHER AUTOBOTS IN THE COURTYARD. NONE OF THEM WERE HIT.
AND NOBODY GOT A GOOD LOOK, BARRICADE?
WHOEVER DID THIS USED E.M.P.S AND SONICS TO BLIND EVERYBODY.
THE WITNESSES COULDN'T EVEN TELL HOW MANY ATTACKERS THERE WERE.
SKRAM, LANDER, DIVER, AND FIREBALL.
ALL BIG NAMES, I'M SURE.
STARSCREAM— IT'S ONE THING IF DECEPTICONS GET OFFED, BUT THIS...
ALL LIFE IS IMPORTANT, SLUG.
YOU'VE BEEN GONE TOO LONG.
THE CYBERTRONIAN PEOPLE MAY NOT HAVE FOND MEMORIES OF THE WAR—
—BUT THEY WON'T STAND FOR DEAD AUTOBOTS.
GET A CREW, BARRICADE.
SIR—?
RAZE THE DECEPTICON GHETTO.
I'VE BEEN LETTING THINGS GET WORSE—MAYBE KNOCKING DOWN SOME BUILDINGS WILL LOOSEN SOME VOCAL PROCESSORS.
NO WAY, STARSCREAM.
I'M A COP. I SIDED WITH A UNITED CYBERTRON BECAUSE I BELIEVE IN IT. BUT THERE'S A REASON I STILL WEAR THE DECEPTICON SIGIL—
—AND I'M SICK OF PEOPLE SAYING I'VE SOLD OUT OR I'M JUST AN— AN AUTOBOT.
I DO WHAT I DO IN THE NAME OF EQUALITY, AND THAT'S ALWAYS BEEN THE DECEPTICON CAUSE.
I'M NOT FOLLOWING YOUR ORDER. AND I DON'T CARE WHAT HAPPENS TO ME.

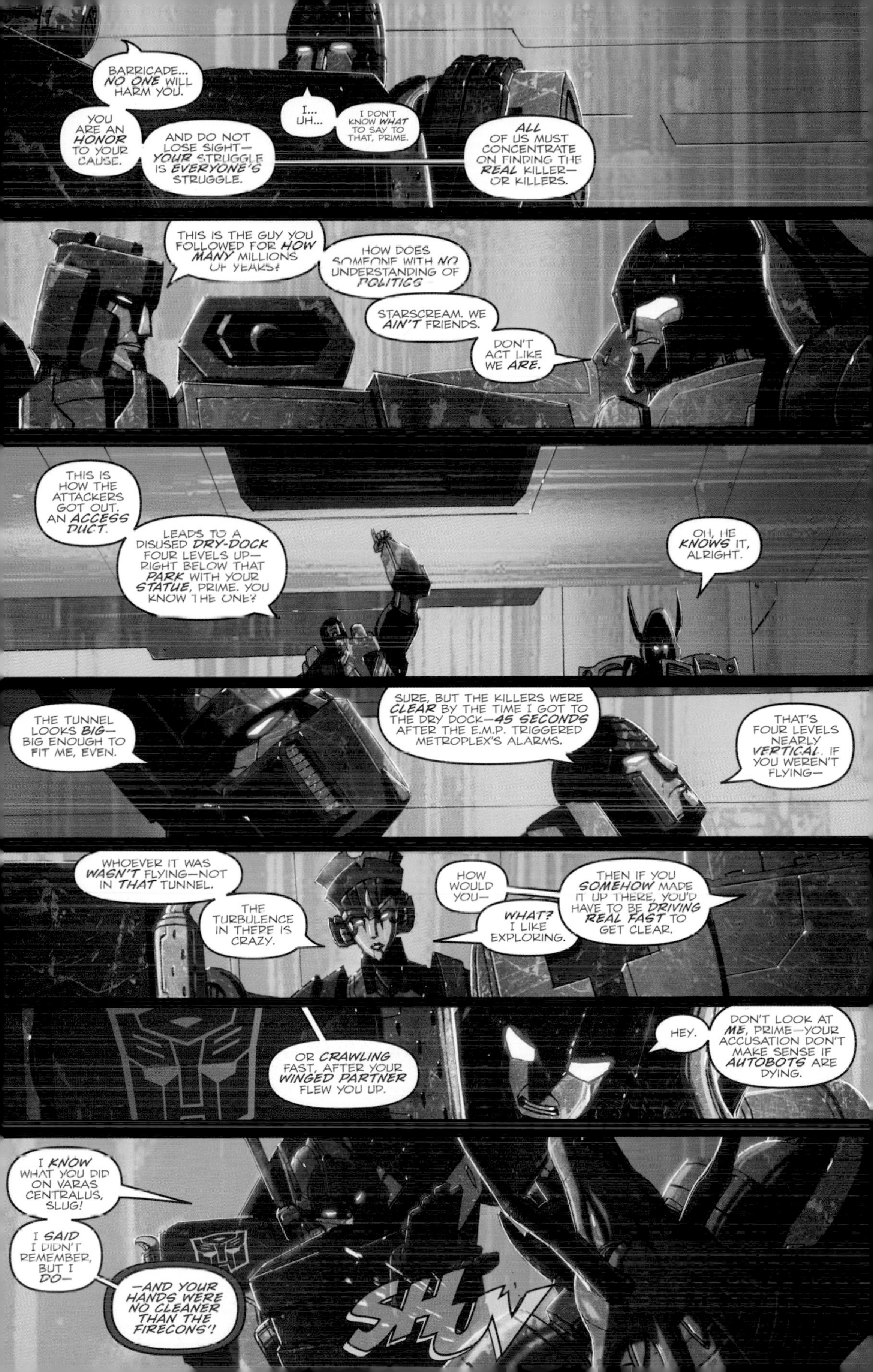
BARRICADE... NO ONE WILL HARM YOU.
YOU ARE AN HONOR TO YOUR CAUSE.
AND DO NOT LOSE SIGHT— YOUR STRUGGLE IS EVERYONE'S STRUGGLE.
I... UH...
I DON'T KNOW WHAT TO SAY TO THAT, PRIME.
ALL OF US MUST CONCENTRATE ON FINDING THE REAL KILLER— OR KILLERS.
THIS IS THE GUY YOU FOLLOWED FOR HOW MANY MILLIONS OF YEARS?
HOW DOES SOMEONE WITH NO UNDERSTANDING OF POLITICS
STARSCREAM. WE AIN'T FRIENDS.
DON'T ACT LIKE WE ARE.
THIS IS HOW THE ATTACKERS GOT OUT. AN ACCESS DUCT.
LEADS TO A DISUSED DRY-DOCK FOUR LEVELS UP— RIGHT BELOW THAT PARK WITH YOUR STATUE, PRIME. YOU KNOW THE ONE?
OH, HE KNOWS IT, ALRIGHT.
THE TUNNEL LOOKS BIG— BIG ENOUGH TO FIT ME, EVEN.
SURE, BUT THE KILLERS WERE CLEAR BY THE TIME I GOT TO THE DRY DOCK—45 SECONDS AFTER THE E.M.P. TRIGGERED METROPLEX'S ALARMS.
THAT'S FOUR LEVELS NEARLY VERTICAL. IF YOU WEREN'T FLYING—
WHOEVER IT WAS WASN'T FLYING—NOT IN THAT TUNNEL.
THE TURBULENCE IN THERE IS CRAZY.
HOW WOULD YOU—
WHAT? I LIKE EXPLORING.
THEN IF YOU SOMEHOW MADE IT UP THERE, YOU'D HAVE TO BE DRIVING REAL FAST TO GET CLEAR.
OR CRAWLING FAST, AFTER YOUR WINGED PARTNER FLEW YOU UP.
HEY.
DON'T LOOK AT ME, PRIME—YOUR ACCUSATION DON'T MAKE SENSE IF AUTOBOTS ARE DYING.
I KNOW WHAT YOU DID ON VARAS CENTRALUS, SLUG!
I SAID I DIDN'T REMEMBER, BUT I DO—
—AND YOUR HANDS WERE NO CLEANER THAN THE FIRECONS'!
SHUN

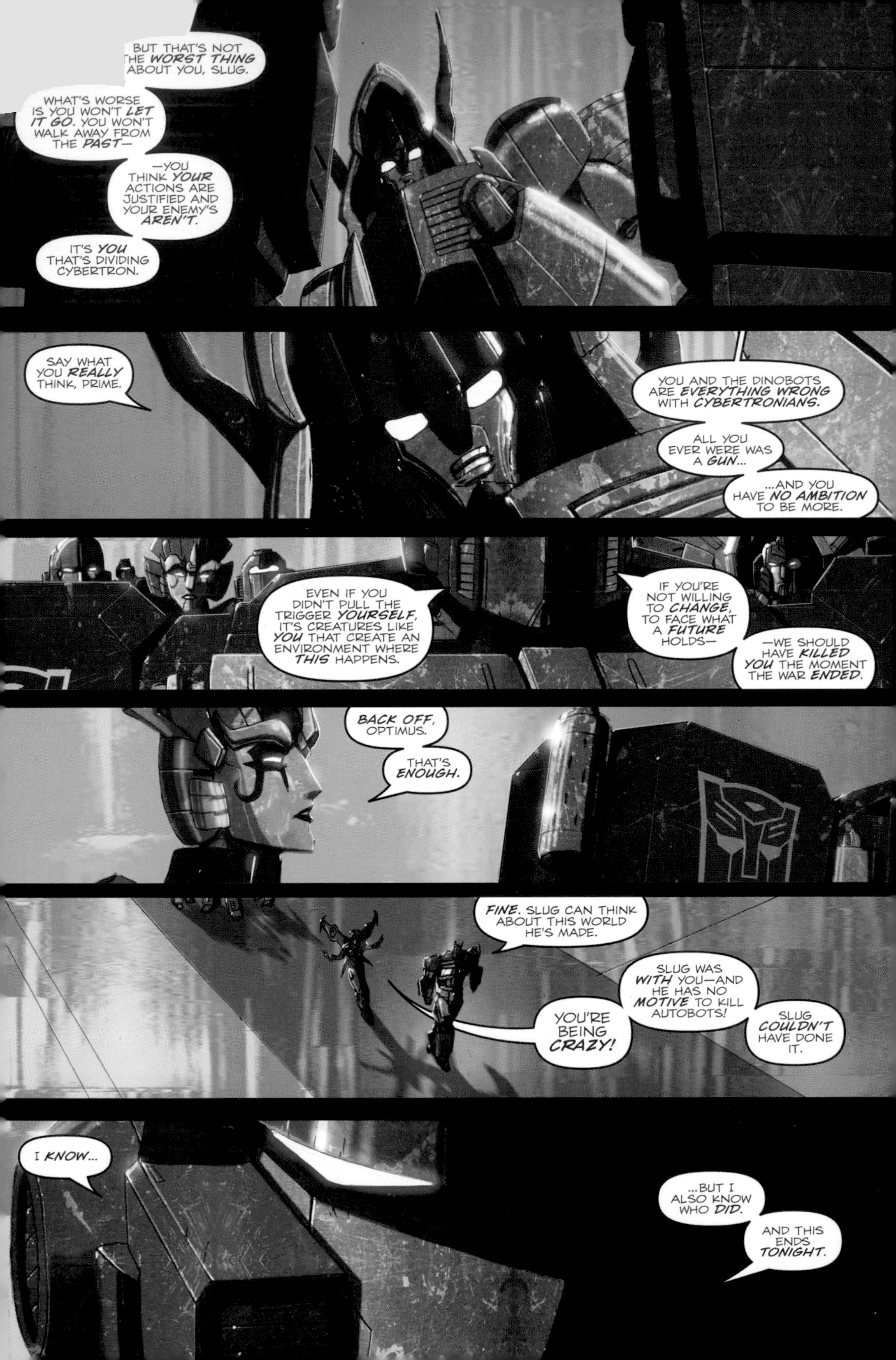
BUT THAT'S NOT THE WORST THING ABOUT YOU, SLUG.
WHAT'S WORSE IS YOU WON'T LET IT GO. YOU WON'T WALK AWAY FROM THE PAST—
—YOU THINK YOUR ACTIONS ARE JUSTIFIED AND YOUR ENEMY'S AREN'T.
IT'S YOU THAT'S DIVIDING CYBERTRON.
SAY WHAT YOU REALLY THINK, PRIME.
YOU AND THE DINOBOTS ARE EVERYTHING WRONG WITH CYBERTRONIANS.
ALL YOU EVER WERE WAS A GUN...
...AND YOU HAVE NO AMBITION TO BE MORE.
EVEN IF YOU DIDN'T PULL THE TRIGGER YOURSELF, IT'S CREATURES LIKE YOU THAT CREATE AN ENVIRONMENT WHERE THIS HAPPENS.
IF YOU'RE NOT WILLING TO CHANGE, TO FACE WHAT A FUTURE HOLDS—
—WE SHOULD HAVE KILLED YOU THE MOMENT THE WAR ENDED.
BACK OFF, OPTIMUS.
THAT'S ENOUGH.
FINE. SLUG CAN THINK ABOUT THIS WORLD HE'S MADE.
YOU'RE BEING CRAZY!
SLUG WAS WITH YOU—AND HE HAS NO MOTIVE TO KILL AUTOBOTS!
SLUG COULDN'T HAVE DONE IT.
I KNOW...
...BUT I ALSO KNOW WHO DID.
AND THIS ENDS TONIGHT.

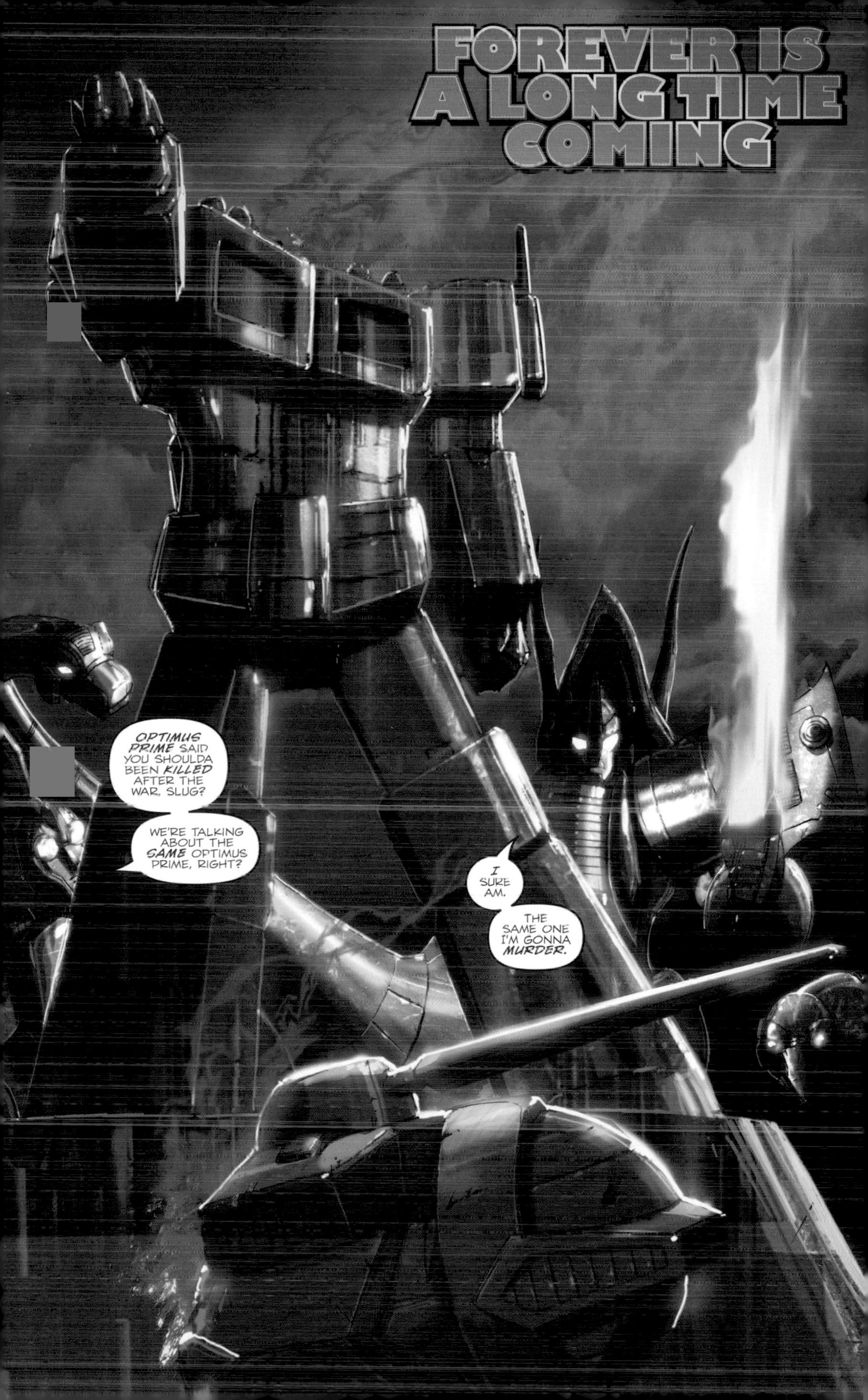
FOREVER IS A LONG TIME COMING
OPTIMUS PRIME SAID YOU SHOULDA BEEN KILLED AFTER THE WAR, SLUG?
WE'RE TALKING ABOUT THE SAME OPTIMUS PRIME, RIGHT?
I SURE AM.
THE SAME ONE I'M GONNA MURDER.

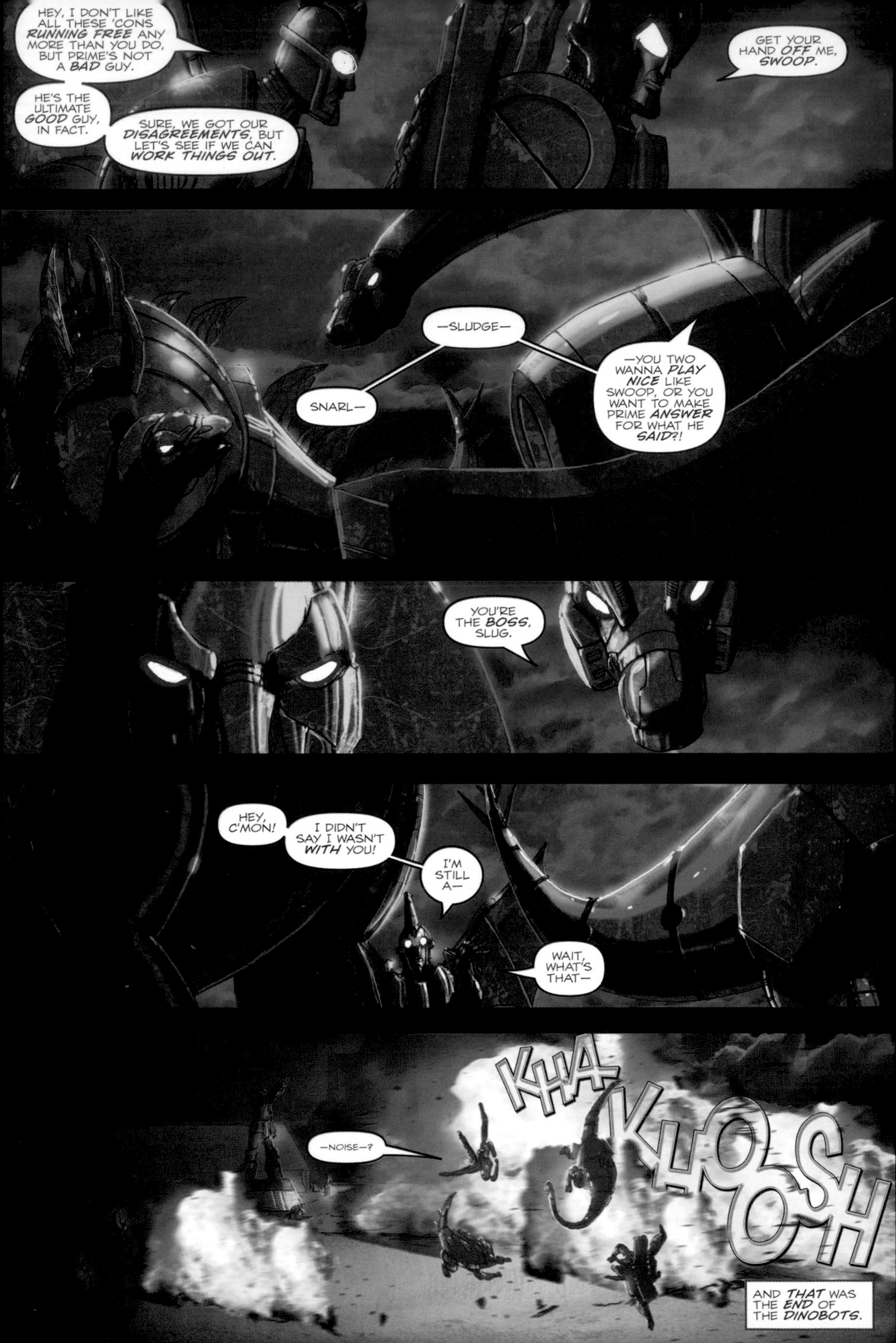
HEY, I DON'T LIKE ALL THESE 'CONS RUNNING FREE ANY MORE THAN YOU DO, BUT PRIME'S NOT A BAD GUY.
HE'S THE ULTIMATE GOOD GUY, IN FACT.
SURE, WE GOT OUR DISAGREEMENTS, BUT LET'S SEE IF WE CAN WORK THINGS OUT.
GET YOUR HAND OFF ME, SWOOP.
SNARL—
—SLUDGE—
—YOU TWO WANNA PLAY NICE LIKE SWOOP, OR YOU WANT TO MAKE PRIME ANSWER FOR WHAT HE SAID?!
YOU'RE THE BOSS, SLUG.
HEY, C'MON!
I DIDN'T SAY I WASN'T WITH YOU!
I'M STILL A—
WAIT, WHAT'S THAT—
—NOISE—?
KHA KHOOSH
AND THAT WAS THE END OF THE DINOBOTS.

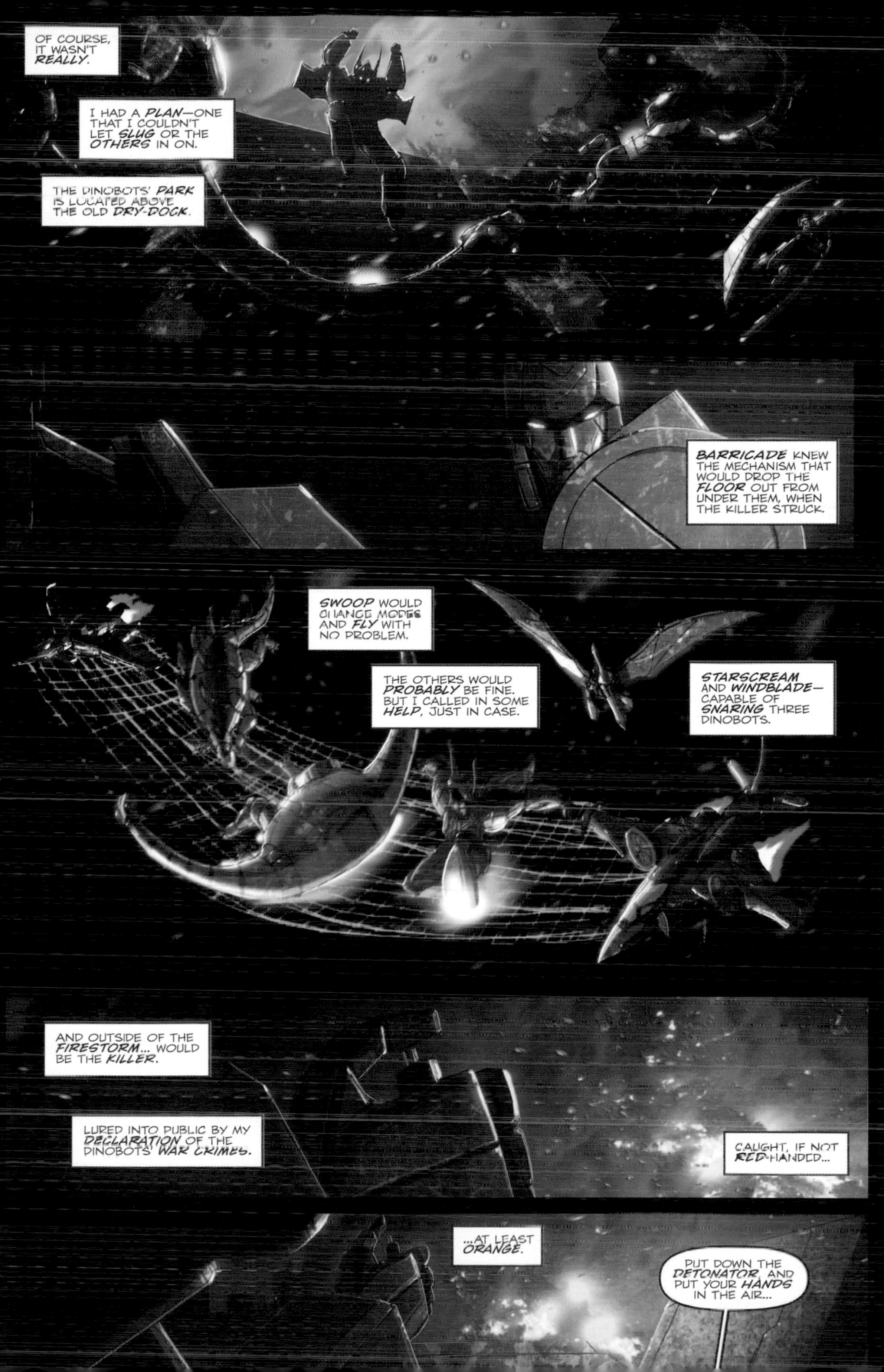
OF COURSE, IT WASN'T REALLY.
I HAD A PLAN—ONE THAT I COULDN'T LET SLUG OR THE OTHERS IN ON.
THE DINOBOTS' PARK IS LOCATED ABOVE THE OLD DRY-DOCK.
BARRICADE KNEW THE MECHANISM THAT WOULD DROP THE FLOOR OUT FROM UNDER THEM, WHEN THE KILLER STRUCK.
SWOOP WOULD CHANGE MODES AND FLY WITH NO PROBLEM.
THE OTHERS WOULD PROBABLY BE FINE. BUT I CALLED IN SOME HELP, JUST IN CASE.
STARSCREAM AND WINDBLADE—CAPABLE OF SNARING THREE DINOBOTS.
AND OUTSIDE OF THE FIRESTORM... WOULD BE THE KILLER.
LURED INTO PUBLIC BY MY DECLARATION OF THE DINOBOTS' WAR CRIMES.
CAUGHT, IF NOT RED-HANDED...
...AT LEAST ORANGE.
PUT DOWN THE DETONATOR, AND PUT YOUR HANDS IN THE AIR...

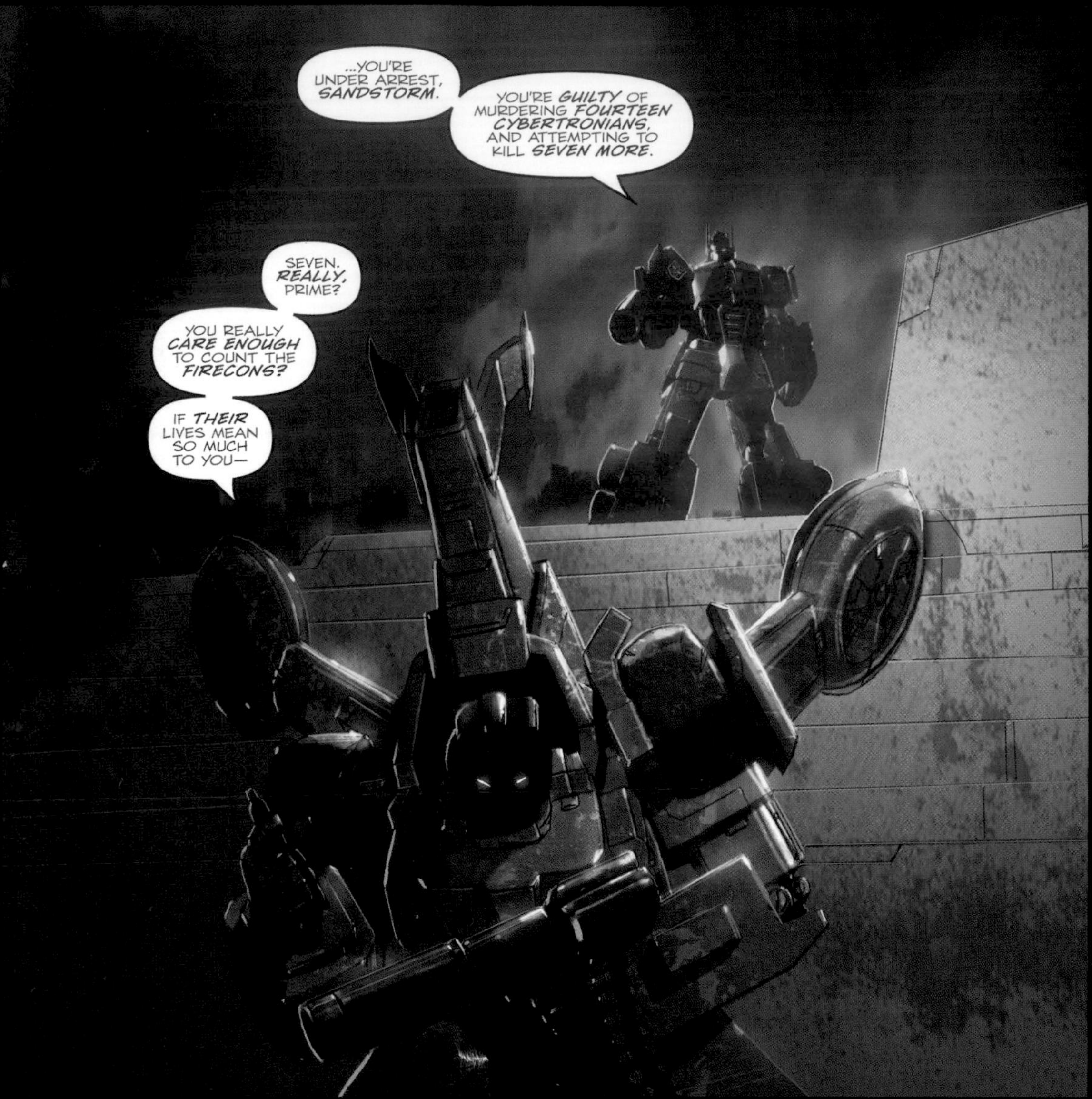
...YOU'RE UNDER ARREST, SANDSTORM.
YOU'RE GUILTY OF MURDERING FOURTEEN CYBERTRONIANS, AND ATTEMPTING TO KILL SEVEN MORE.
SEVEN. REALLY, PRIME?
YOU REALLY CARE ENOUGH TO COUNT THE FIRECONS?
IF THEIR LIVES MEAN SO MUCH TO YOU—

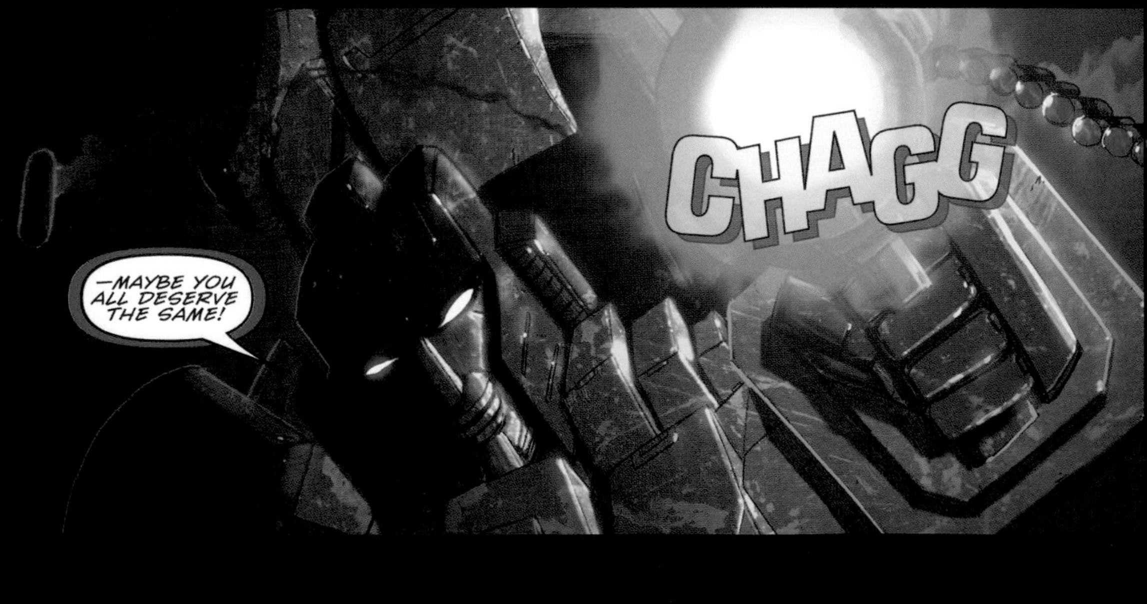
CHAGG
—MAYBE YOU ALL DESERVE THE SAME!

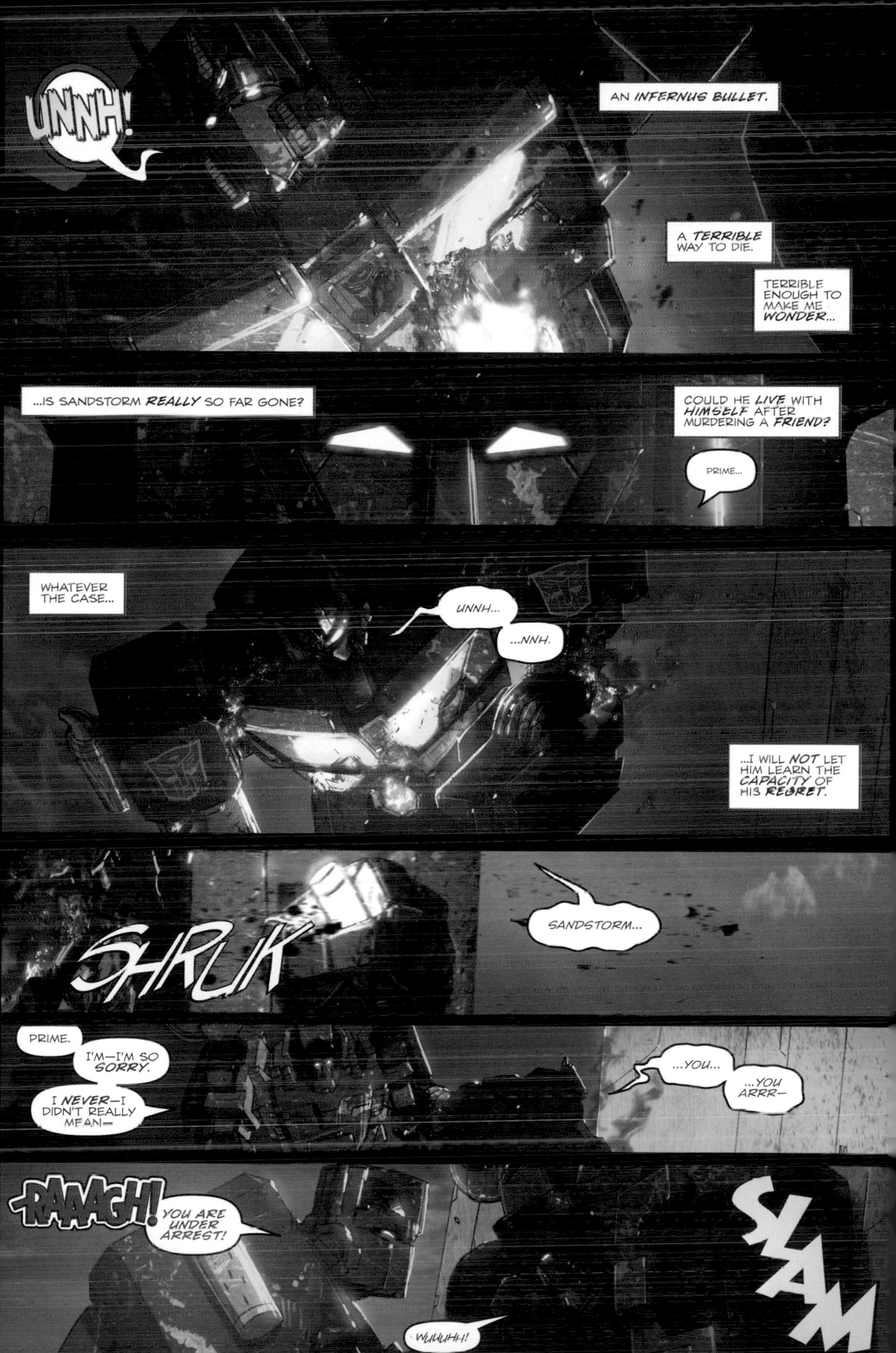
UNNH!
AN INFERNUS BULLET.
A TERRIBLE WAY TO DIE.
TERRIBLE ENOUGH TO MAKE ME WONDER...
...IS SANDSTORM REALLY SO FAR GONE?
COULD HE LIVE WITH HIMSELF AFTER MURDERING A FRIEND?
PRIME...
WHATEVER THE CASE...
UNNH...
...NNH.
...I WILL NOT LET HIM LEARN THE CAPACITY OF HIS REGRET.
SHRUK
SANDSTORM...
PRIME.
I'M—I'M SO SORRY.
I NEVER—I DIDN'T REALLY MEAN—
...YOU...
...YOU ARRR—
RAAAGH!
YOU ARE UNDER ARREST!
SLAM
WUUUHH!

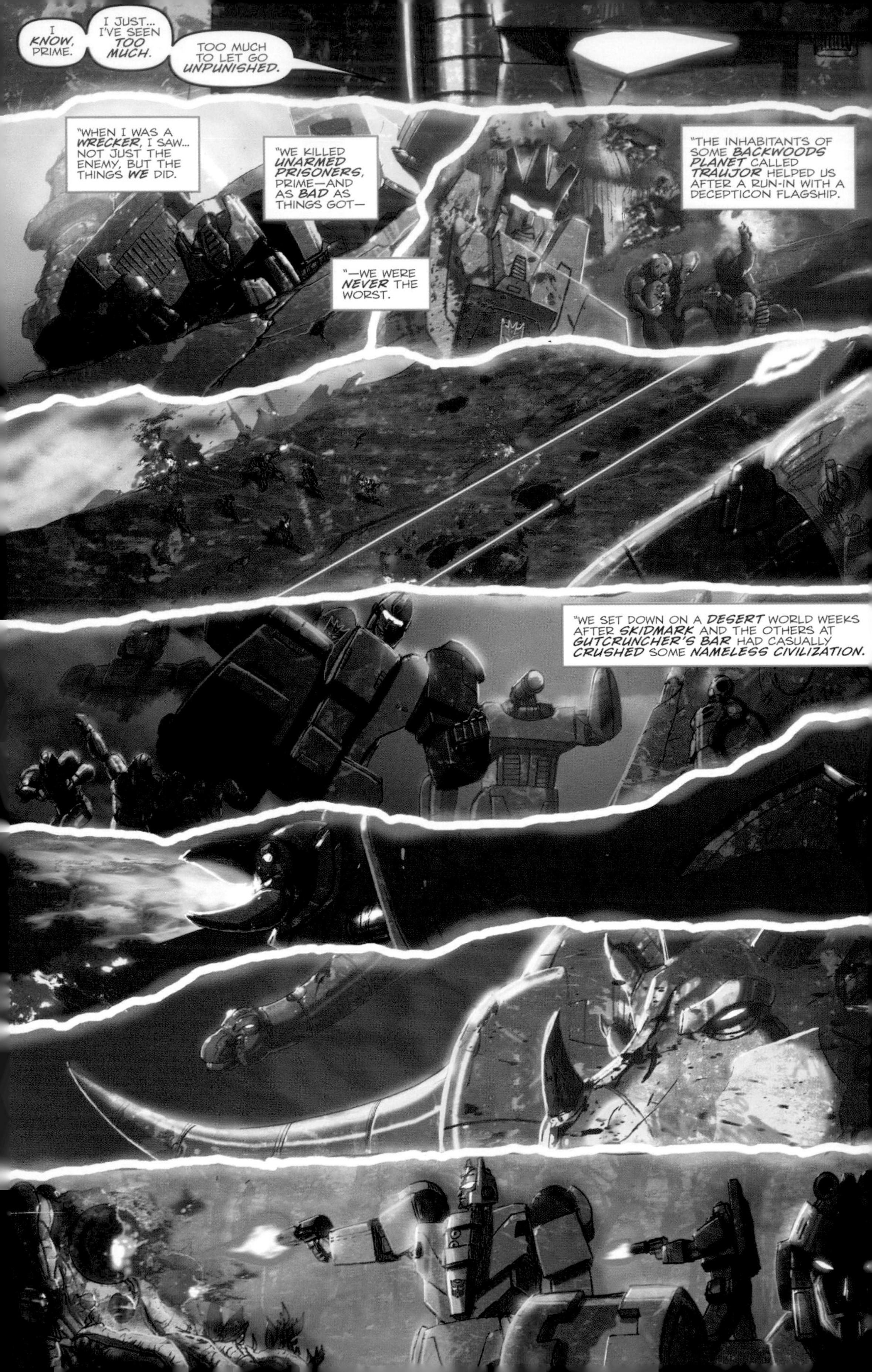

I KNOW, PRIME.
I JUST... I'VE SEEN TOO MUCH.
TOO MUCH TO LET GO UNPUNISHED.
"WHEN I WAS A WRECKER, I SAW... NOT JUST THE ENEMY, BUT THE THINGS WE DID.
"WE KILLED UNARMED PRISONERS, PRIME—AND AS BAD AS THINGS GOT—
"—WE WERE NEVER THE WORST.
"THE INHABITANTS OF SOME BACKWOODS PLANET CALLED TRAUJOR HELPED US AFTER A RUN-IN WITH A DECEPTICON FLAGSHIP.
"WE SET DOWN ON A DESERT WORLD WEEKS AFTER SKIDMARK AND THE OTHERS AT GUTCRUNCHER'S BAR HAD CASUALLY CRUSHED SOME NAMELESS CIVILIZATION.

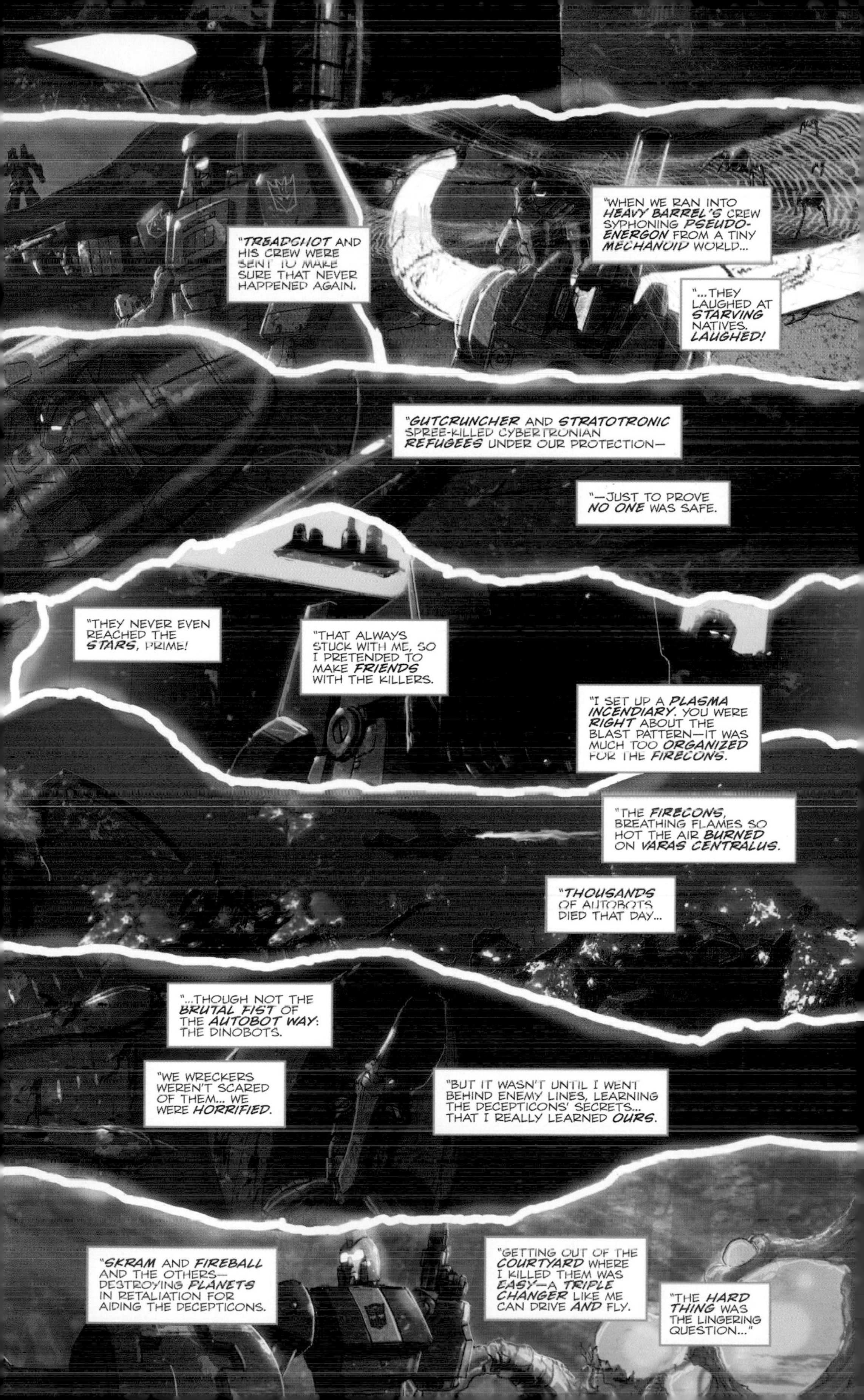
"TREADSHOT AND HIS CREW WERE SENT TO MAKE SURE THAT NEVER HAPPENED AGAIN.
"WHEN WE RAN INTO HEAVY BARREL'S CREW SYPHONING PSEUDO-ENERGON FROM A TINY MECHANOID WORLD...
"...THEY LAUGHED AT STARVING NATIVES. LAUGHED!
"GUTCRUNCHER AND STRATOTRONIC SPREE-KILLED CYBERTRONIAN REFUGEES UNDER OUR PROTECTION—
"—JUST TO PROVE NO ONE WAS SAFE.
"THEY NEVER EVEN REACHED THE STARS, PRIME!
"THAT ALWAYS STUCK WITH ME, SO I PRETENDED TO MAKE FRIENDS WITH THE KILLERS.
"I SET UP A PLASMA INCENDIARY. YOU WERE RIGHT ABOUT THE BLAST PATTERN—IT WAS MUCH TOO ORGANIZED FOR THE FIRECONS.
"THE FIRECONS, BREATHING FLAMES SO HOT THE AIR BURNED ON VARAS CENTRALUS.
"THOUSANDS OF AUTOBOTS DIED THAT DAY...
"...THOUGH NOT THE BRUTAL FIST OF THE AUTOBOT WAY: THE DINOBOTS.
"WE WRECKERS WEREN'T SCARED OF THEM... WE WERE HORRIFIED.
"BUT IT WASN'T UNTIL I WENT BEHIND ENEMY LINES, LEARNING THE DECEPTICONS' SECRETS... THAT I REALLY LEARNED OURS.
"SKRAM AND FIREBALL AND THE OTHERS—DESTROYING PLANETS IN RETALIATION FOR AIDING THE DECEPTICONS.
"GETTING OUT OF THE COURTYARD WHERE I KILLED THEM WAS EASY—A TRIPLE CHANGER LIKE ME CAN DRIVE AND FLY.
"THE HARD THING WAS THE LINGERING QUESTION..."

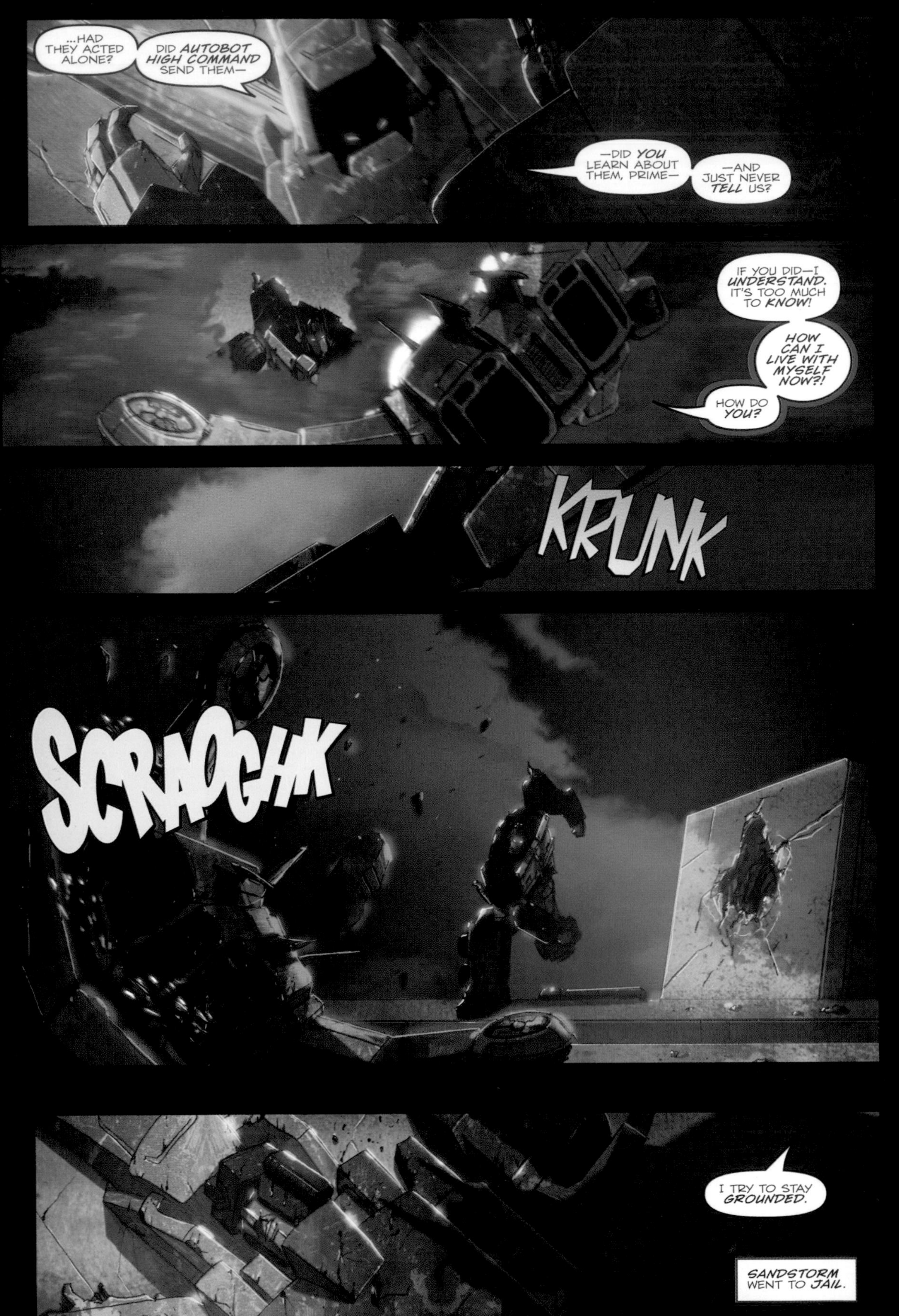
...HAD THEY ACTED ALONE?
DID AUTOBOT HIGH COMMAND SEND THEM—
—DID YOU LEARN ABOUT THEM, PRIME—
—AND JUST NEVER TELL US?
IF YOU DID—I UNDERSTAND. IT'S TOO MUCH TO KNOW!
HOW CAN I LIVE WITH MYSELF NOW?!
HOW DO YOU?
KRUNK
SCRAOGHK
I TRY TO STAY GROUNDED.
SANDSTORM WENT TO JAIL.

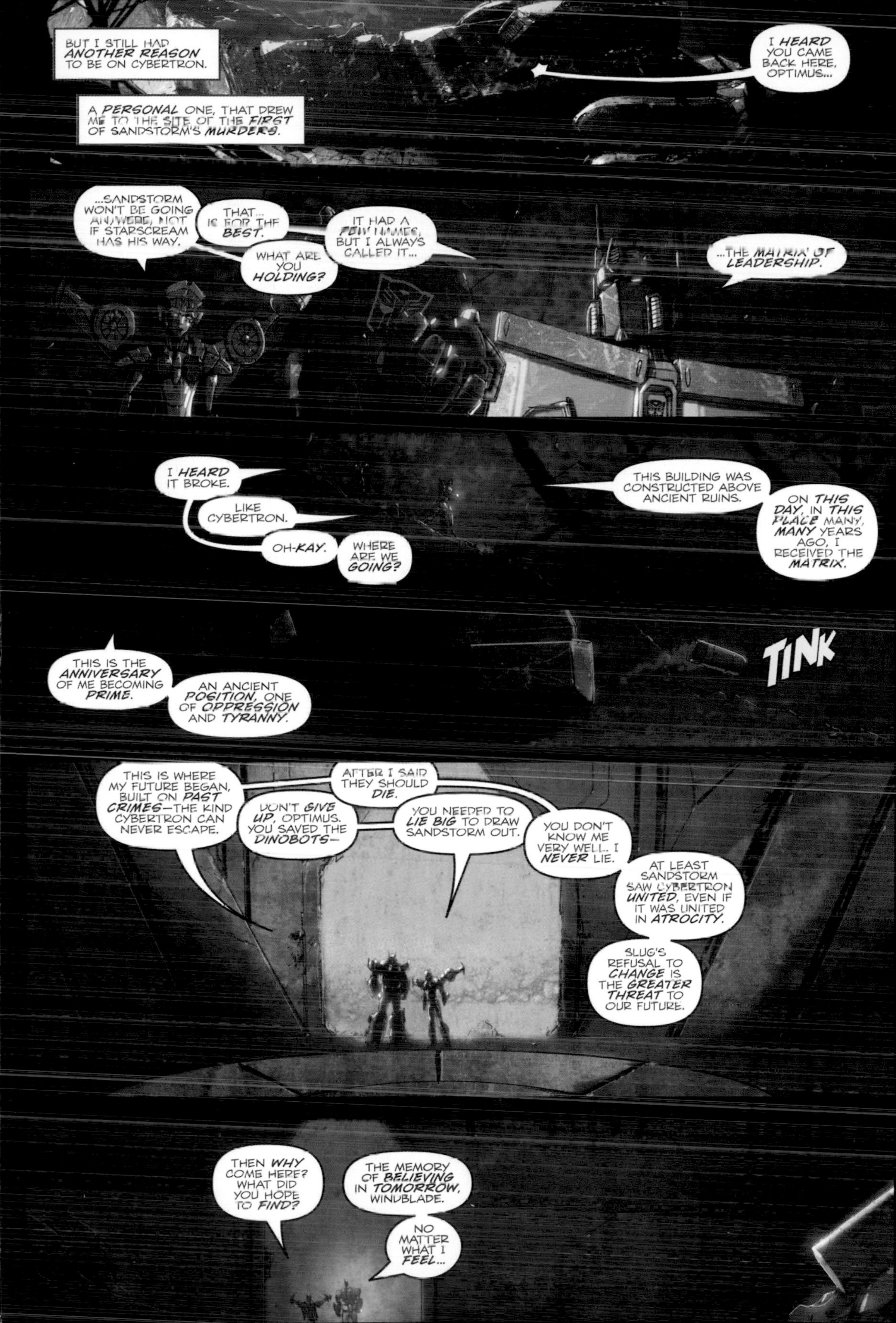
BUT I STILL HAD ANOTHER REASON TO BE ON CYBERTRON.
I HEARD YOU CAME BACK HERE, OPTIMUS...
A PERSONAL ONE, THAT DREW ME TO THE SITE OF THE FIRST OF SANDSTORM'S MURDERS.
...SANDSTORM WON'T BE GOING ANYWHERE, NOT IF STARSCREAM HAS HIS WAY.
THAT... IS FOR THE BEST.
WHAT ARE YOU HOLDING?
IT HAD A FEW NAMES, BUT I ALWAYS CALLED IT...
...THE MATRIX OF LEADERSHIP.
I HEARD IT BROKE.
LIKE CYBERTRON.
OH-KAY.
WHERE ARE WE GOING?
THIS BUILDING WAS CONSTRUCTED ABOVE ANCIENT RUINS.
ON THIS DAY, IN THIS PLACE MANY, MANY YEARS AGO, I RECEIVED THE MATRIX.
THIS IS THE ANNIVERSARY OF ME BECOMING PRIME.
AN ANCIENT POSITION, ONE OF OPPRESSION AND TYRANNY.
TINK
THIS IS WHERE MY FUTURE BEGAN, BUILT ON PAST CRIMES—THE KIND CYBERTRON CAN NEVER ESCAPE.
DON'T GIVE UP, OPTIMUS. YOU SAVED THE DINOBOTS—
AFTER I SAID THEY SHOULD DIE.
YOU NEEDED TO LIE BIG TO DRAW SANDSTORM OUT.
YOU DON'T KNOW ME VERY WELL.. I NEVER LIE.
AT LEAST SANDSTORM SAW CYBERTRON UNITED, EVEN IF IT WAS UNITED IN ATROCITY.
SLUG'S REFUSAL TO CHANGE IS THE GREATER THREAT TO OUR FUTURE.
THEN WHY COME HERE? WHAT DID YOU HOPE TO FIND?
THE MEMORY OF BELIEVING IN TOMORROW, WINDBLADE.
NO MATTER WHAT I FEEL...

...CYBERTRON NEEDS ME TO HOLD ON TO THAT.

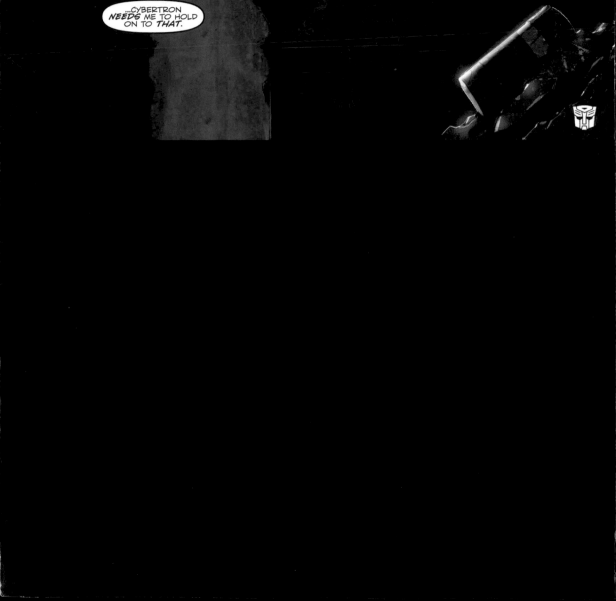

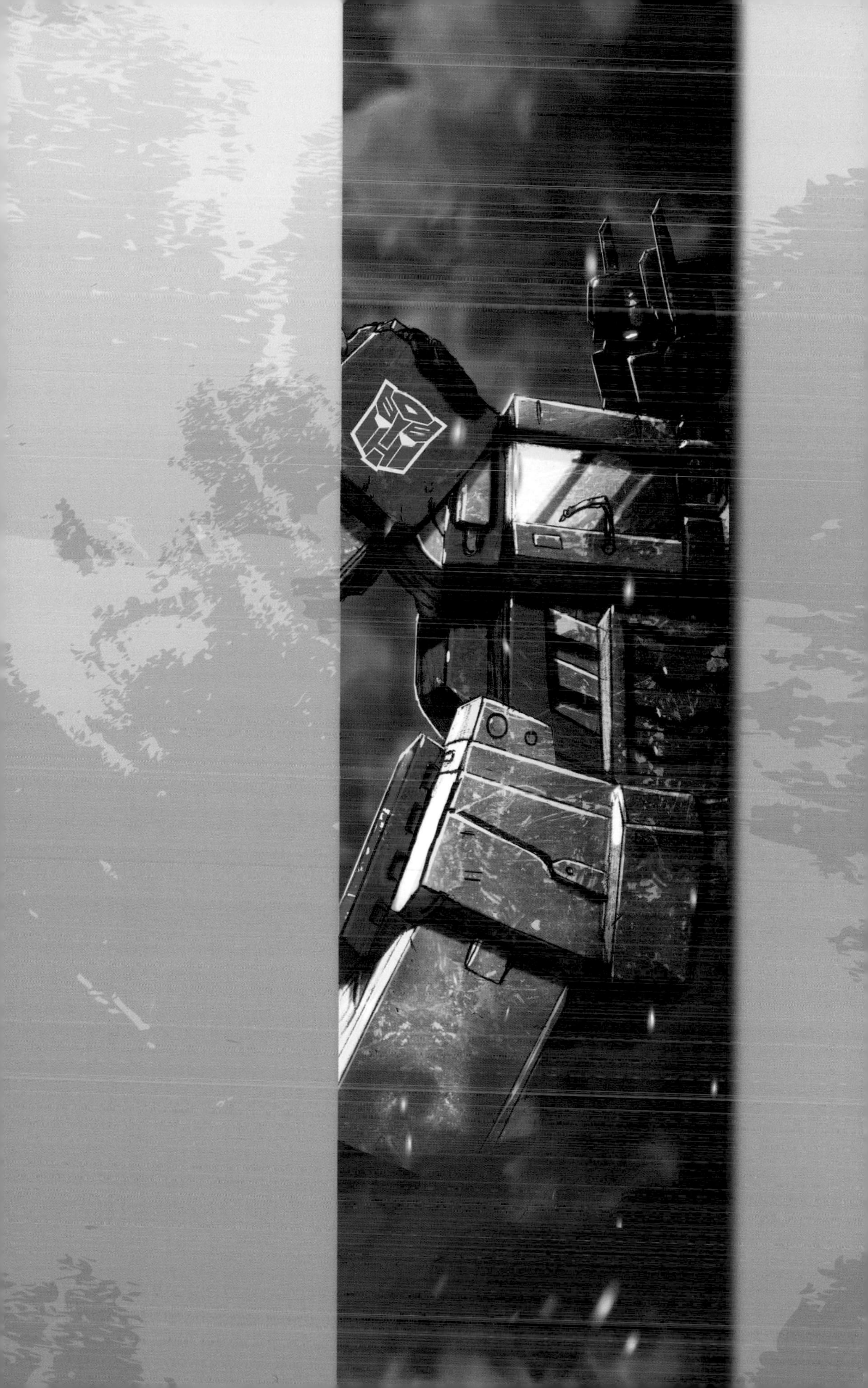

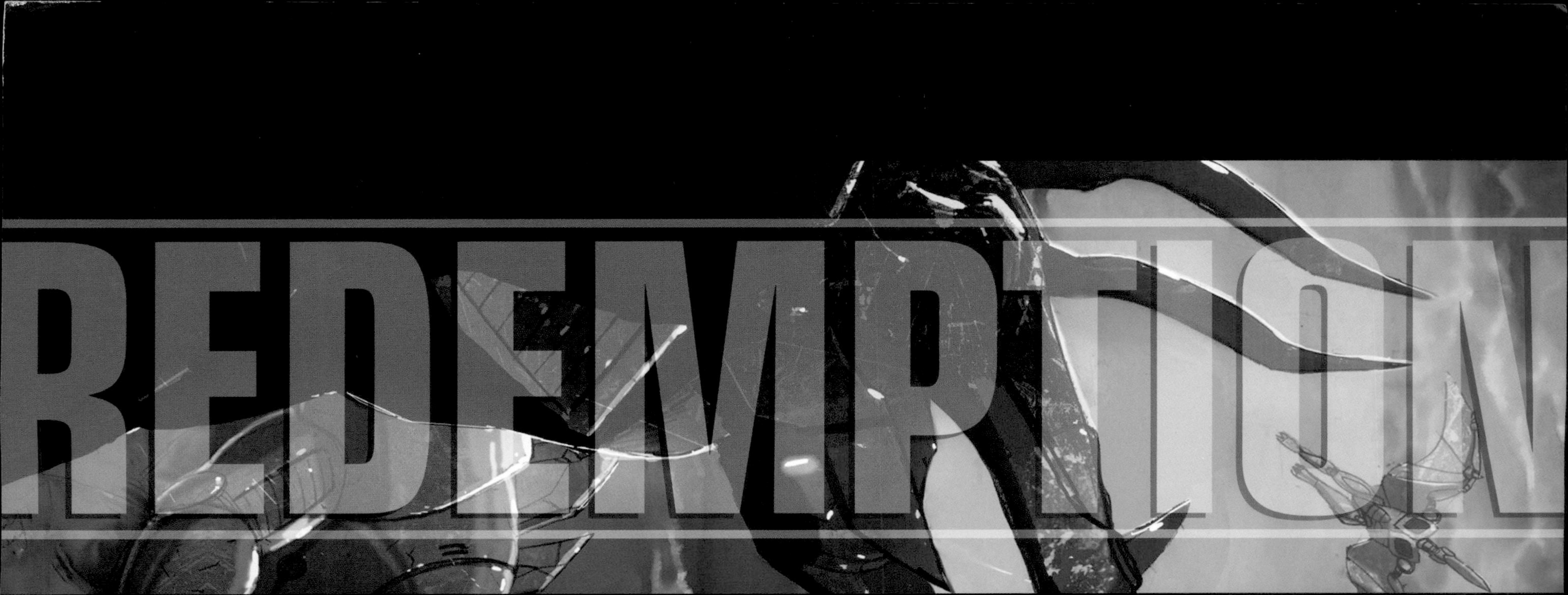
REDEMPTION

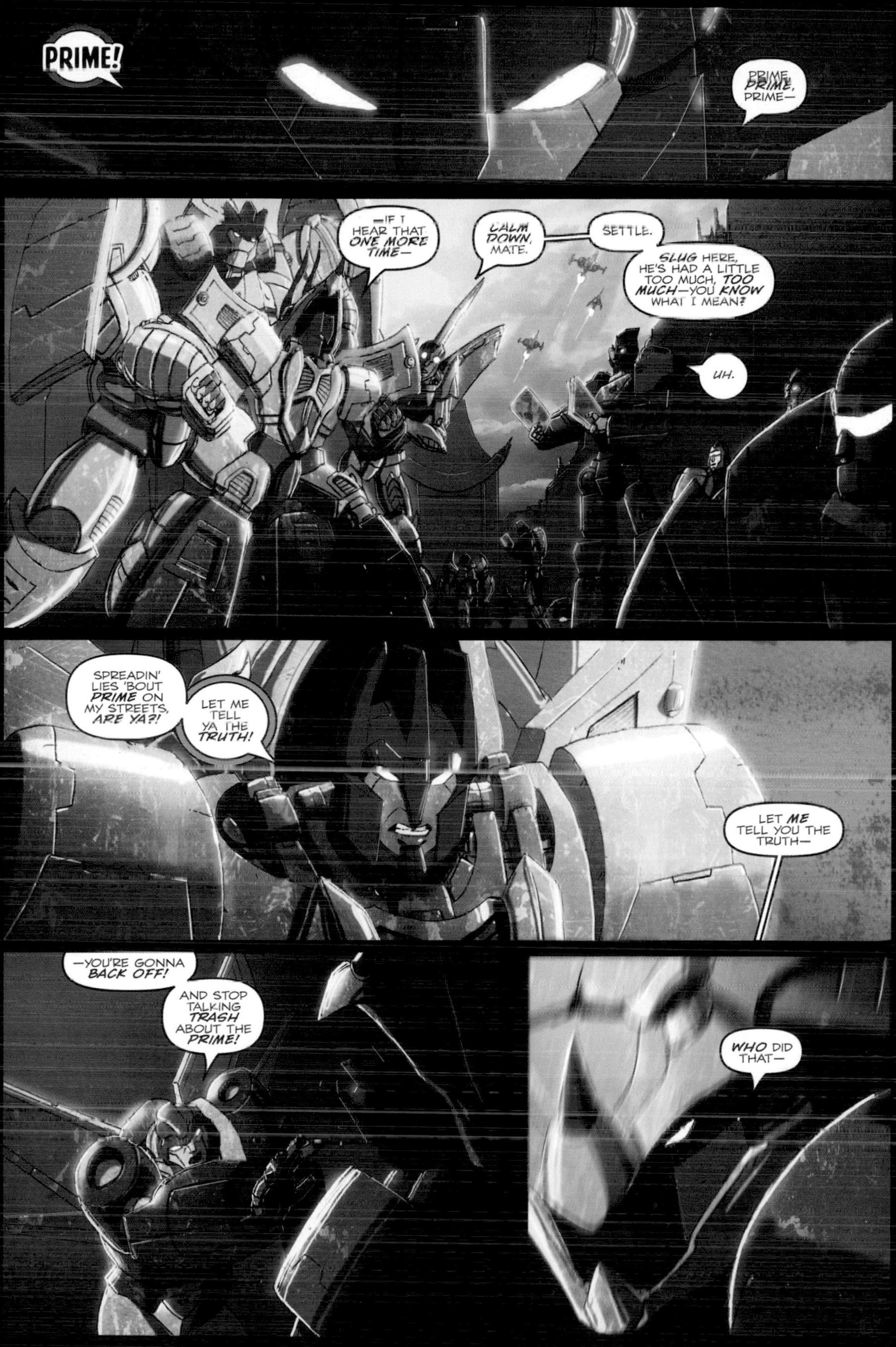
PRIME!
PRIME, PRIME, PRIME—
—IF I HEAR THAT ONE MORE TIME—
CALM DOWN, MATE.
SETTLE.
SLUG HERE, HE'S HAD A LITTLE TOO MUCH, TOO MUCH—YOU KNOW WHAT I MEAN?
UH.
SPREADIN' LIES 'BOUT PRIME ON MY STREETS, ARE YA?!
LET ME TELL YA THE TRUTH!
LET ME TELL YOU THE TRUTH—
—YOU'RE GONNA BACK OFF!
AND STOP TALKING TRASH ABOUT THE PRIME!
WHO DID THAT—

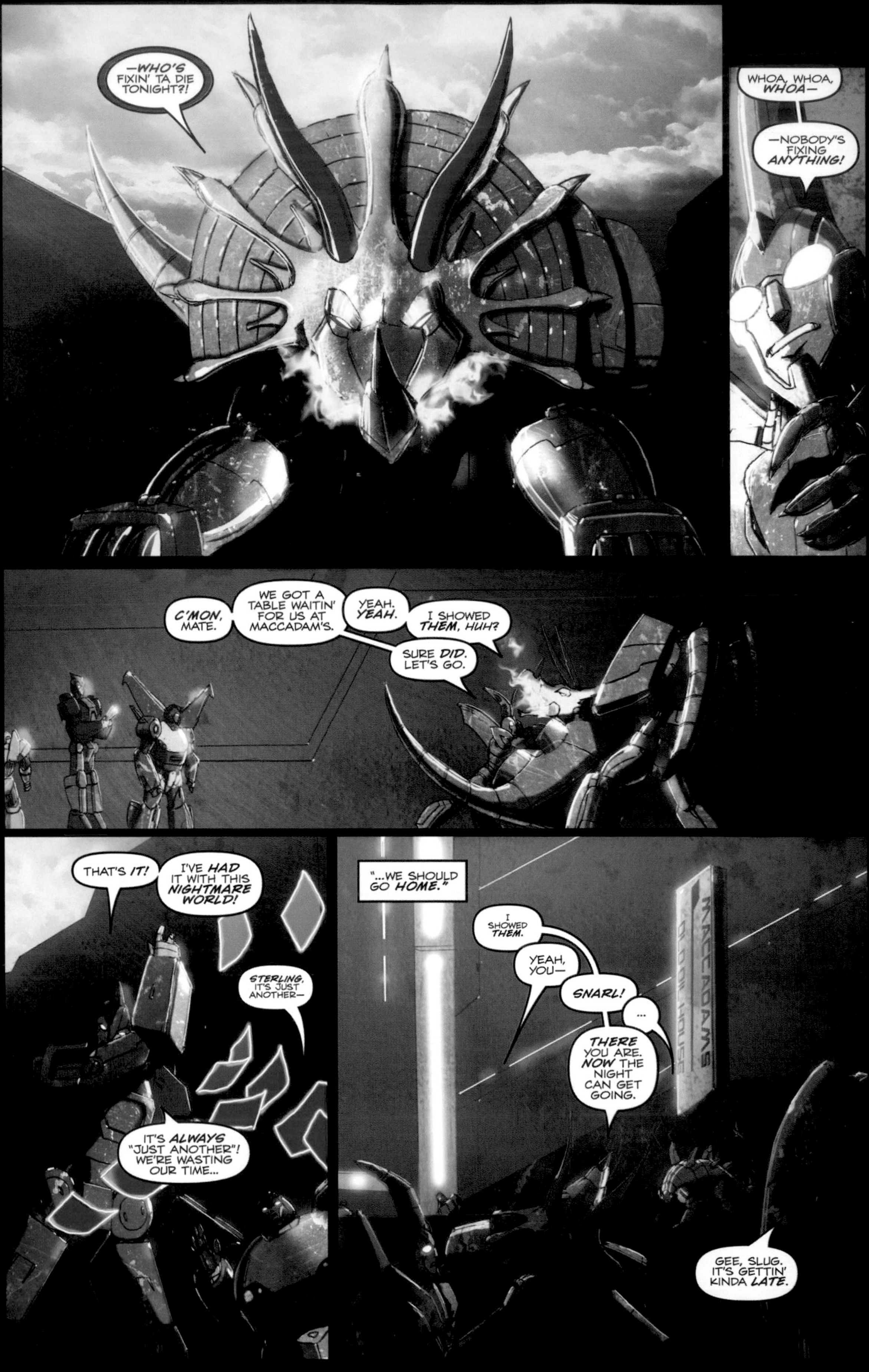

—WHO'S FIXIN' TA DIE TONIGHT?!
WHOA, WHOA, WHOA—
—NOBODY'S FIXING ANYTHING!
C'MON, MATE.
WE GOT A TABLE WAITIN' FOR US AT MACCADAM'S.
YEAH. YEAH.
I SHOWED THEM, HUH?
SURE DID. LET'S GO.
THAT'S IT!
I'VE HAD IT WITH THIS NIGHTMARE WORLD!
STERLING, IT'S JUST ANOTHER—
IT'S ALWAYS "JUST ANOTHER"! WE'RE WASTING OUR TIME...
"...WE SHOULD GO HOME."
I SHOWED THEM.
YEAH, YOU—
SNARL!
...
THERE YOU ARE. NOW THE NIGHT CAN GET GOING.
MACCADAM'S OLD OIL HOUSE
GEE, SLUG. IT'S GETTIN' KINDA LATE.

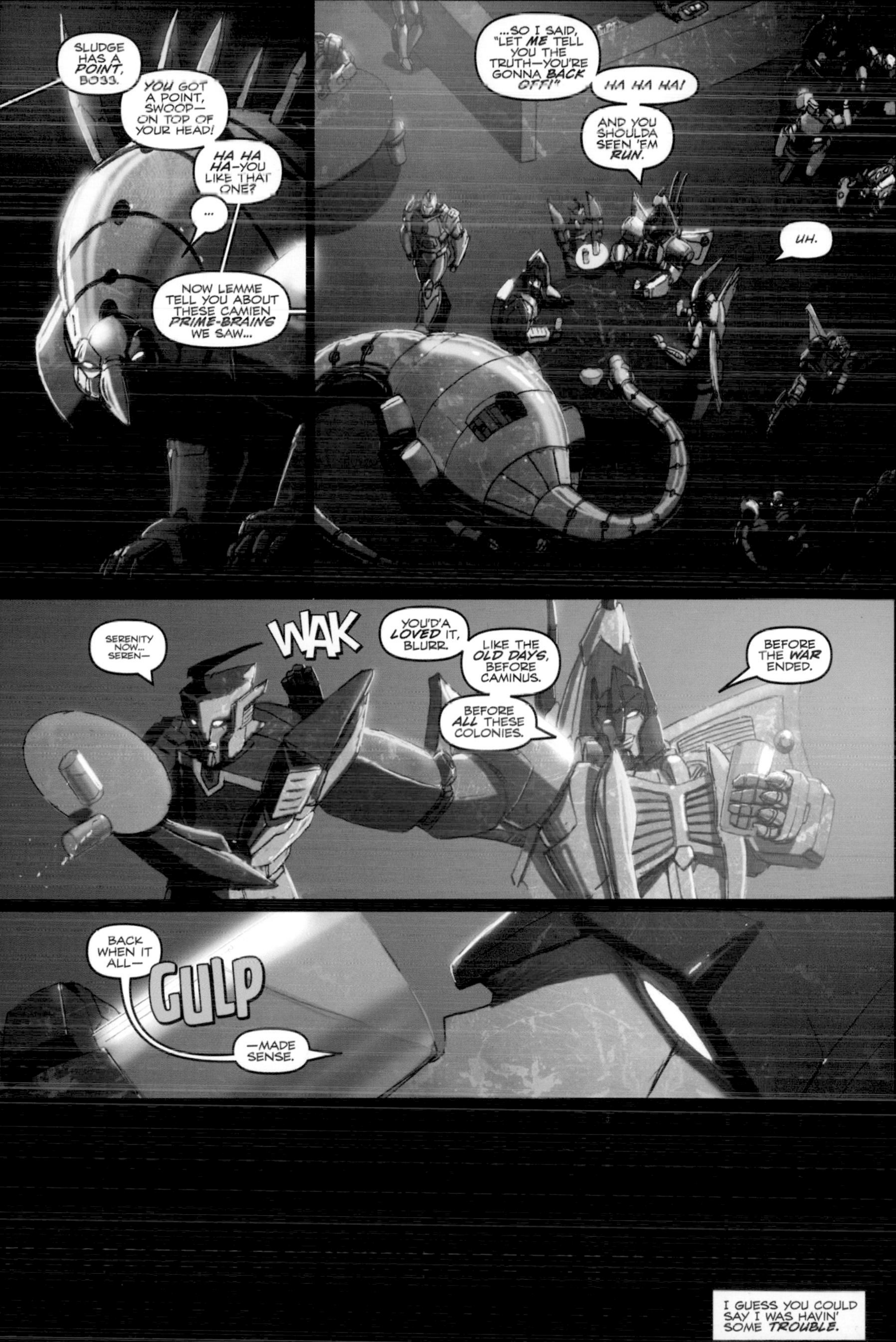
SLUDGE HAS A POINT, BOSS.
YOU GOT A POINT, SWOOP— ON TOP OF YOUR HEAD!
HA HA HA–YOU LIKE THAT ONE?
...
NOW LEMME TELL YOU ABOUT THESE CAMIEN PRIME-BRAINS WE SAW...
...SO I SAID, "LET ME TELL YOU THE TRUTH—YOU'RE GONNA BACK OFF!"
HA HA HA!
AND YOU SHOULDA SEEN 'EM RUN.
UH.
SERENITY NOW... SEREN—
WAK
YOU'D'A LOVED IT, BLURR.
LIKE THE OLD DAYS, BEFORE CAMINUS.
BEFORE ALL THESE COLONIES.
BEFORE THE WAR ENDED.
BACK WHEN IT ALL—
GULP
—MADE SENSE.
I GUESS YOU COULD SAY I WAS HAVIN' SOME TROUBLE.

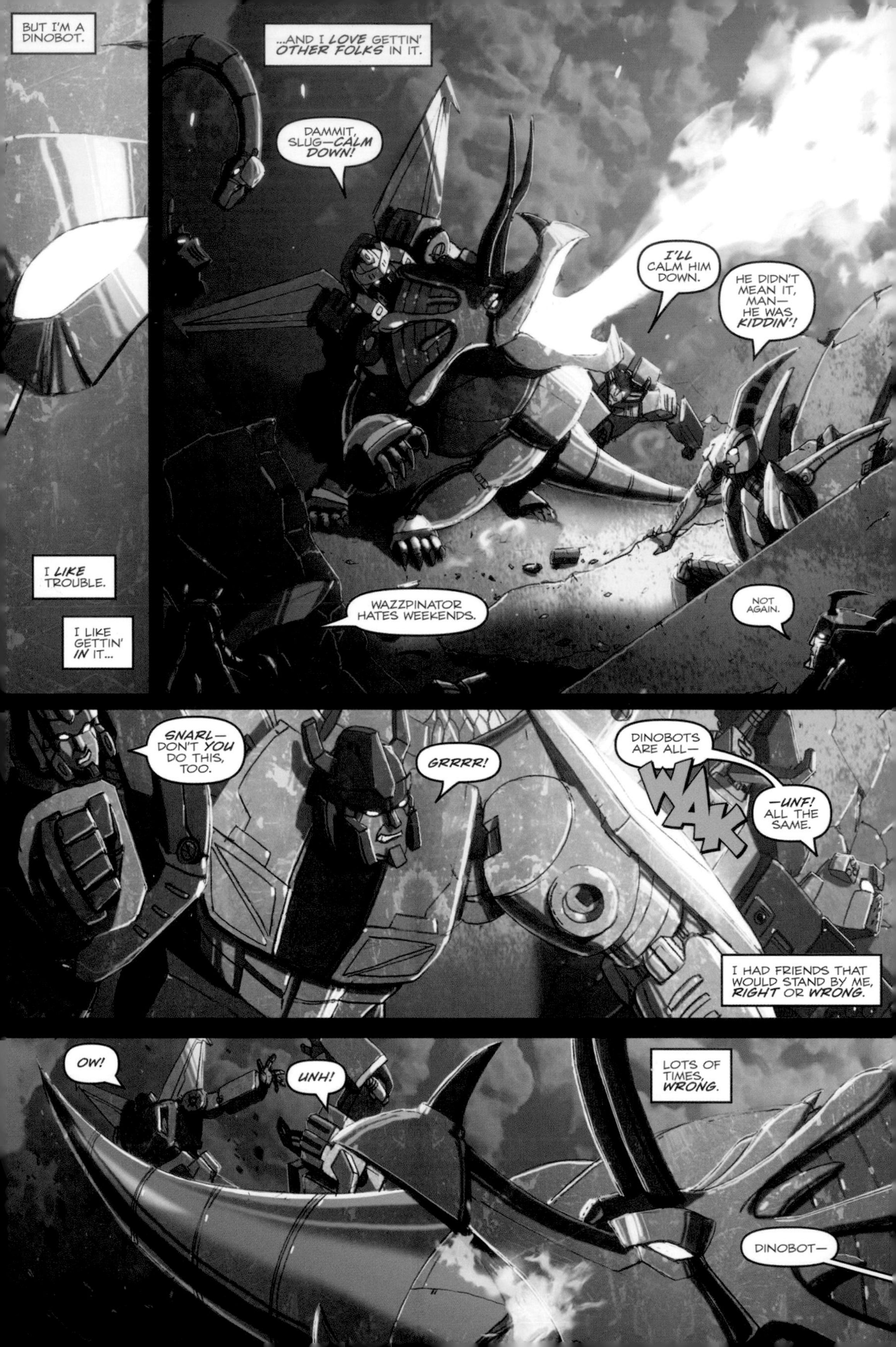
BUT I'M A DINOBOT.
I LIKE TROUBLE.
I LIKE GETTIN' IN IT...
...AND I LOVE GETTIN' OTHER FOLKS IN IT.
DAMMIT, SLUG—CALM DOWN!
I'LL CALM HIM DOWN.
HE DIDN'T MEAN IT, MAN—HE WAS KIDDIN'!
WAZZPINATOR HATES WEEKENDS.
NOT AGAIN.
SNARL—DON'T YOU DO THIS, TOO.
GRRRR!
DINOBOTS ARE ALL—
WAK
—UNF! ALL THE SAME.
I HAD FRIENDS THAT WOULD STAND BY ME, RIGHT OR WRONG.
OW!
UNH!
LOTS OF TIMES, WRONG.
DINOBOT—

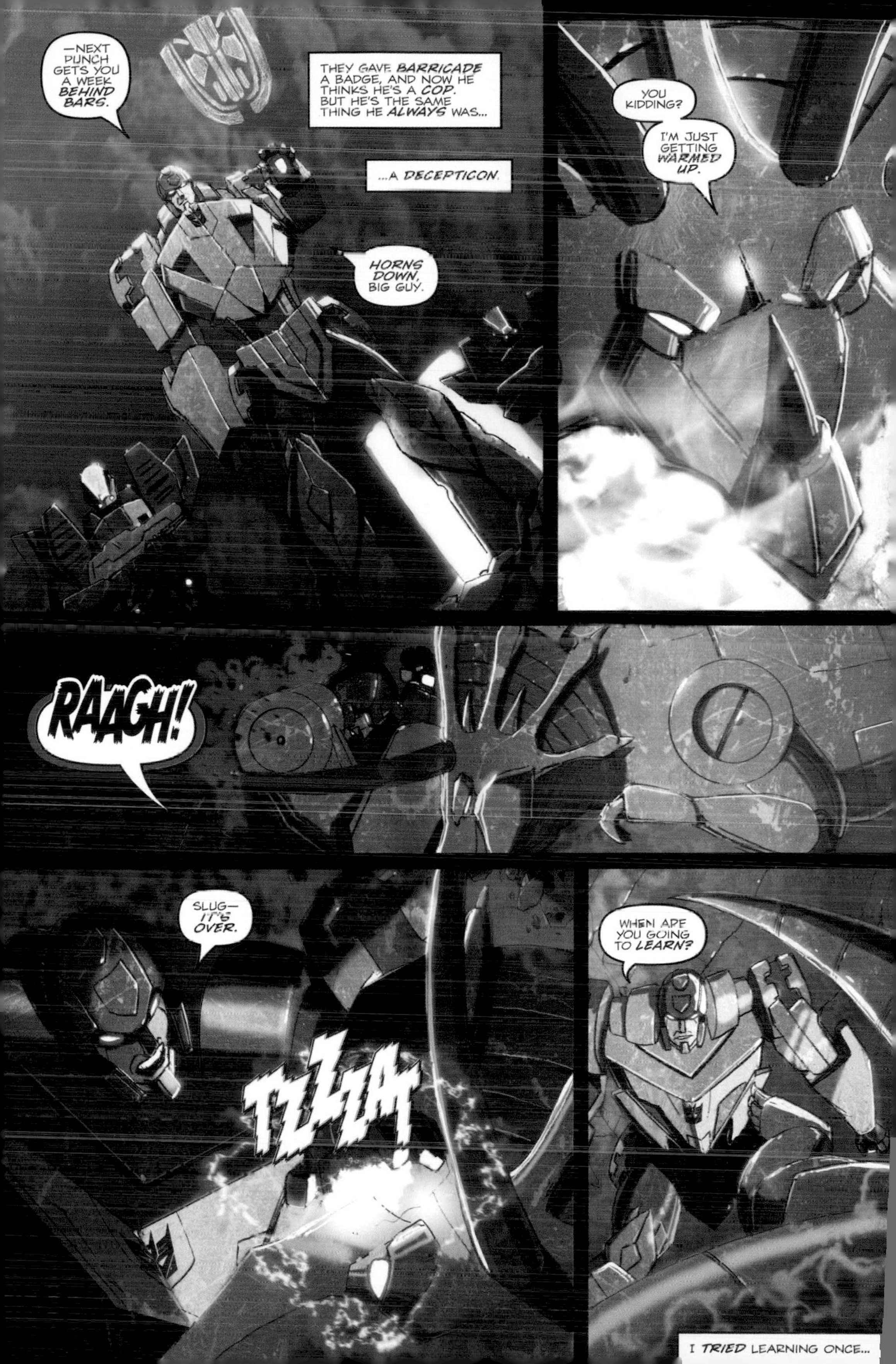
—NEXT PUNCH GETS YOU A WEEK BEHIND BARS.
THEY GAVE BARRICADE A BADGE, AND NOW HE THINKS HE'S A COP. BUT HE'S THE SAME THING HE ALWAYS WAS...
...A DECEPTICON.
HORNS DOWN, BIG GUY.
YOU KIDDING?
I'M JUST GETTING WARMED UP.
RAAGH!
SLUG— IT'S OVER.
TZZZAT
WHEN ARE YOU GOING TO LEARN?
I TRIED LEARNING ONCE...

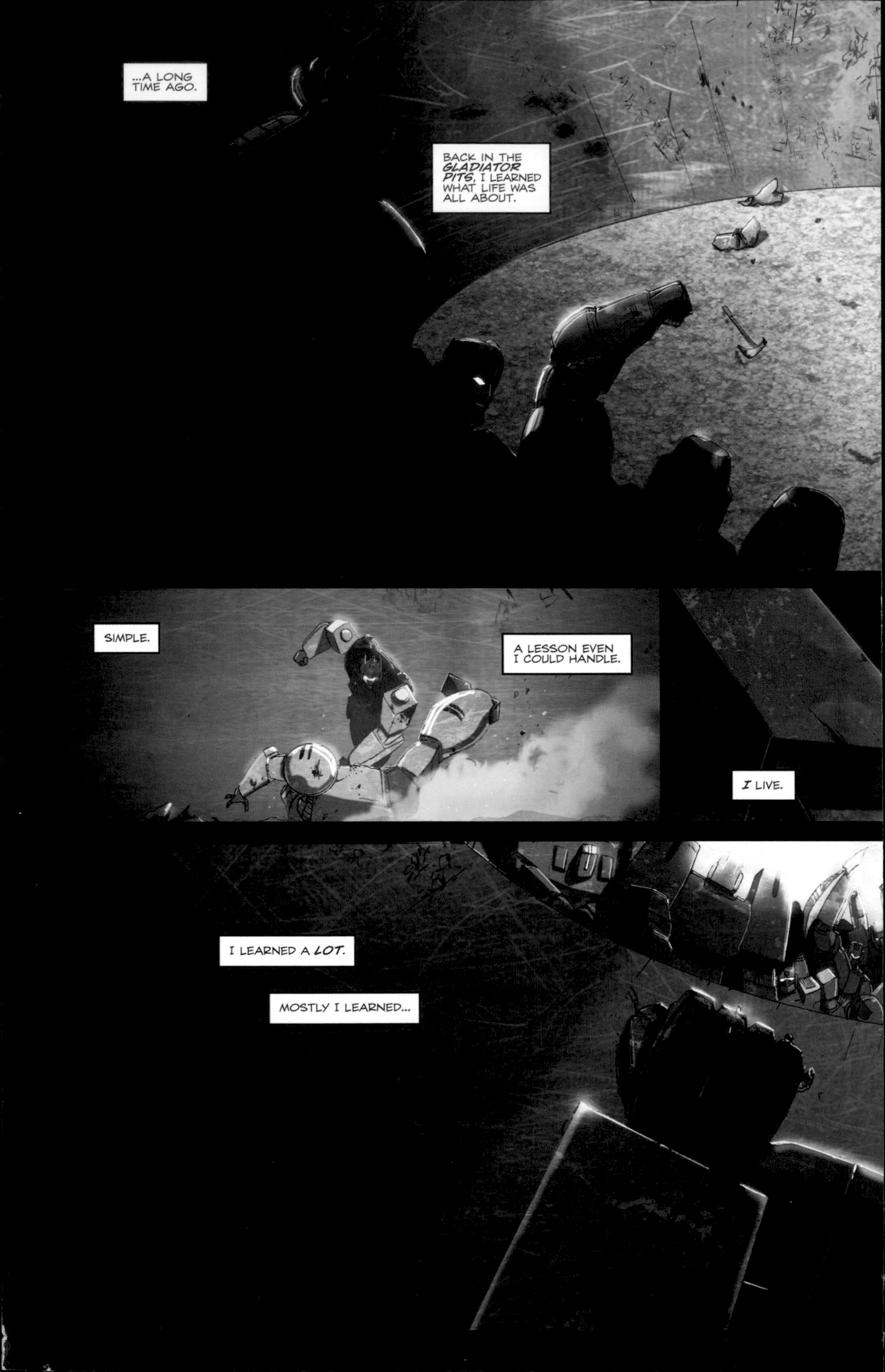
...A LONG TIME AGO.
BACK IN THE *GLADIATOR PITS*, I LEARNED WHAT LIFE WAS ALL ABOUT.
SIMPLE.
A LESSON EVEN I COULD HANDLE.
*I* LIVE.
I LEARNED A *LOT*.
MOSTLY I LEARNED...

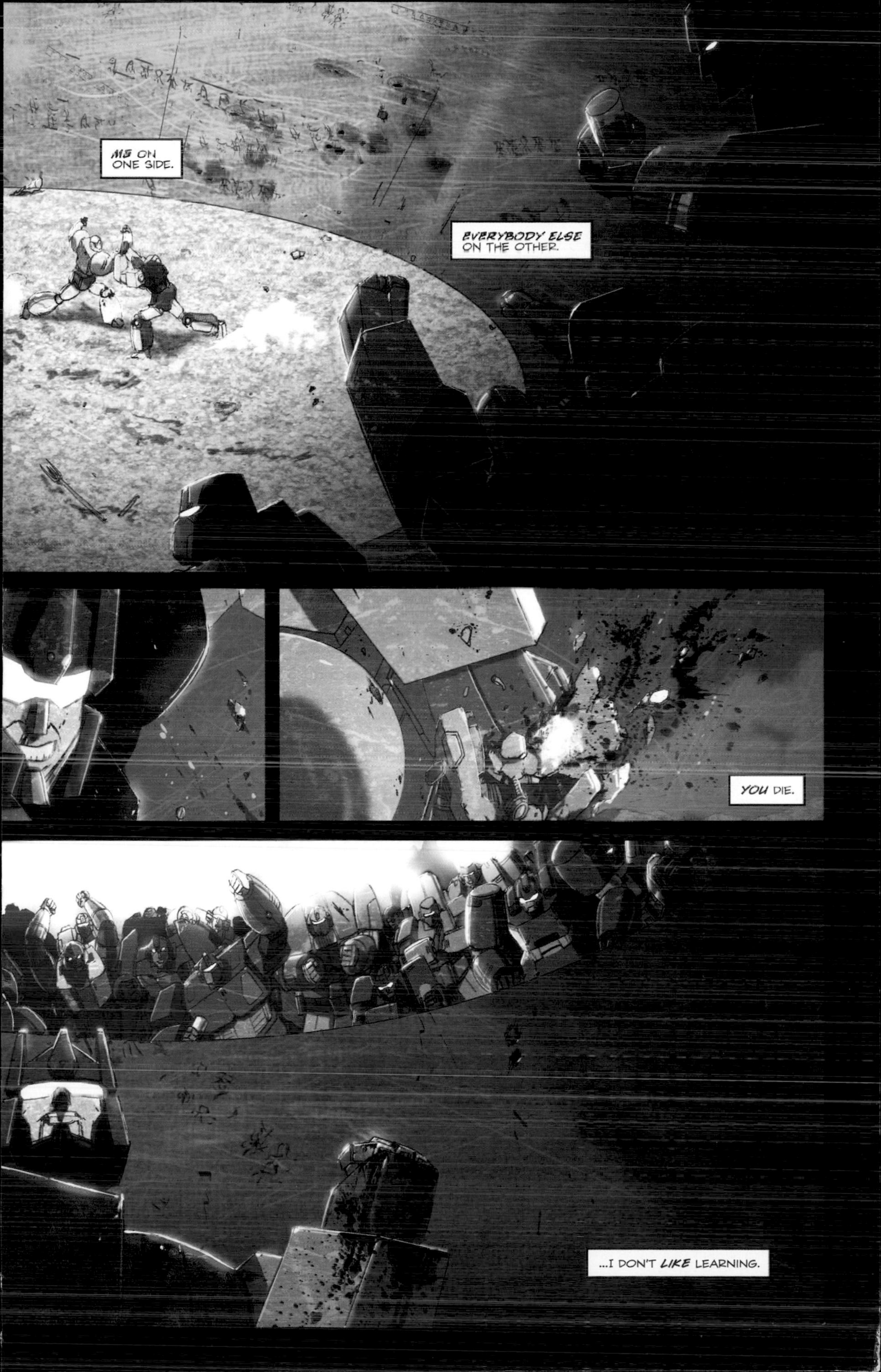

ME ON ONE SIDE.
EVERYBODY ELSE ON THE OTHER.
YOU DIE.
...I DON'T LIKE LEARNING.

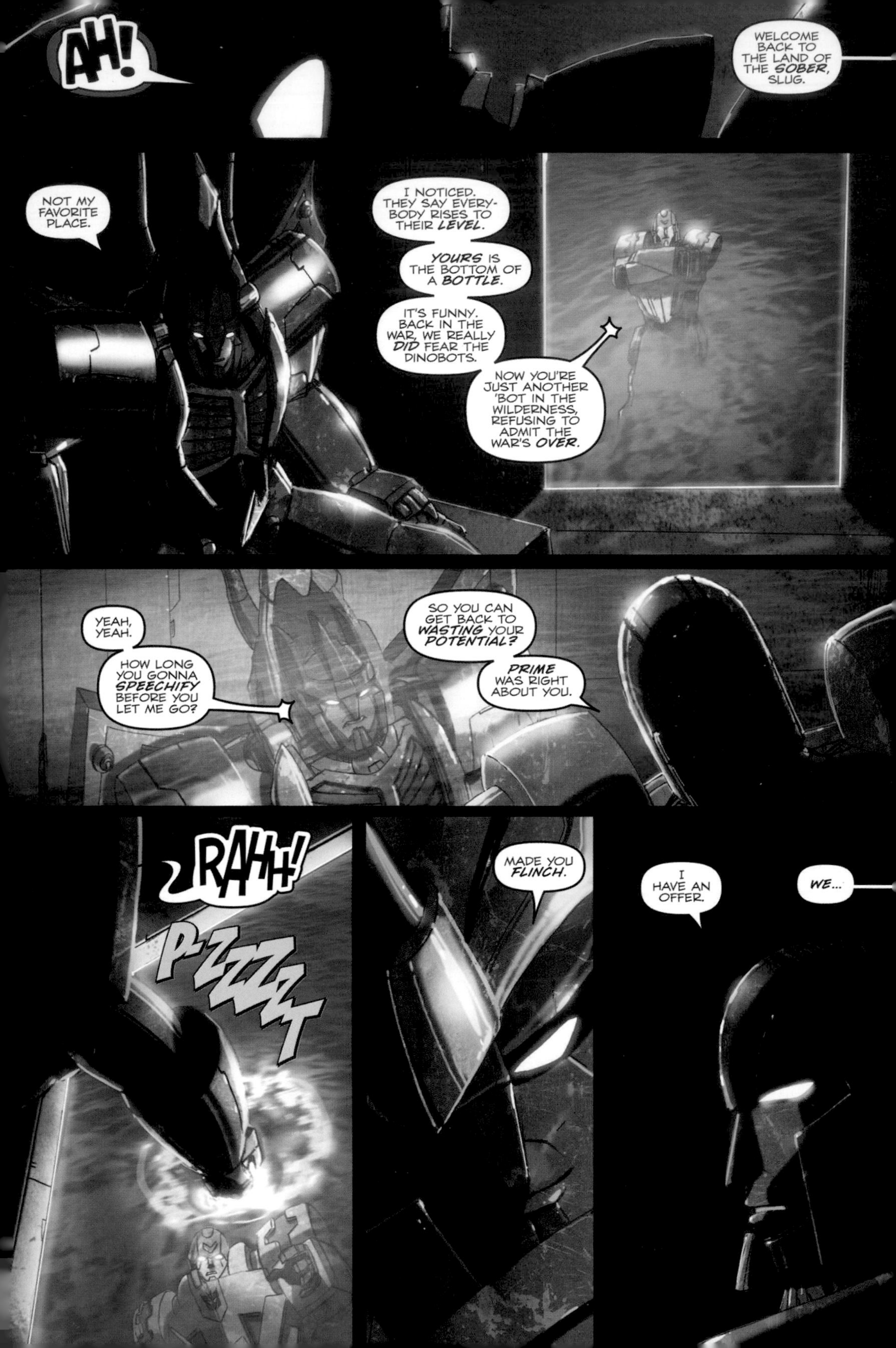
AH!
WELCOME BACK TO THE LAND OF THE SOBER, SLUG.
NOT MY FAVORITE PLACE.
I NOTICED. THEY SAY EVERY-BODY RISES TO THEIR LEVEL.
YOURS IS THE BOTTOM OF A BOTTLE.
IT'S FUNNY. BACK IN THE WAR, WE REALLY DID FEAR THE DINOBOTS.
NOW YOU'RE JUST ANOTHER 'BOT IN THE WILDERNESS, REFUSING TO ADMIT THE WAR'S OVER.
YEAH, YEAH.
HOW LONG YOU GONNA SPEECHIFY BEFORE YOU LET ME GO?
SO YOU CAN GET BACK TO WASTING YOUR POTENTIAL?
PRIME WAS RIGHT ABOUT YOU.
RAHH!
PZZZZT
MADE YOU FLINCH.
I HAVE AN OFFER.
WE...

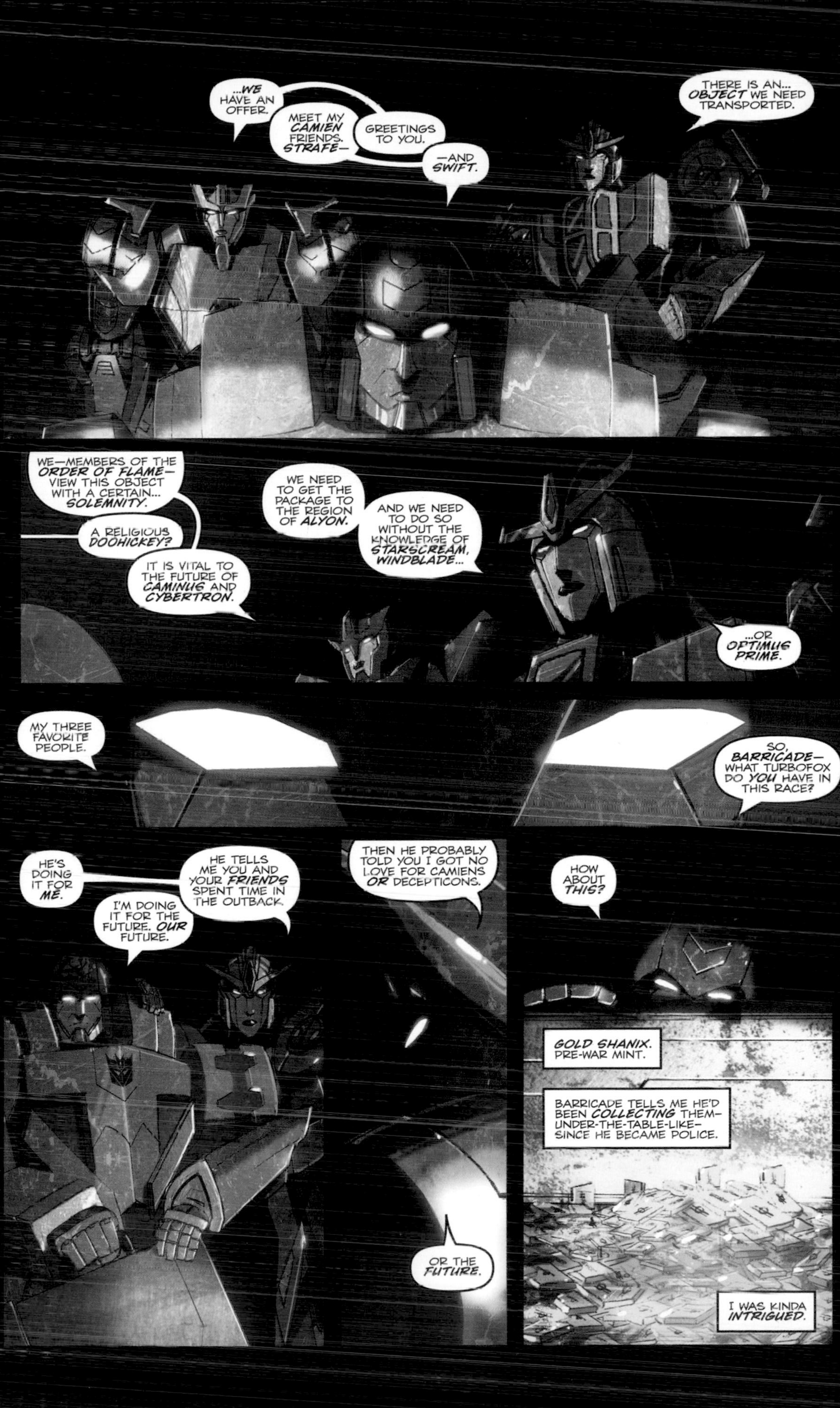
...WE HAVE AN OFFER.
MEET MY CAMIEN FRIENDS. STRAFE—
GREETINGS TO YOU.
—AND SWIFT.
THERE IS AN... OBJECT WE NEED TRANSPORTED.
WE—MEMBERS OF THE ORDER OF FLAME—VIEW THIS OBJECT WITH A CERTAIN... SOLEMNITY.
A RELIGIOUS DOOHICKEY?
IT IS VITAL TO THE FUTURE OF CAMINUS AND CYBERTRON.
WE NEED TO GET THE PACKAGE TO THE REGION OF ALYON.
AND WE NEED TO DO SO WITHOUT THE KNOWLEDGE OF STARSCREAM, WINDBLADE...
...OR OPTIMUS PRIME.
MY THREE FAVORITE PEOPLE.
SO, BARRICADE—WHAT TURBOFOX DO YOU HAVE IN THIS RACE?
HE'S DOING IT FOR ME.
HE TELLS ME YOU AND YOUR FRIENDS SPENT TIME IN THE OUTBACK.
I'M DOING IT FOR THE FUTURE. OUR FUTURE.
THEN HE PROBABLY TOLD YOU I GOT NO LOVE FOR CAMIENS OR DECEPTICONS.
OR THE FUTURE.
HOW ABOUT THIS?
GOLD SHANIX. PRE-WAR MINT.
BARRICADE TELLS ME HE'D BEEN COLLECTING THEM—UNDER-THE-TABLE-LIKE—SINCE HE BECAME POLICE.
I WAS KINDA INTRIGUED.

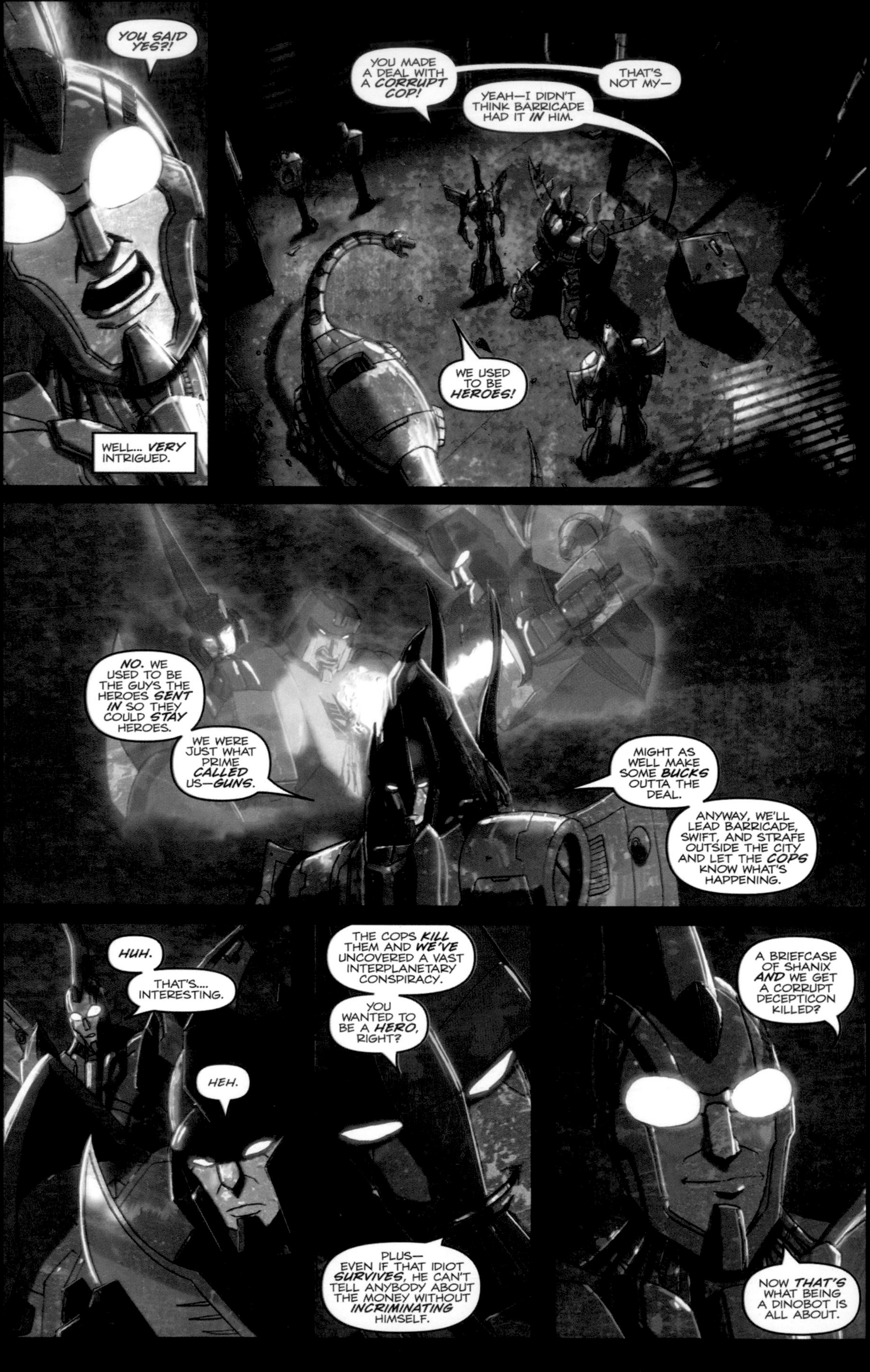
YOU SAID YES?!
WELL... VERY INTRIGUED.
YOU MADE A DEAL WITH A CORRUPT COP!
THAT'S NOT MY—
YEAH—I DIDN'T THINK BARRICADE HAD IT IN HIM.
WE USED TO BE HEROES!
NO. WE USED TO BE THE GUYS THE HEROES SENT IN SO THEY COULD STAY HEROES.
WE WERE JUST WHAT PRIME CALLED US—GUNS.
MIGHT AS WELL MAKE SOME BUCKS OUTTA THE DEAL.
ANYWAY, WE'LL LEAD BARRICADE, SWIFT, AND STRAFE OUTSIDE THE CITY AND LET THE COPS KNOW WHAT'S HAPPENING.
HUH.
THAT'S.... INTERESTING.
HEH.
THE COPS KILL THEM AND WE'VE UNCOVERED A VAST INTERPLANETARY CONSPIRACY.
YOU WANTED TO BE A HERO, RIGHT?
PLUS— EVEN IF THAT IDIOT SURVIVES, HE CAN'T TELL ANYBODY ABOUT THE MONEY WITHOUT INCRIMINATING HIMSELF.
A BRIEFCASE OF SHANIX AND WE GET A CORRUPT DECEPTICON KILLED?
NOW THAT'S WHAT BEING A DINOBOT IS ALL ABOUT.

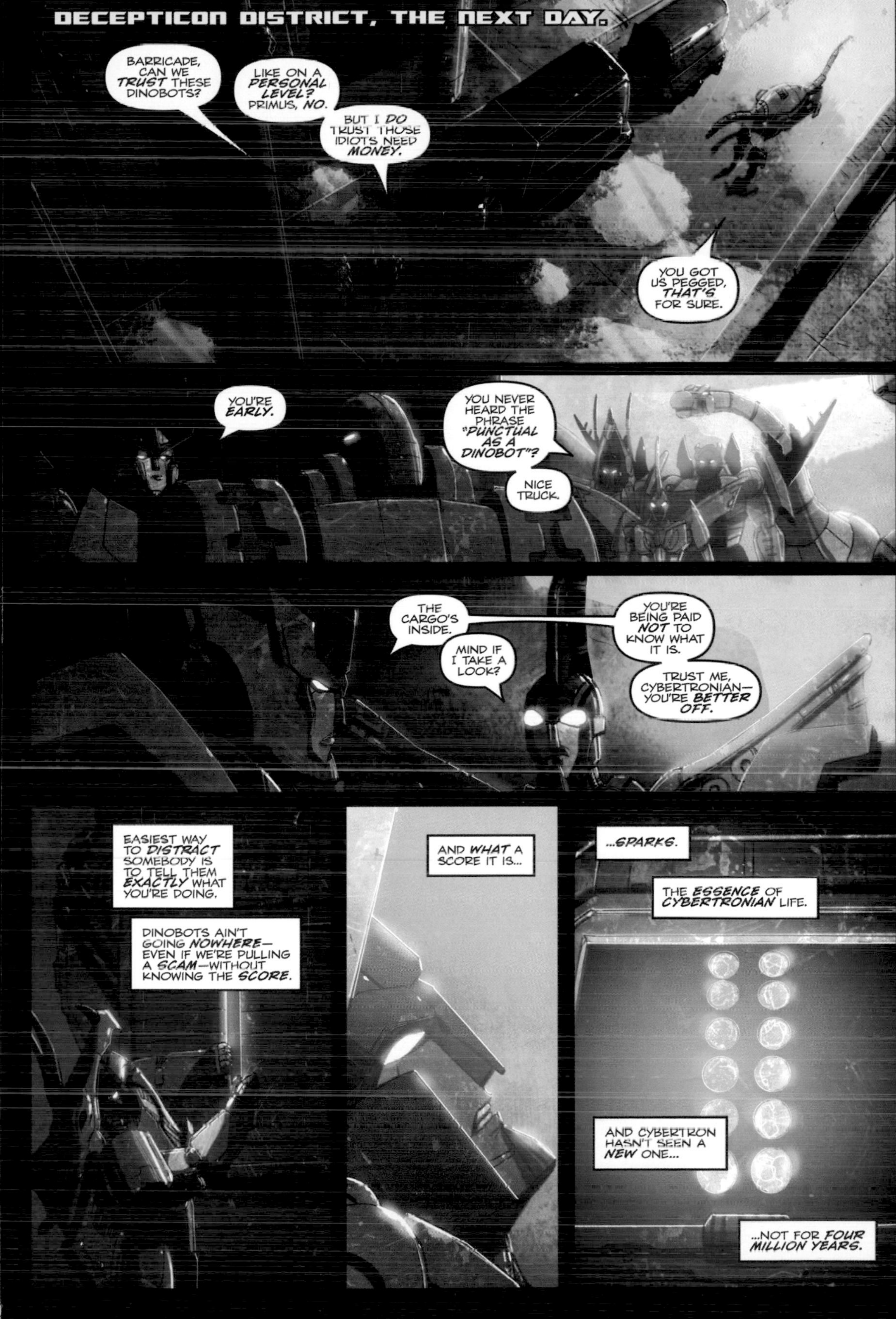
DECEPTICON DISTRICT, THE NEXT DAY.
BARRICADE, CAN WE TRUST THESE DINOBOTS?
LIKE ON A PERSONAL LEVEL? PRIMUS, NO.
BUT I DO TRUST THOSE IDIOTS NEED MONEY.
YOU GOT US PEGGED, THAT'S FOR SURE.
YOU'RE EARLY.
YOU NEVER HEARD THE PHRASE "PUNCTUAL AS A DINOBOT"?
NICE TRUCK.
THE CARGO'S INSIDE.
MIND IF I TAKE A LOOK?
YOU'RE BEING PAID NOT TO KNOW WHAT IT IS.
TRUST ME, CYBERTRONIAN— YOU'RE BETTER OFF.
EASIEST WAY TO DISTRACT SOMEBODY IS TO TELL THEM EXACTLY WHAT YOU'RE DOING.
DINOBOTS AIN'T GOING NOWHERE— EVEN IF WE'RE PULLING A SCAM—WITHOUT KNOWING THE SCORE.
AND WHAT A SCORE IT IS...
...SPARKS.
THE ESSENCE OF CYBERTRONIAN LIFE.
AND CYBERTRON HASN'T SEEN A NEW ONE...
...NOT FOR FOUR MILLION YEARS.

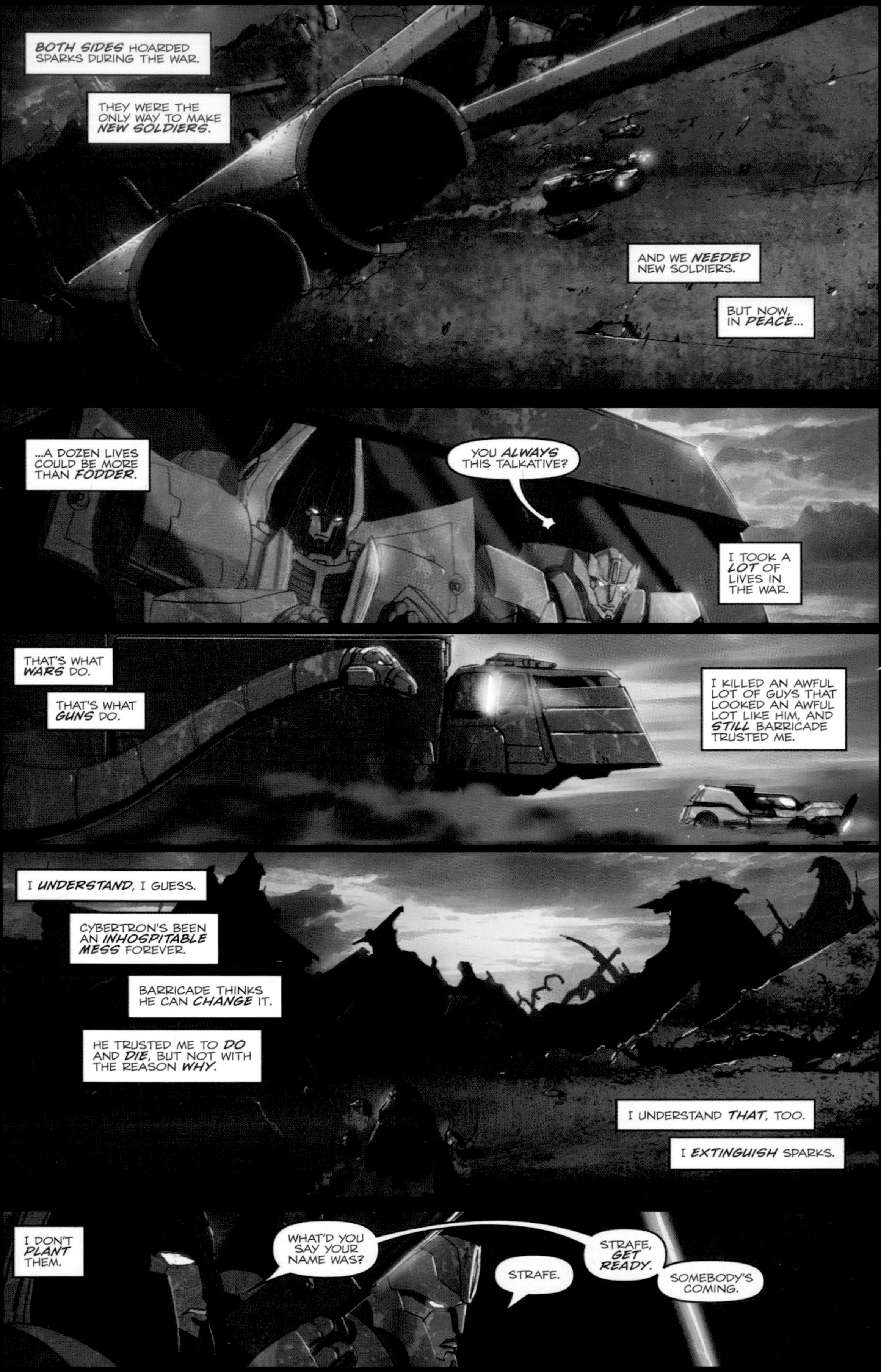
BOTH SIDES HOARDED SPARKS DURING THE WAR.
THEY WERE THE ONLY WAY TO MAKE NEW SOLDIERS.
AND WE NEEDED NEW SOLDIERS.
BUT NOW, IN PEACE...
...A DOZEN LIVES COULD BE MORE THAN FODDER.
YOU ALWAYS THIS TALKATIVE?
I TOOK A LOT OF LIVES IN THE WAR.
THAT'S WHAT WARS DO.
THAT'S WHAT GUNS DO.
I KILLED AN AWFUL LOT OF GUYS THAT LOOKED AN AWFUL LOT LIKE HIM, AND STILL BARRICADE TRUSTED ME.
I UNDERSTAND, I GUESS.
CYBERTRON'S BEEN AN INHOSPITABLE MESS FOREVER.
BARRICADE THINKS HE CAN CHANGE IT.
HE TRUSTED ME TO DO AND DIE, BUT NOT WITH THE REASON WHY.
I UNDERSTAND THAT, TOO.
I EXTINGUISH SPARKS.
I DON'T PLANT THEM.
WHAT'D YOU SAY YOUR NAME WAS?
STRAFE.
STRAFE, GET READY.
SOMEBODY'S COMING.

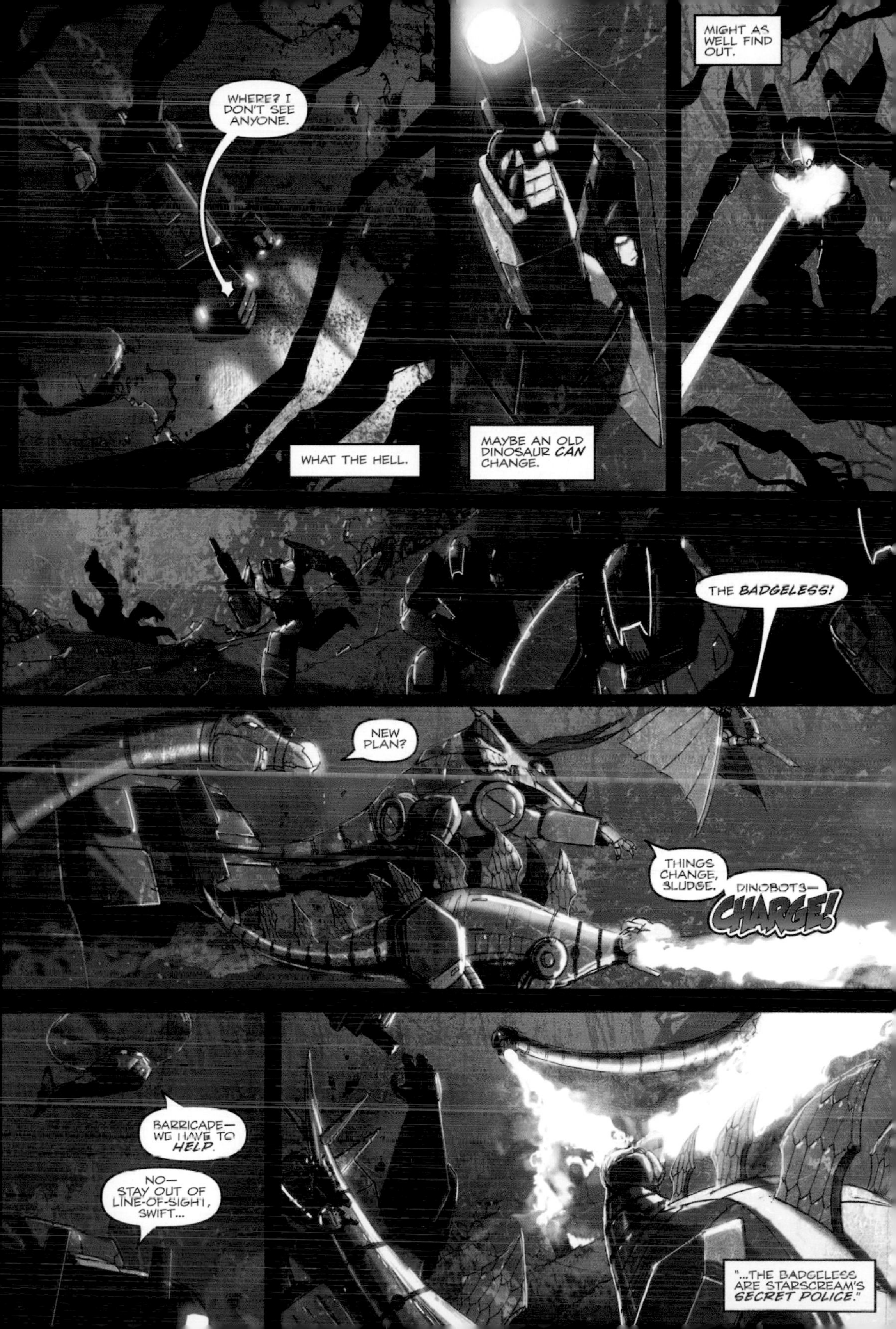

WHERE? I DON'T SEE ANYONE.
WHAT THE HELL.
MAYBE AN OLD DINOSAUR *CAN* CHANGE.
MIGHT AS WELL FIND OUT.
THE *BADGELESS!*
NEW PLAN?
THINGS CHANGE, SLUDGE.
DINOBOTS—
CHARGE!
BARRICADE— WE HAVE TO *HELP*.
NO— STAY OUT OF LINE-OF-SIGHT, SWIFT...
"...THE BADGELESS ARE STARSCREAM'S *SECRET POLICE*."

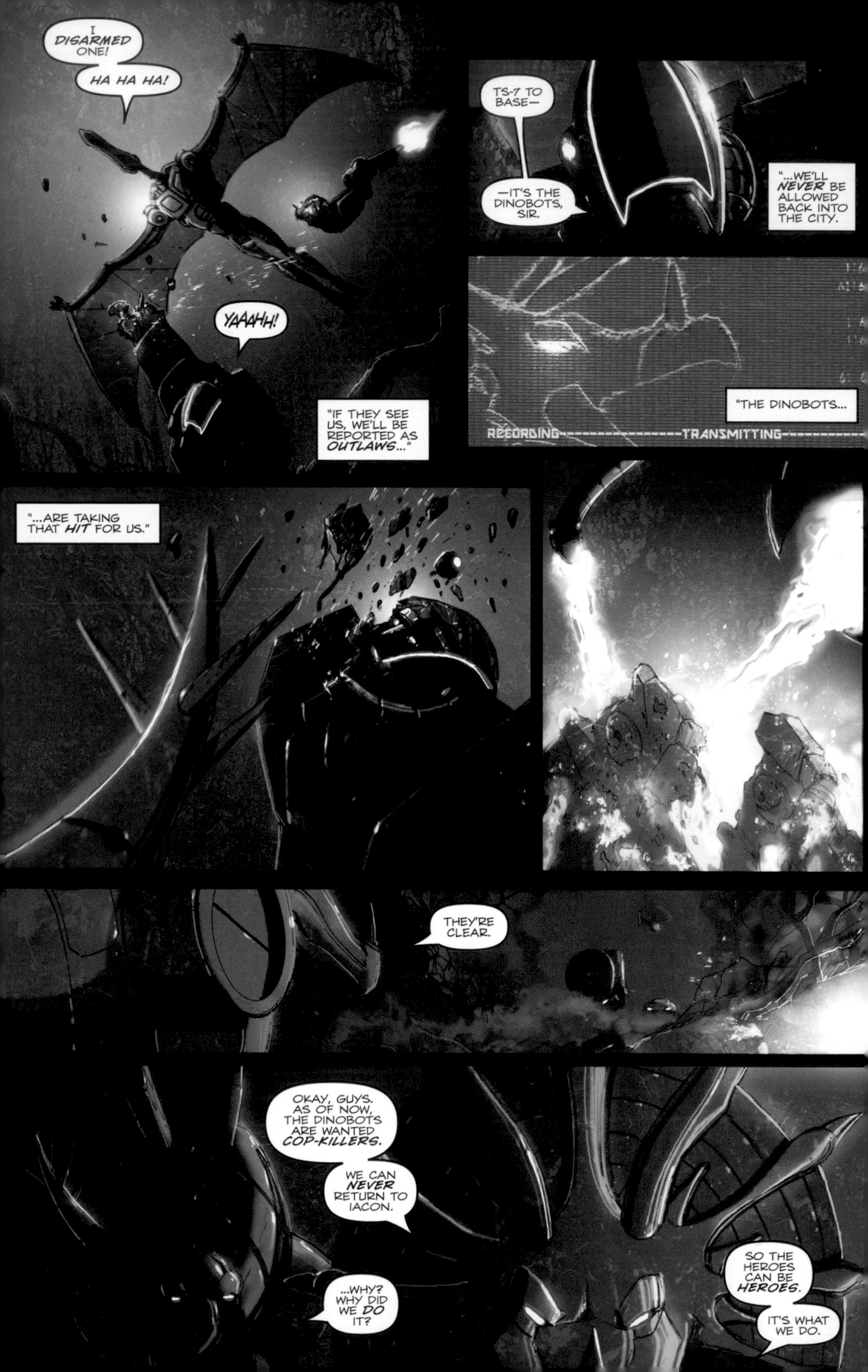
I DISARMED ONE!
HA HA HA!
YAAAHH!
"IF THEY SEE US, WE'LL BE REPORTED AS OUTLAWS..."
TS-7 TO BASE—
—IT'S THE DINOBOTS, SIR.
"...WE'LL NEVER BE ALLOWED BACK INTO THE CITY.
"THE DINOBOTS...
RECORDING
TRANSMITTING
"...ARE TAKING THAT HIT FOR US."
THEY'RE CLEAR.
OKAY, GUYS. AS OF NOW, THE DINOBOTS ARE WANTED COP-KILLERS.
WE CAN NEVER RETURN TO IACON.
...WHY? WHY DID WE DO IT?
SO THE HEROES CAN BE HEROES.
IT'S WHAT WE DO.

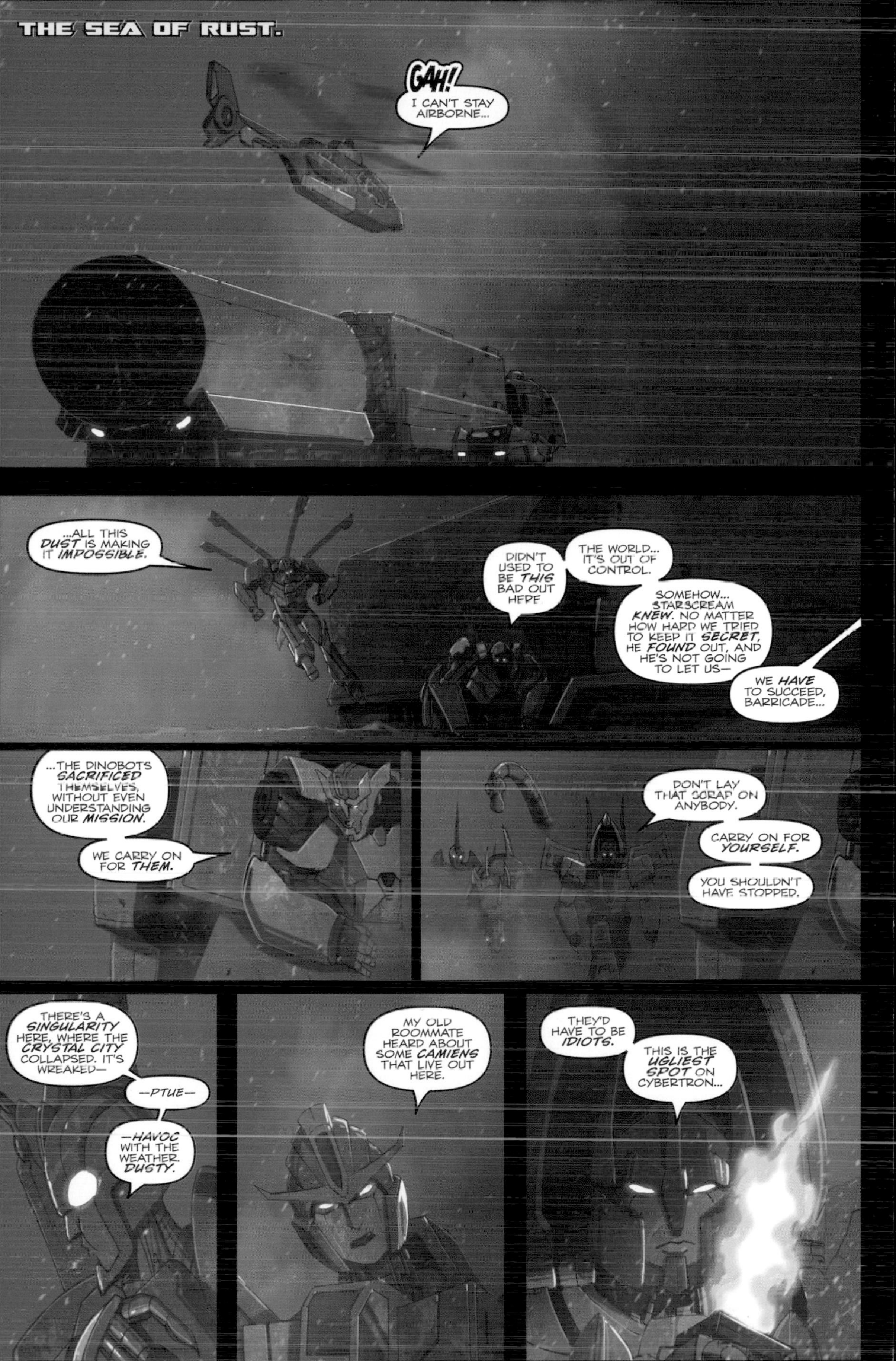
THE SEA OF RUST.
GAH!
I CAN'T STAY AIRBORNE...
...ALL THIS DUST IS MAKING IT IMPOSSIBLE.
DIDN'T USED TO BE THIS BAD OUT HERE.
THE WORLD... IT'S OUT OF CONTROL.
SOMEHOW... STARSCREAM KNEW. NO MATTER HOW HARD WE TRIED TO KEEP IT SECRET, HE FOUND OUT, AND HE'S NOT GOING TO LET US—
WE HAVE TO SUCCEED, BARRICADE...
...THE DINOBOTS SACRIFICED THEMSELVES, WITHOUT EVEN UNDERSTANDING OUR MISSION.
WE CARRY ON FOR THEM.
DON'T LAY THAT SCRAP ON ANYBODY.
CARRY ON FOR YOURSELF.
YOU SHOULDN'T HAVE STOPPED.
THERE'S A SINGULARITY HERE, WHERE THE CRYSTAL CITY COLLAPSED. IT'S WREAKED—
—PTUE—
—HAVOC WITH THE WEATHER. DUSTY.
MY OLD ROOMMATE HEARD ABOUT SOME CAMIENS THAT LIVE OUT HERE.
THEY'D HAVE TO BE IDIOTS.
THIS IS THE UGLIEST SPOT ON CYBERTRON...

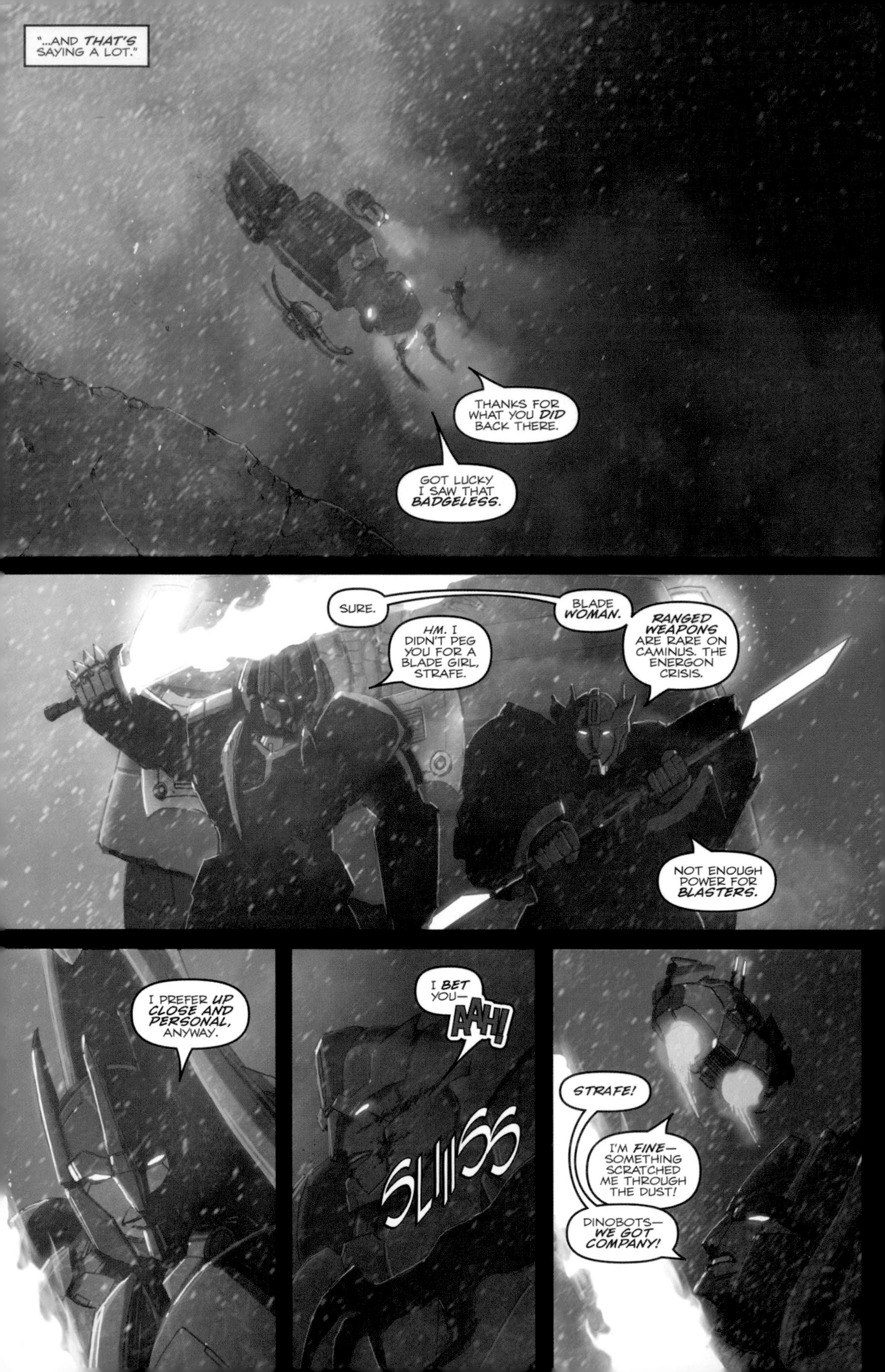
"...AND THAT'S SAYING A LOT."
THANKS FOR WHAT YOU DID BACK THERE.
GOT LUCKY I SAW THAT BADGELESS.
SURE.
BLADE WOMAN.
HM. I DIDN'T PEG YOU FOR A BLADE GIRL, STRAFE.
RANGED WEAPONS ARE RARE ON CAMINUS. THE ENERGON CRISIS.
NOT ENOUGH POWER FOR BLASTERS.
I PREFER UP CLOSE AND PERSONAL, ANYWAY.
I BET YOU—
AAH!
SLIISS
STRAFE!
I'M FINE— SOMETHING SCRATCHED ME THROUGH THE DUST!
DINOBOTS— WE GOT COMPANY!

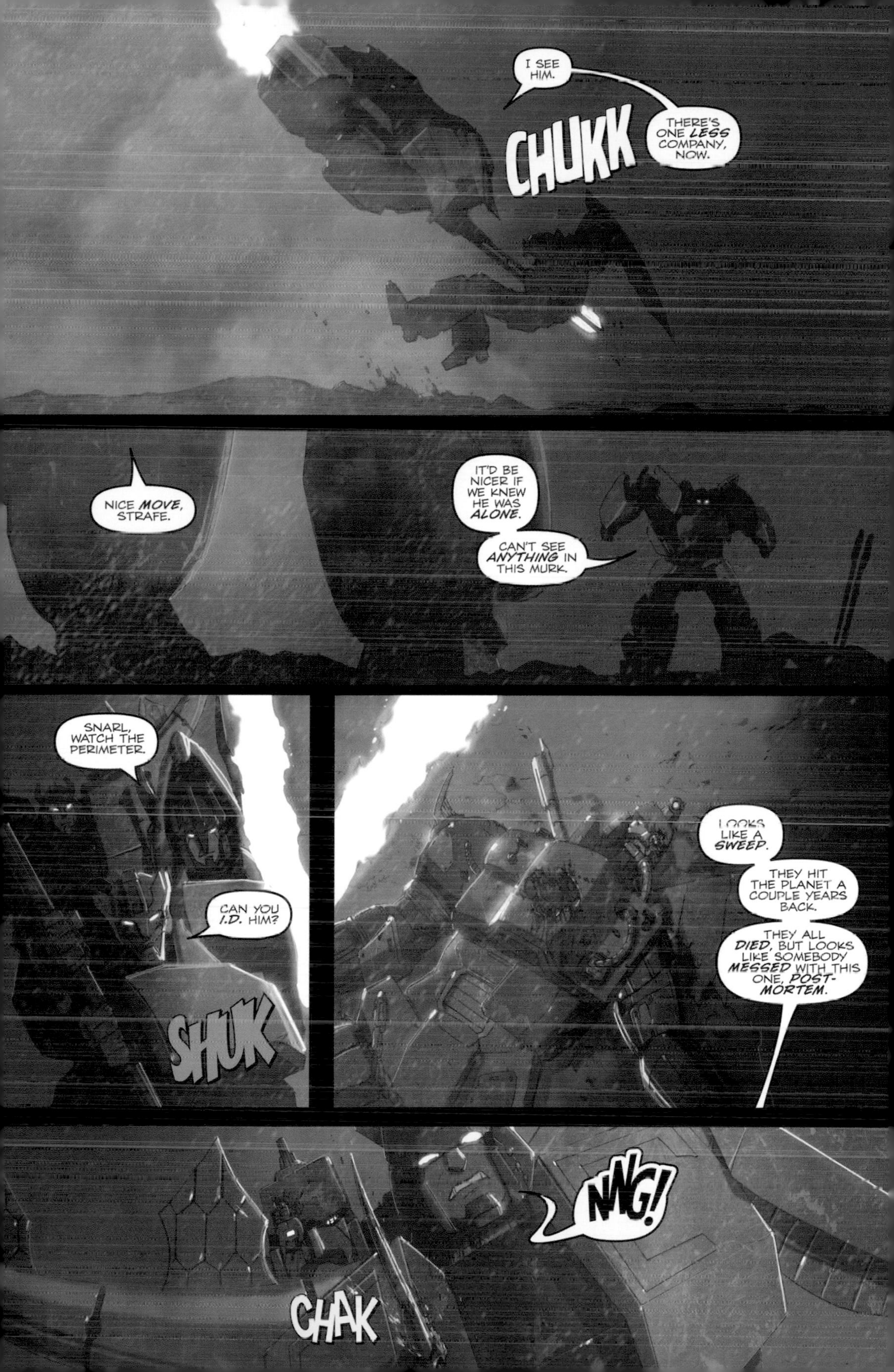
I SEE HIM.
CHUKK
THERE'S ONE LESS COMPANY, NOW.
NICE MOVE, STRAFE.
IT'D BE NICER IF WE KNEW HE WAS ALONE.
CAN'T SEE ANYTHING IN THIS MURK.
SNARL, WATCH THE PERIMETER.
CAN YOU I.D. HIM?
SHUK
LOOKS LIKE A SWEEP.
THEY HIT THE PLANET A COUPLE YEARS BACK.
THEY ALL DIED, BUT LOOKS LIKE SOMEBODY MESSED WITH THIS ONE, POST-MORTEM.
NNG!
CHAK

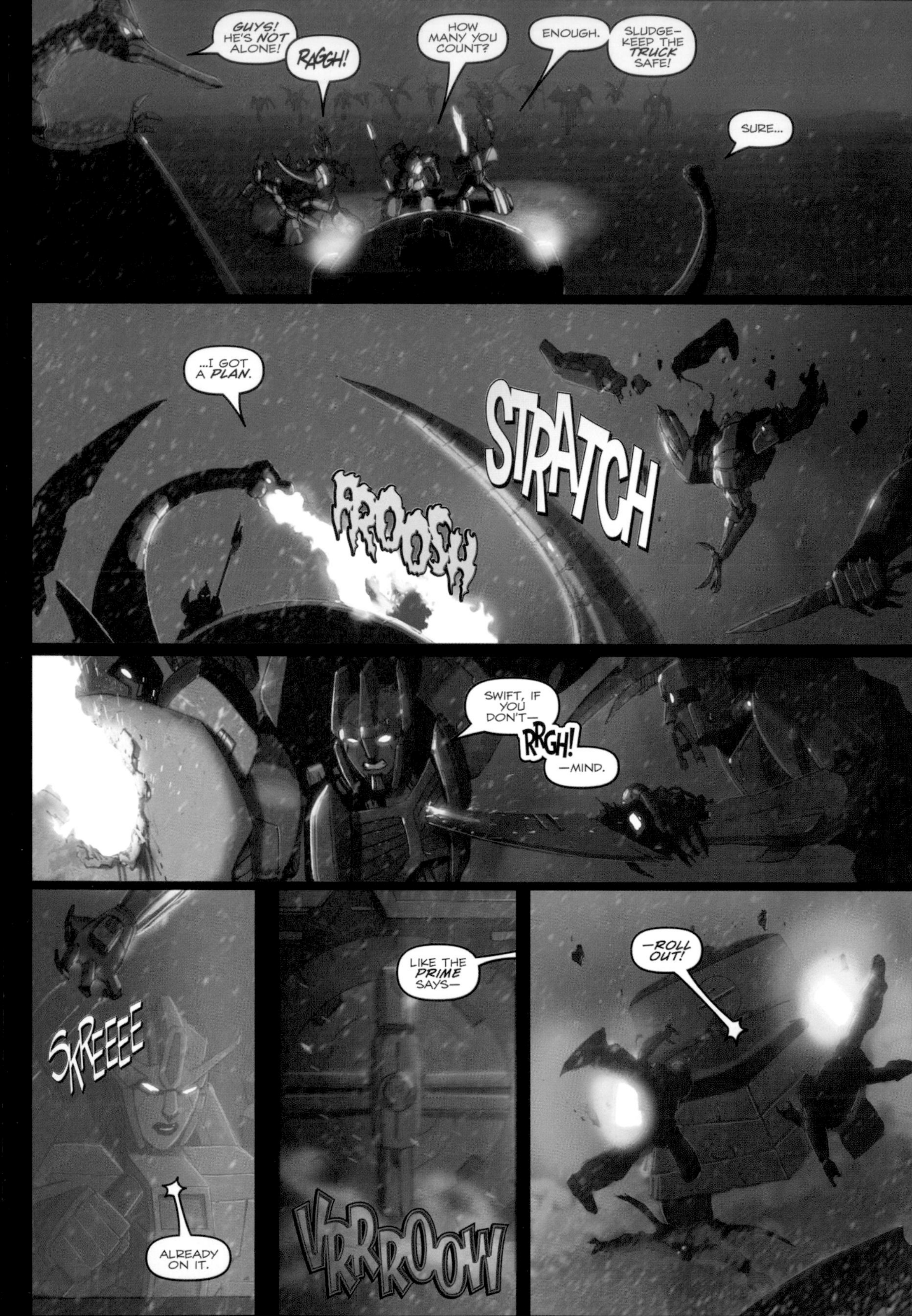
GUYS! HE'S NOT ALONE!
RAGGH!
HOW MANY YOU COUNT?
ENOUGH.
SLUDGE-KEEP THE TRUCK SAFE!
SURE...
...I GOT A PLAN.
STRATCH
PROOSH
SWIFT, IF YOU DON'T—
RRGH!
—MIND.
SKREEEE
ALREADY ON IT.
LIKE THE PRIME SAYS—
VRRROOW
—ROLL OUT!

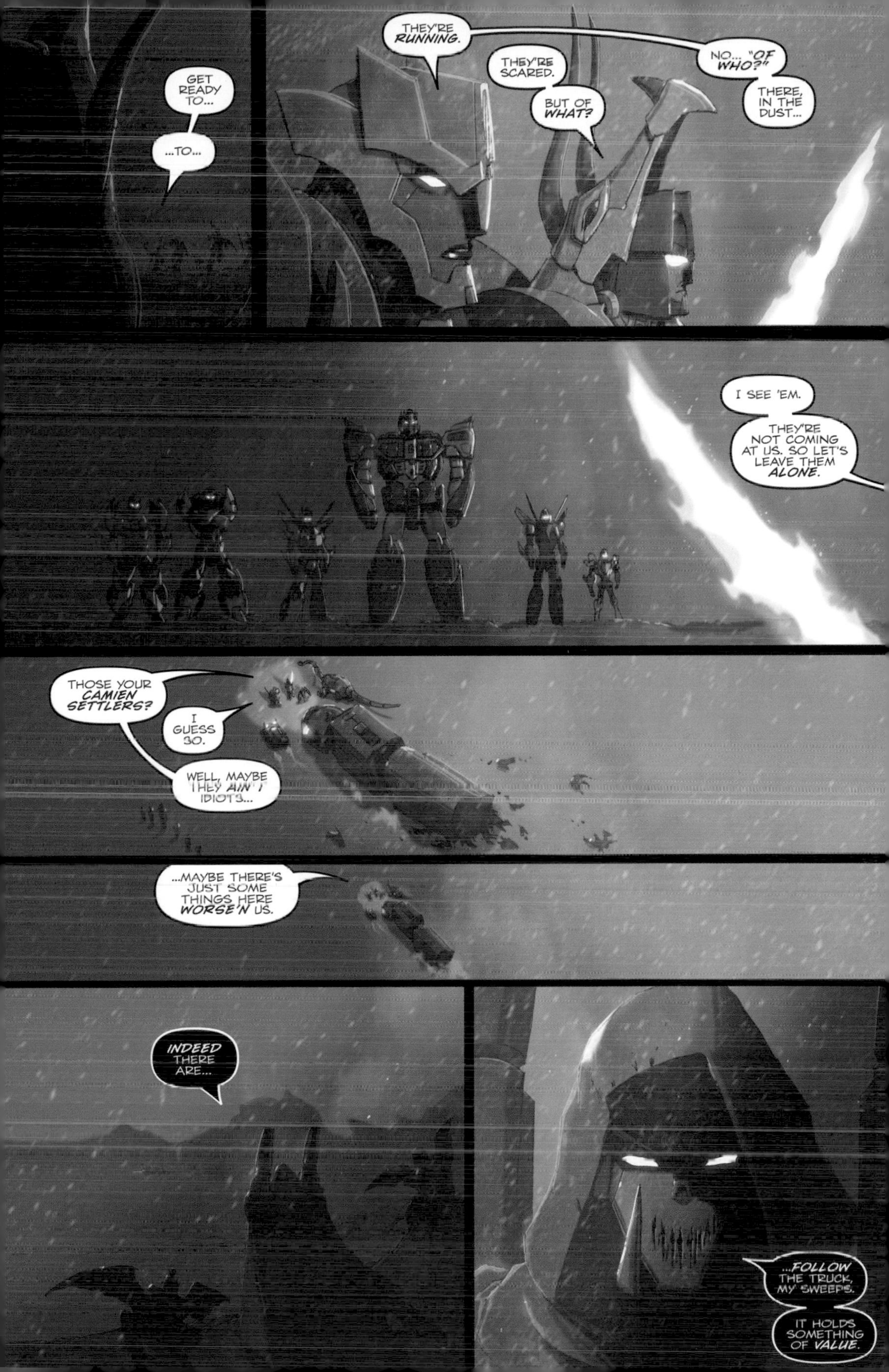

GET READY TO...
...TO...
THEY'RE *RUNNING*.
THEY'RE SCARED.
BUT OF *WHAT?*
NO... *"OF WHO?"*
THERE, IN THE DUST...
I SEE 'EM.
THEY'RE NOT COMING AT US. SO LET'S LEAVE THEM *ALONE*.
THOSE YOUR *CAMIEN SETTLERS?*
I GUESS SO.
WELL, MAYBE THEY *AIN'T* IDIOTS...
...MAYBE THERE'S JUST SOME THINGS HERE *WORSE'N* US.
*INDEED* THERE ARE...
...*FOLLOW* THE TRUCK, MY SWEEPS.
IT HOLDS SOMETHING OF *VALUE*.

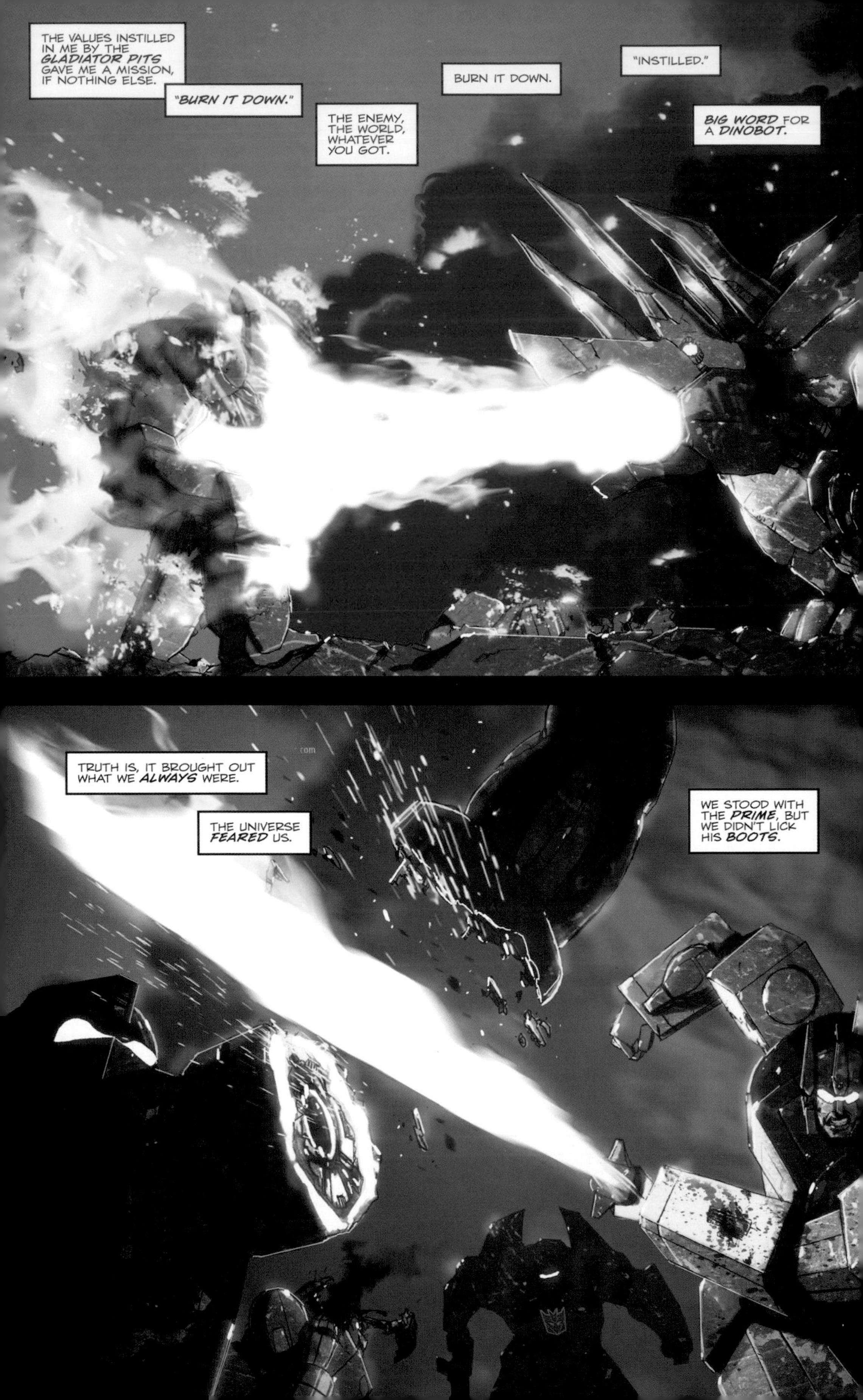
THE VALUES INSTILLED IN ME BY THE ***GLADIATOR PITS*** GAVE ME A MISSION, IF NOTHING ELSE.
"***BURN IT DOWN.***"
THE ENEMY, THE WORLD, WHATEVER YOU GOT.
BURN IT DOWN.
"INSTILLED."
***BIG WORD*** FOR A ***DINOBOT***.
TRUTH IS, IT BROUGHT OUT WHAT WE ***ALWAYS*** WERE.
THE UNIVERSE ***FEARED*** US.
WE STOOD WITH THE ***PRIME***, BUT WE DIDN'T LICK HIS ***BOOTS***.

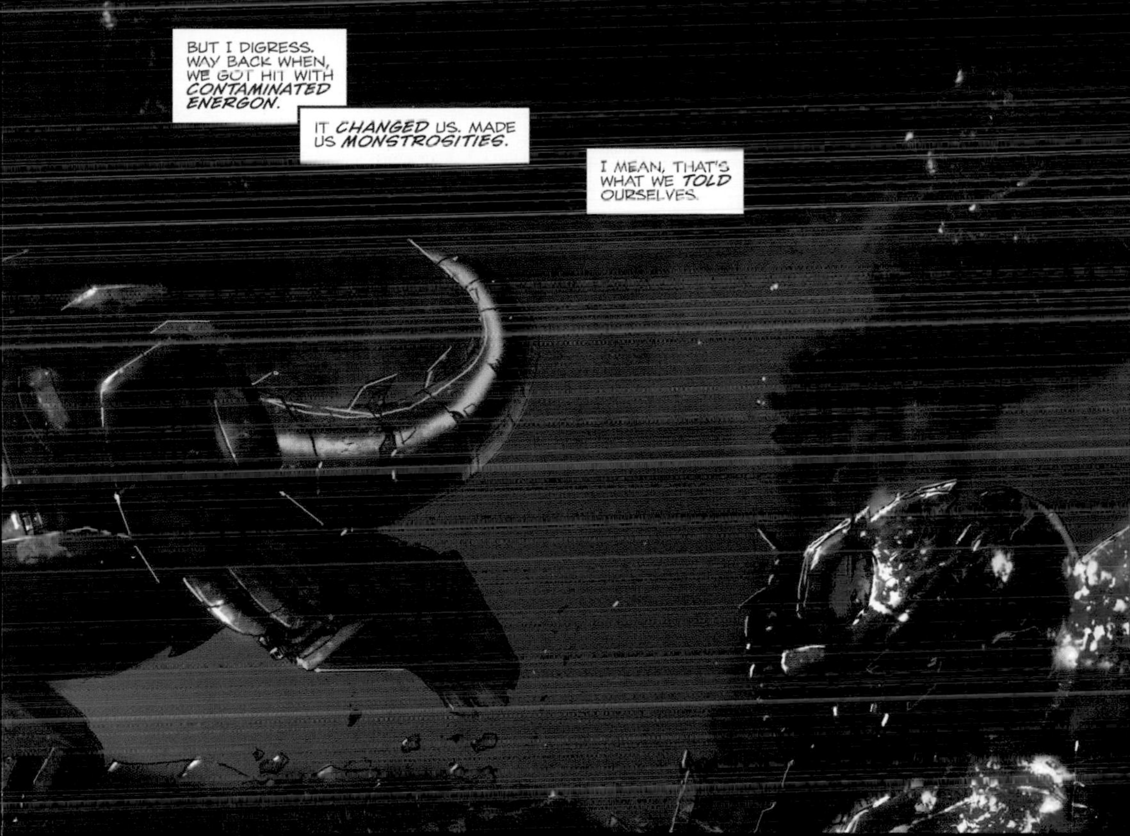
BUT I DIGRESS. WAY BACK WHEN, WE GOT HIT WITH CONTAMINATED ENERGON.
IT CHANGED US. MADE US MONSTROSITIES.
I MEAN, THAT'S WHAT WE TOLD OURSELVES.

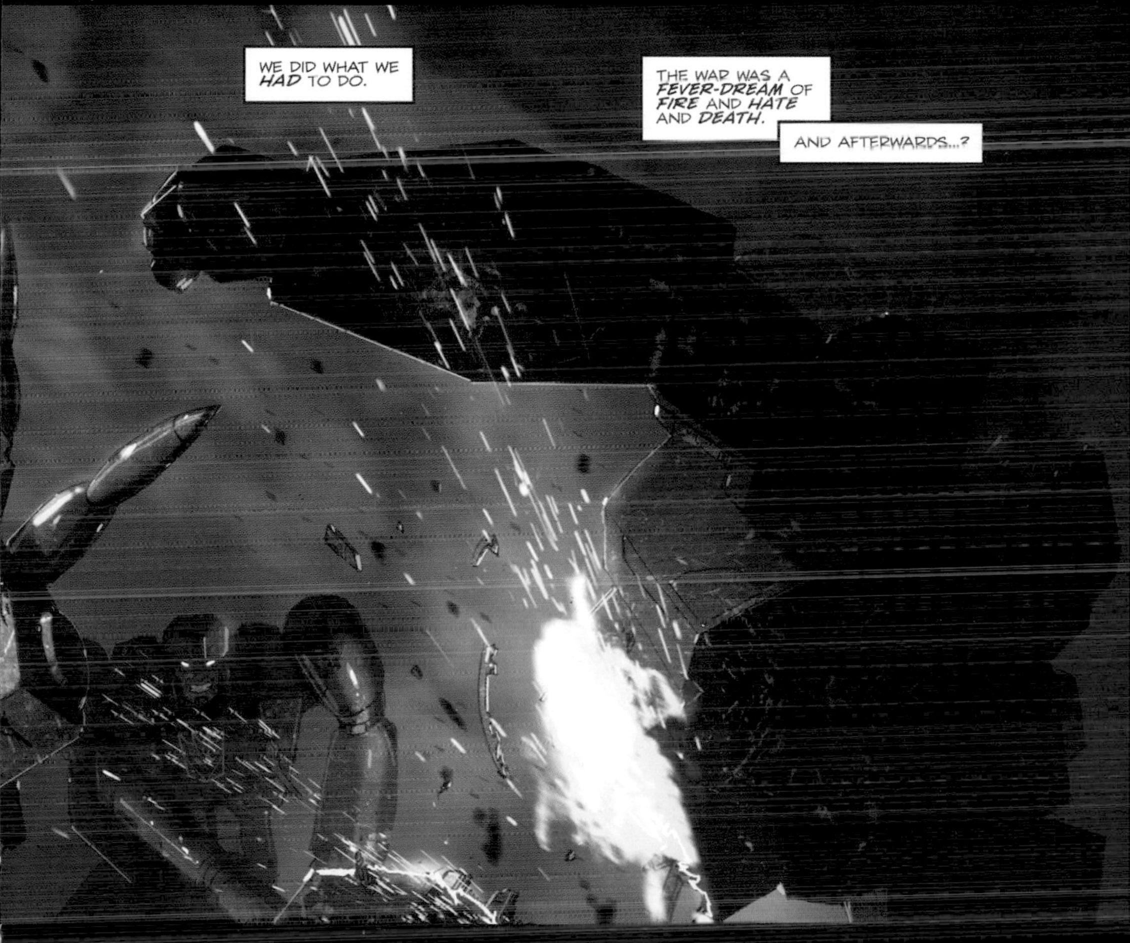
WE DID WHAT WE HAD TO DO.
THE WAR WAS A FEVER-DREAM OF FIRE AND HATE AND DEATH.
AND AFTERWARDS...?

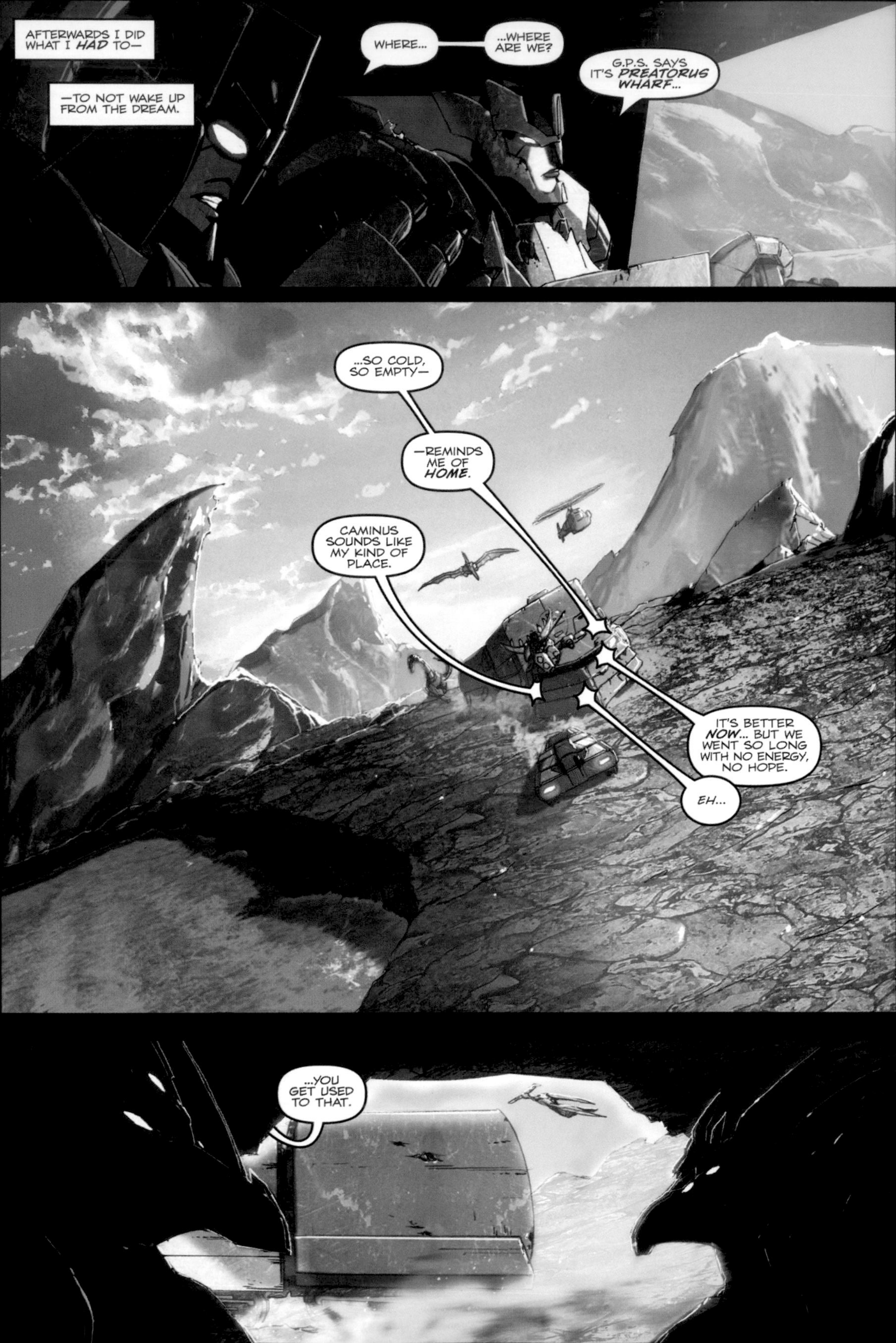
AFTERWARDS I DID WHAT I HAD TO—
—TO NOT WAKE UP FROM THE DREAM.
WHERE...
...WHERE ARE WE?
G.P.S. SAYS IT'S PREATORUS WHARF...
...SO COLD, SO EMPTY—
—REMINDS ME OF HOME.
CAMINUS SOUNDS LIKE MY KIND OF PLACE.
IT'S BETTER NOW... BUT WE WENT SO LONG WITH NO ENERGY, NO HOPE.
EH...
...YOU GET USED TO THAT.

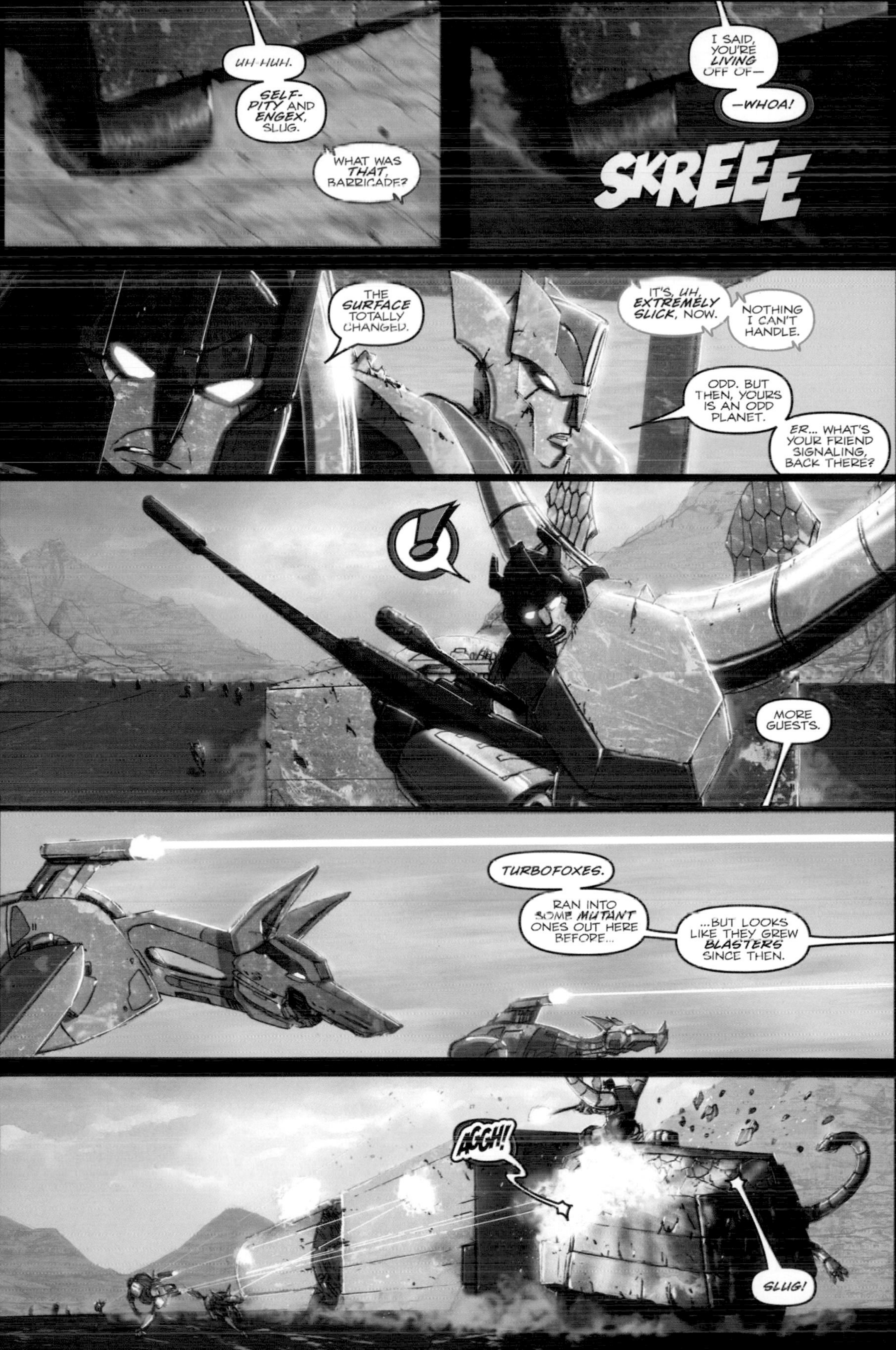
UH-HUH.
SELF-PITY AND ENGEX, SLUG.
WHAT WAS THAT, BARRICADE?
I SAID, YOU'RE LIVING OFF OF—
—WHOA!
SKREEEE
THE SURFACE TOTALLY CHANGED.
IT'S, UH, EXTREMELY SLICK, NOW.
NOTHING I CAN'T HANDLE.
ODD. BUT THEN, YOURS IS AN ODD PLANET.
ER... WHAT'S YOUR FRIEND SIGNALING, BACK THERE?
!
MORE GUESTS.
TURBOFOXES.
RAN INTO SOME MUTANT ONES OUT HERE BEFORE...
...BUT LOOKS LIKE THEY GREW BLASTERS SINCE THEN.
AGGH!
SLUG!

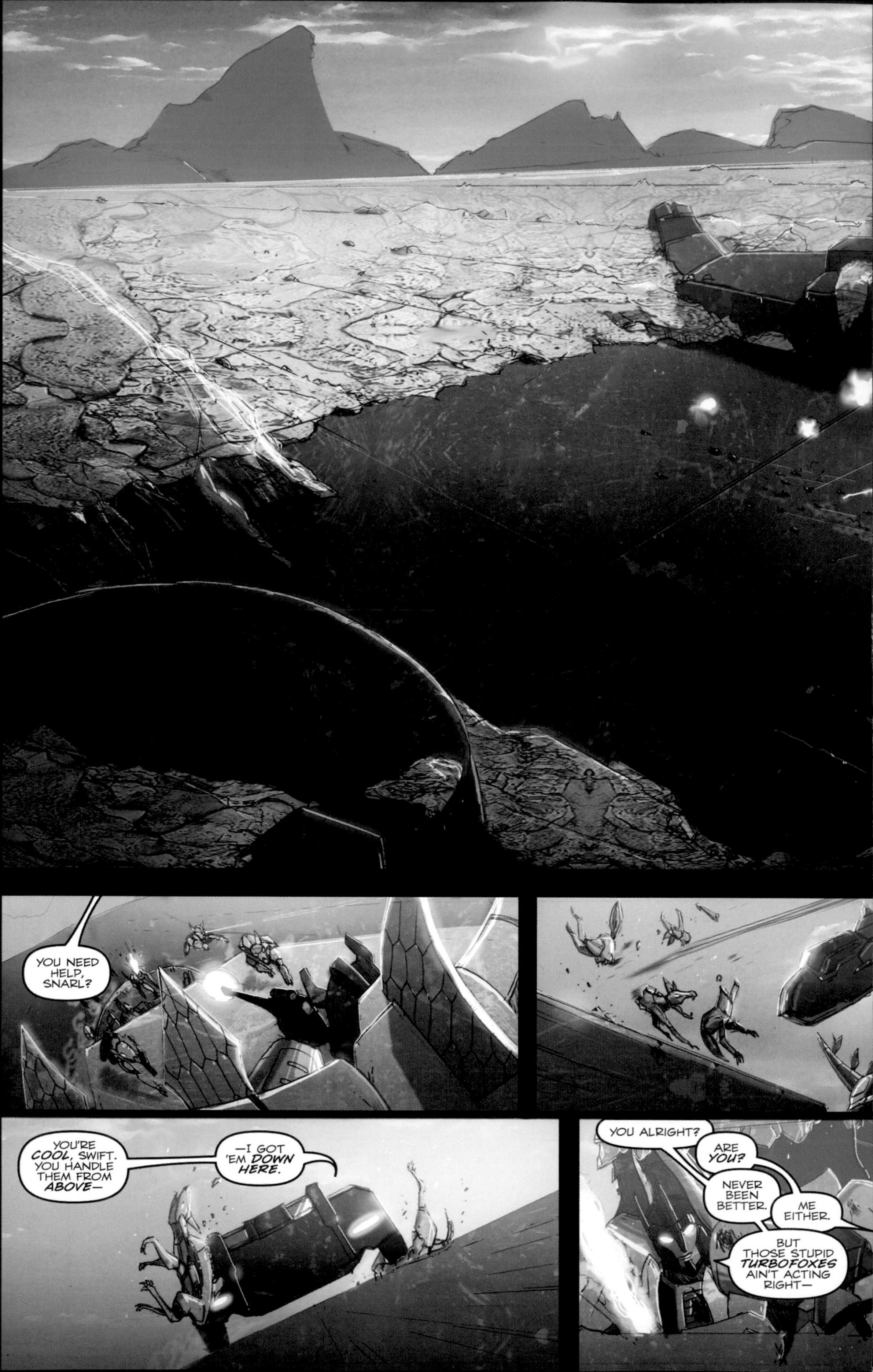
YOU NEED HELP, SNARL?
YOU'RE COOL, SWIFT. YOU HANDLE THEM FROM ABOVE—
—I GOT 'EM DOWN HERE.
YOU ALRIGHT?
ARE YOU?
NEVER BEEN BETTER.
ME EITHER.
BUT THOSE STUPID TURBOFOXES AIN'T ACTING RIGHT—

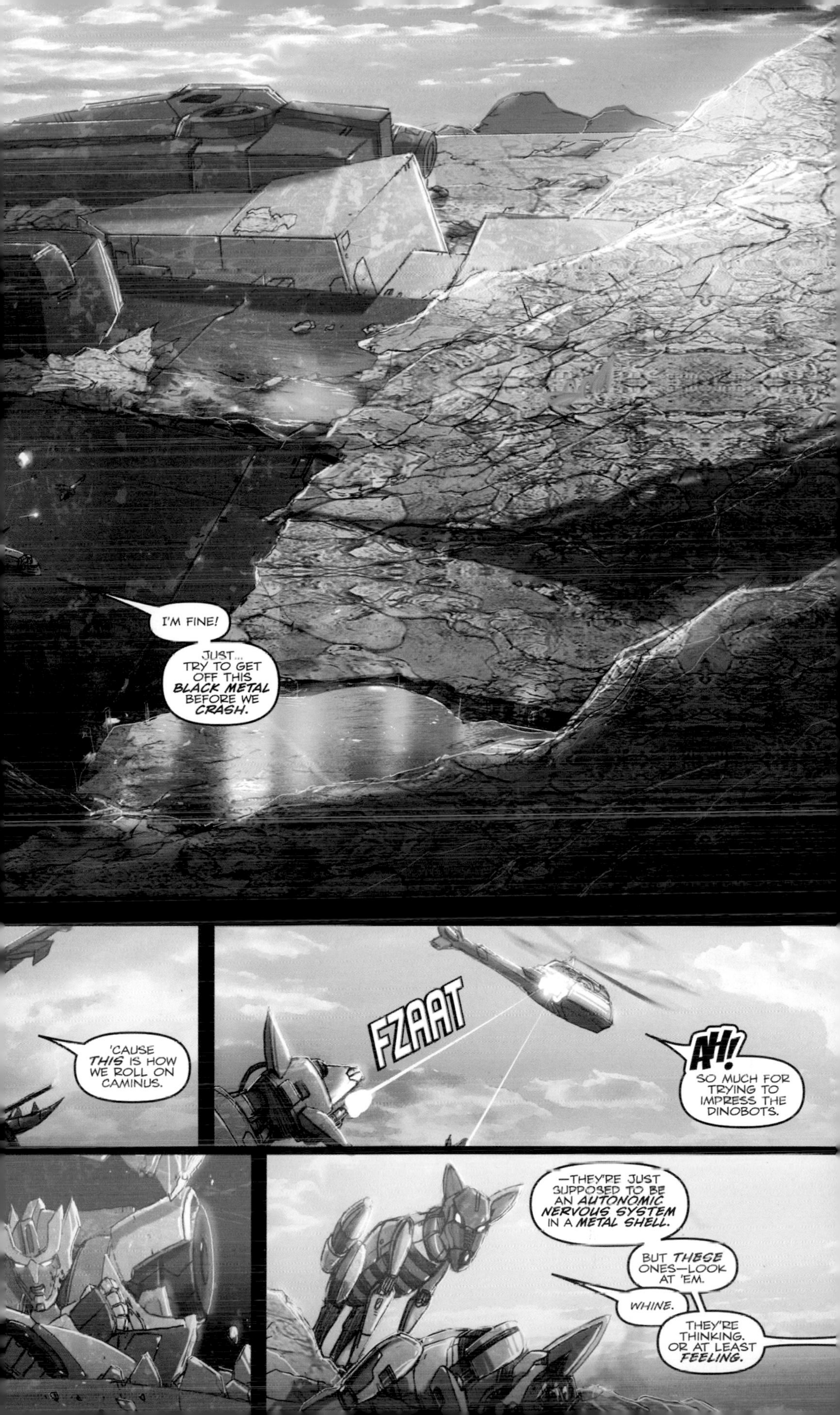
I'M FINE!
JUST... TRY TO GET OFF THIS BLACK METAL BEFORE WE CRASH.
'CAUSE THIS IS HOW WE ROLL ON CAMINUS.
FZAAT
AH! SO MUCH FOR TRYING TO IMPRESS THE DINOBOTS.
—THEY'RE JUST SUPPOSED TO BE AN AUTONOMIC NERVOUS SYSTEM IN A METAL SHELL.
BUT THESE ONES—LOOK AT 'EM.
WHINE.
THEY'RE THINKING. OR AT LEAST FEELING.

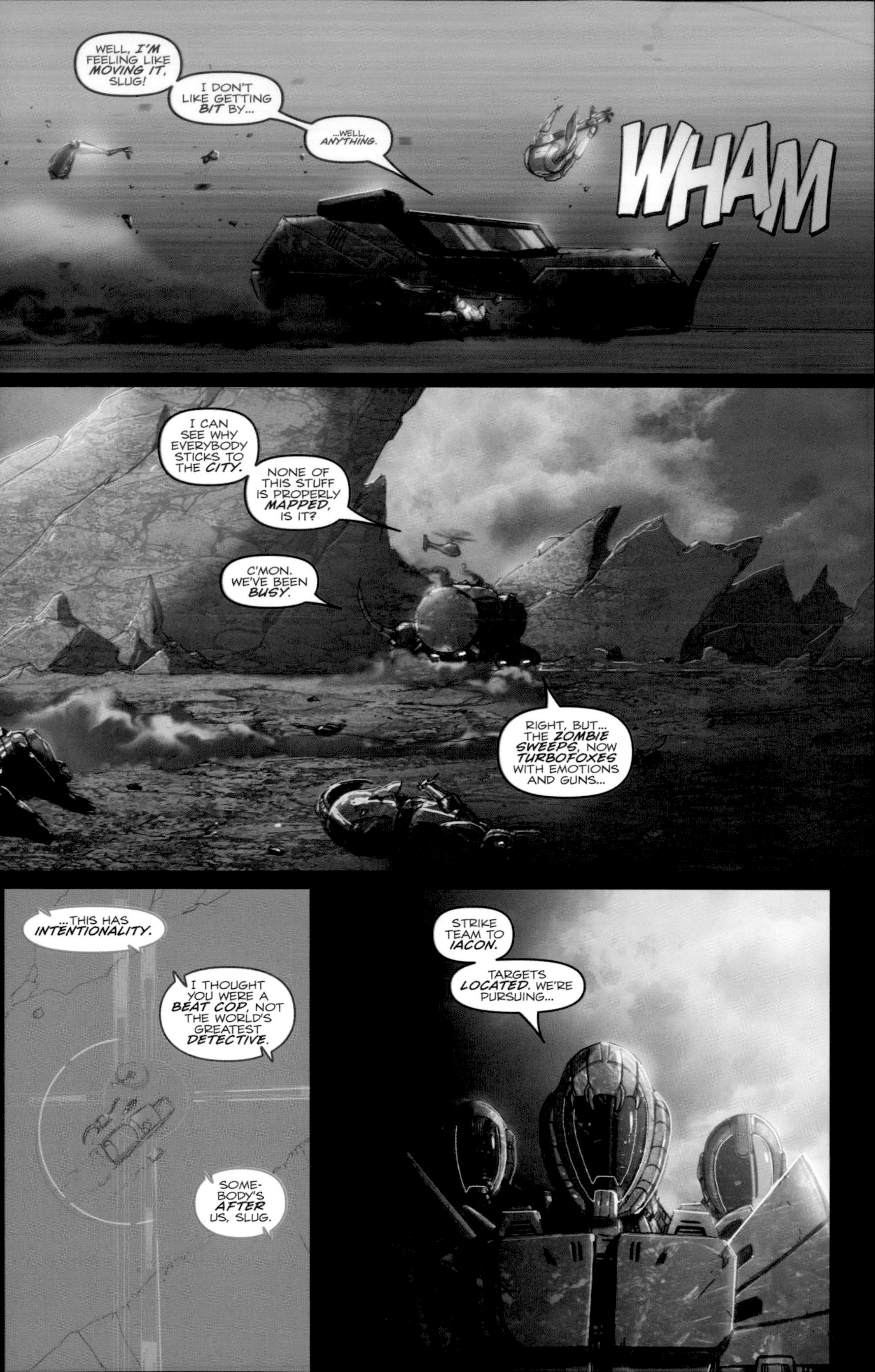
WELL, I'M FEELING LIKE MOVING IT, SLUG!
I DON'T LIKE GETTING BIT BY...
...WELL, ANYTHING.
WHAM
I CAN SEE WHY EVERYBODY STICKS TO THE CITY.
NONE OF THIS STUFF IS PROPERLY MAPPED, IS IT?
C'MON. WE'VE BEEN BUSY.
RIGHT, BUT... THE ZOMBIE SWEEPS, NOW TURBOFOXES WITH EMOTIONS AND GUNS...
...THIS HAS INTENTIONALITY.
I THOUGHT YOU WERE A BEAT COP, NOT THE WORLD'S GREATEST DETECTIVE.
SOMEBODY'S AFTER US, SLUG.
STRIKE TEAM TO IACON.
TARGETS LOCATED. WE'RE PURSUING...

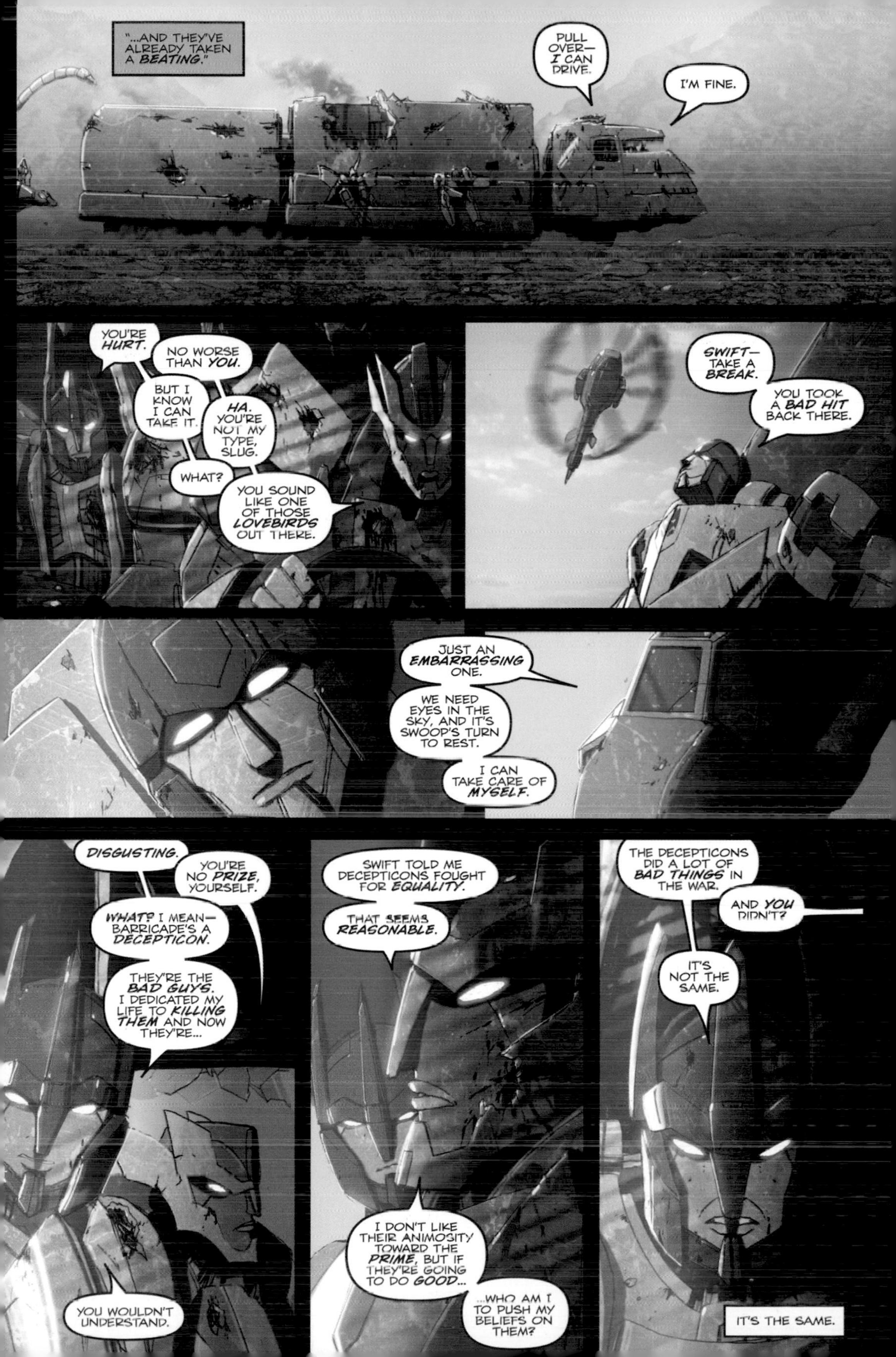
"...AND THEY'VE ALREADY TAKEN A BEATING."
PULL OVER— I CAN DRIVE.
I'M FINE.
YOU'RE HURT.
NO WORSE THAN YOU.
BUT I KNOW I CAN TAKE IT.
HA. YOU'RE NOT MY TYPE, SLUG.
WHAT?
YOU SOUND LIKE ONE OF THOSE LOVEBIRDS OUT THERE.
SWIFT— TAKE A BREAK.
YOU TOOK A BAD HIT BACK THERE.
JUST AN EMBARRASSING ONE.
WE NEED EYES IN THE SKY, AND IT'S SWOOP'S TURN TO REST.
I CAN TAKE CARE OF MYSELF.
DISGUSTING.
YOU'RE NO PRIZE, YOURSELF.
WHAT? I MEAN—BARRICADE'S A DECEPTICON.
THEY'RE THE BAD GUYS. I DEDICATED MY LIFE TO KILLING THEM AND NOW THEY'RE...
YOU WOULDN'T UNDERSTAND.
SWIFT TOLD ME DECEPTICONS FOUGHT FOR EQUALITY.
THAT SEEMS REASONABLE.
I DON'T LIKE THEIR ANIMOSITY TOWARD THE PRIME, BUT IF THEY'RE GOING TO DO GOOD...
...WHO AM I TO PUSH MY BELIEFS ON THEM?
THE DECEPTICONS DID A LOT OF BAD THINGS IN THE WAR.
AND YOU DIDN'T?
IT'S NOT THE SAME.
IT'S THE SAME.

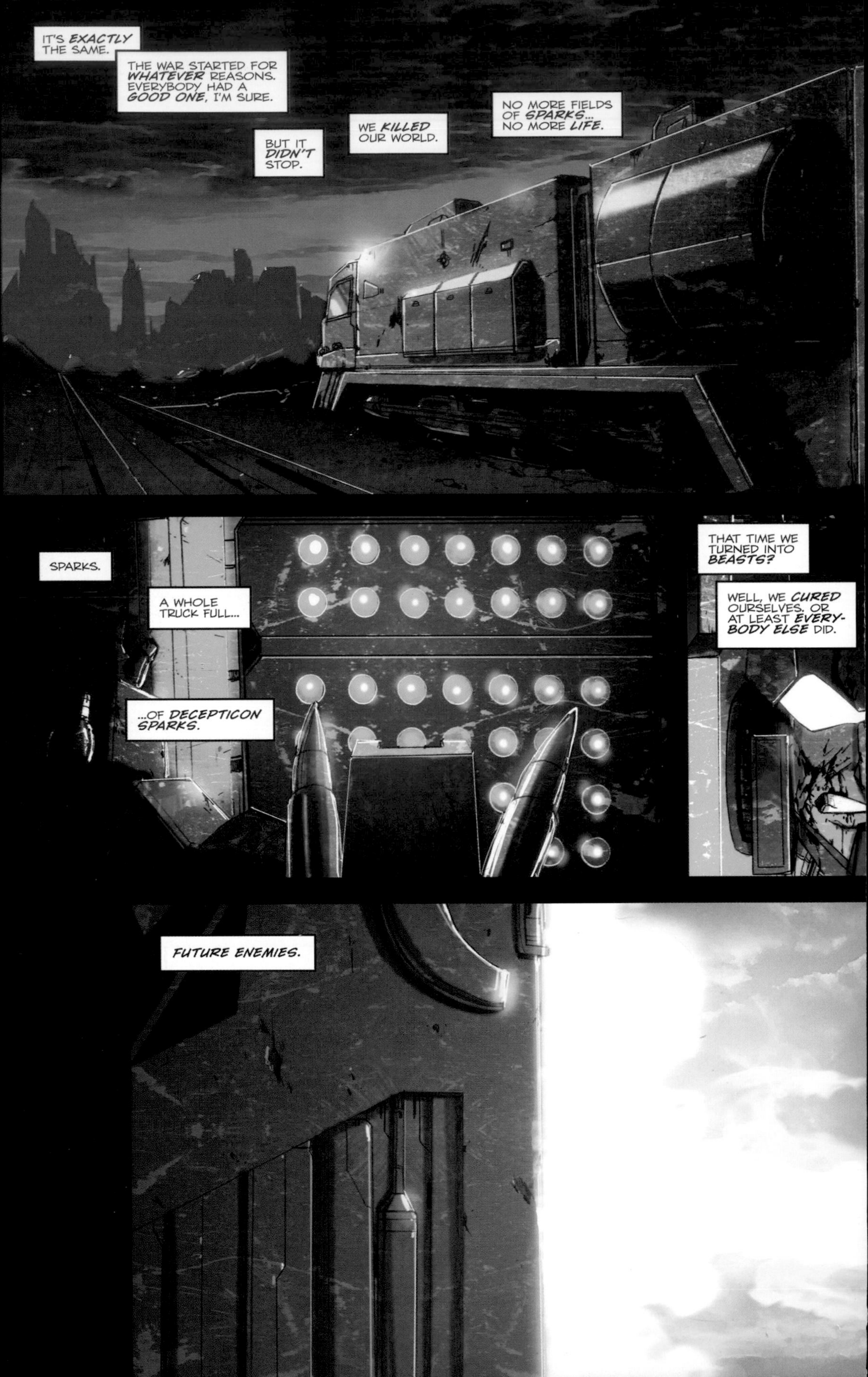
IT'S EXACTLY THE SAME.
THE WAR STARTED FOR WHATEVER REASONS. EVERYBODY HAD A GOOD ONE, I'M SURE.
BUT IT DIDN'T STOP.
WE KILLED OUR WORLD.
NO MORE FIELDS OF SPARKS... NO MORE LIFE.
SPARKS.
A WHOLE TRUCK FULL...
...OF DECEPTICON SPARKS.
THAT TIME WE TURNED INTO BEASTS?
WELL, WE CURED OURSELVES. OR AT LEAST EVERY-BODY ELSE DID.
FUTURE ENEMIES.

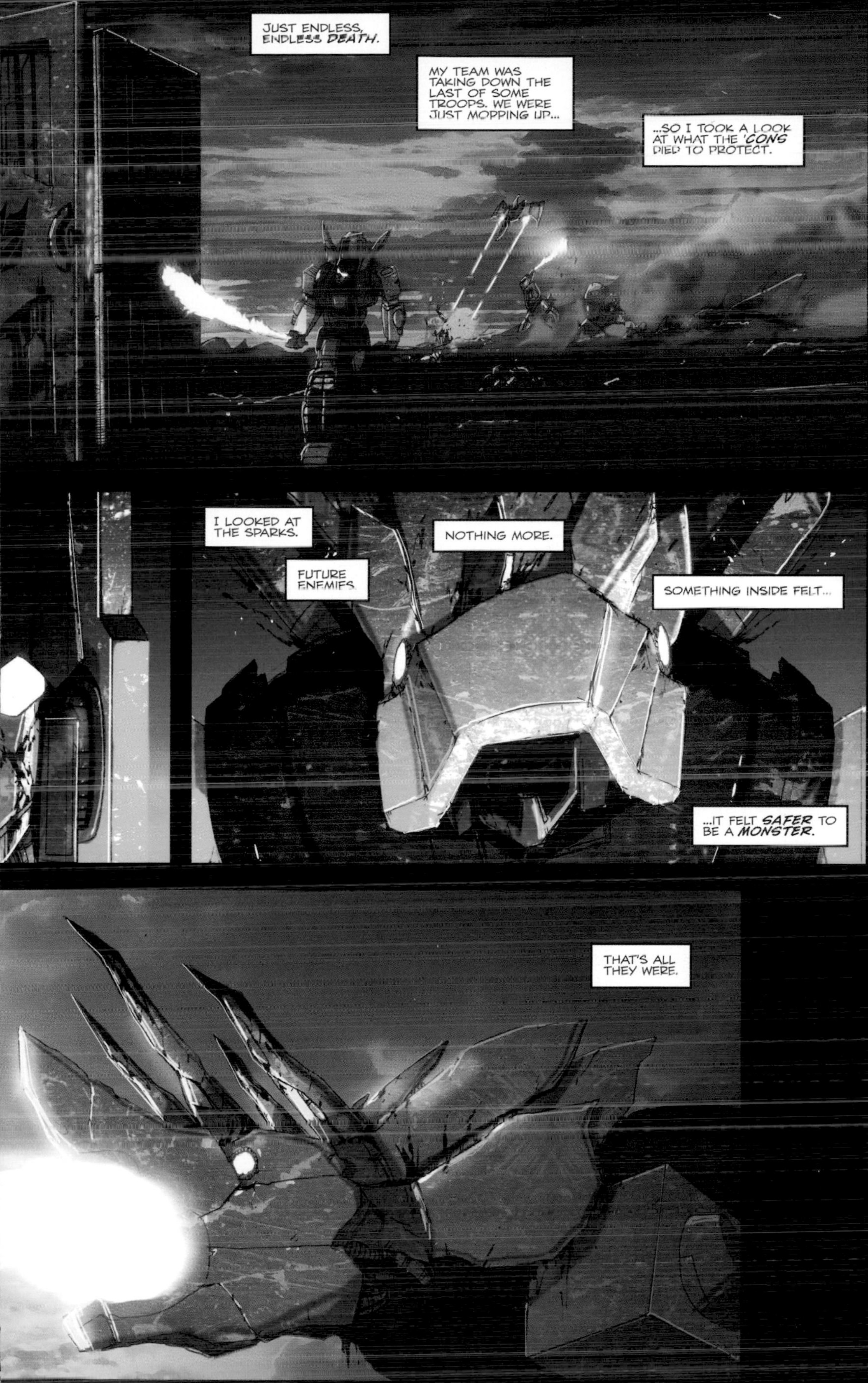
JUST ENDLESS, ENDLESS DEATH.
MY TEAM WAS TAKING DOWN THE LAST OF SOME TROOPS. WE WERE JUST MOPPING UP...
...SO I TOOK A LOOK AT WHAT THE 'CONS DIED TO PROTECT.
I LOOKED AT THE SPARKS.
FUTURE ENEMIES.
NOTHING MORE.
SOMETHING INSIDE FELT...
...IT FELT SAFER TO BE A MONSTER.
THAT'S ALL THEY WERE.

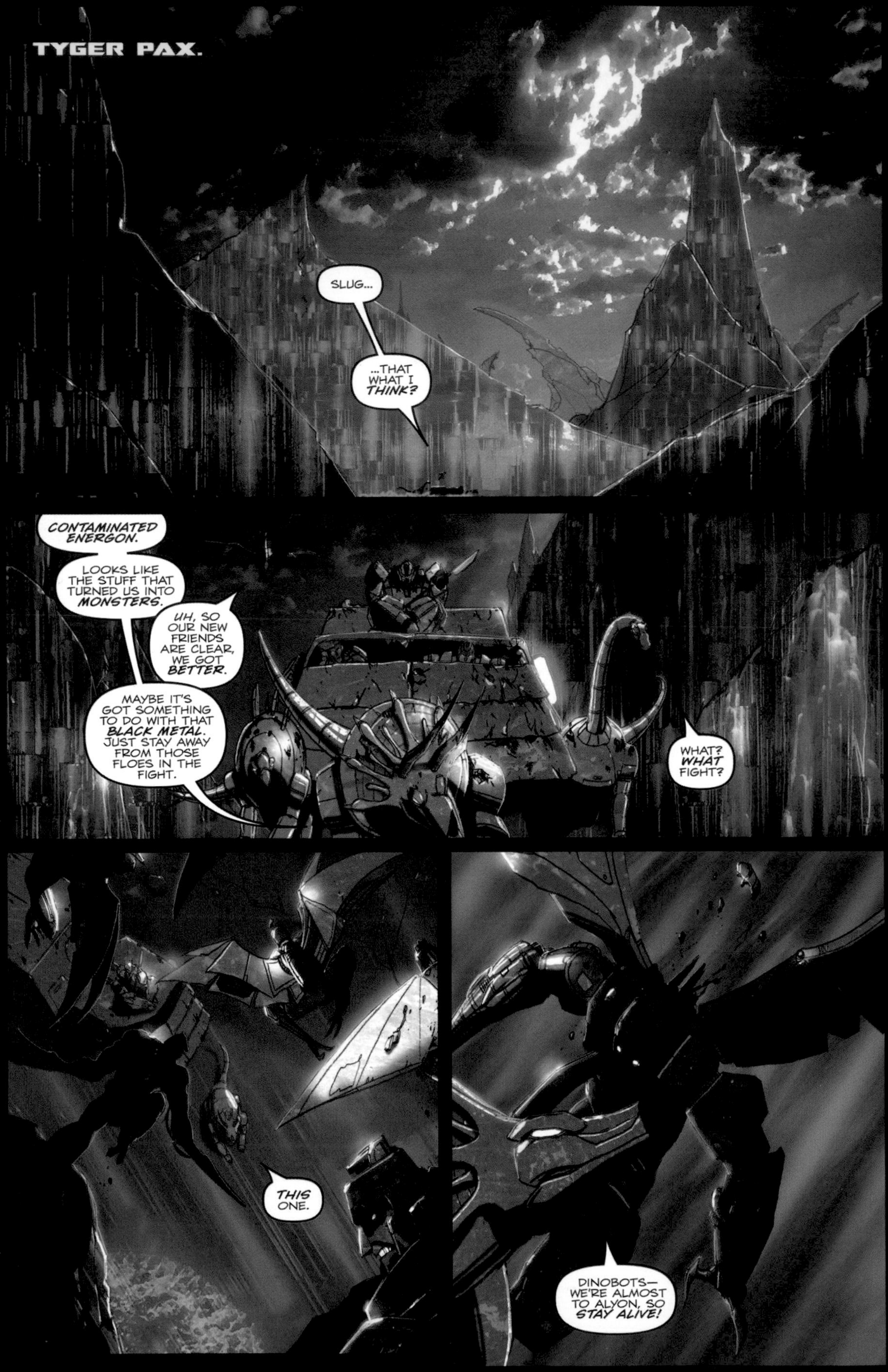

TYGER PAX.
SLUG...
...THAT WHAT I THINK?
CONTAMINATED ENERGON.
LOOKS LIKE THE STUFF THAT TURNED US INTO MONSTERS.
UH, SO OUR NEW FRIENDS ARE CLEAR, WE GOT BETTER.
MAYBE IT'S GOT SOMETHING TO DO WITH THAT BLACK METAL. JUST STAY AWAY FROM THOSE FLOES IN THE FIGHT.
WHAT? WHAT FIGHT?
THIS ONE.
DINOBOTS— WE'RE ALMOST TO ALYON, SO STAY ALIVE!

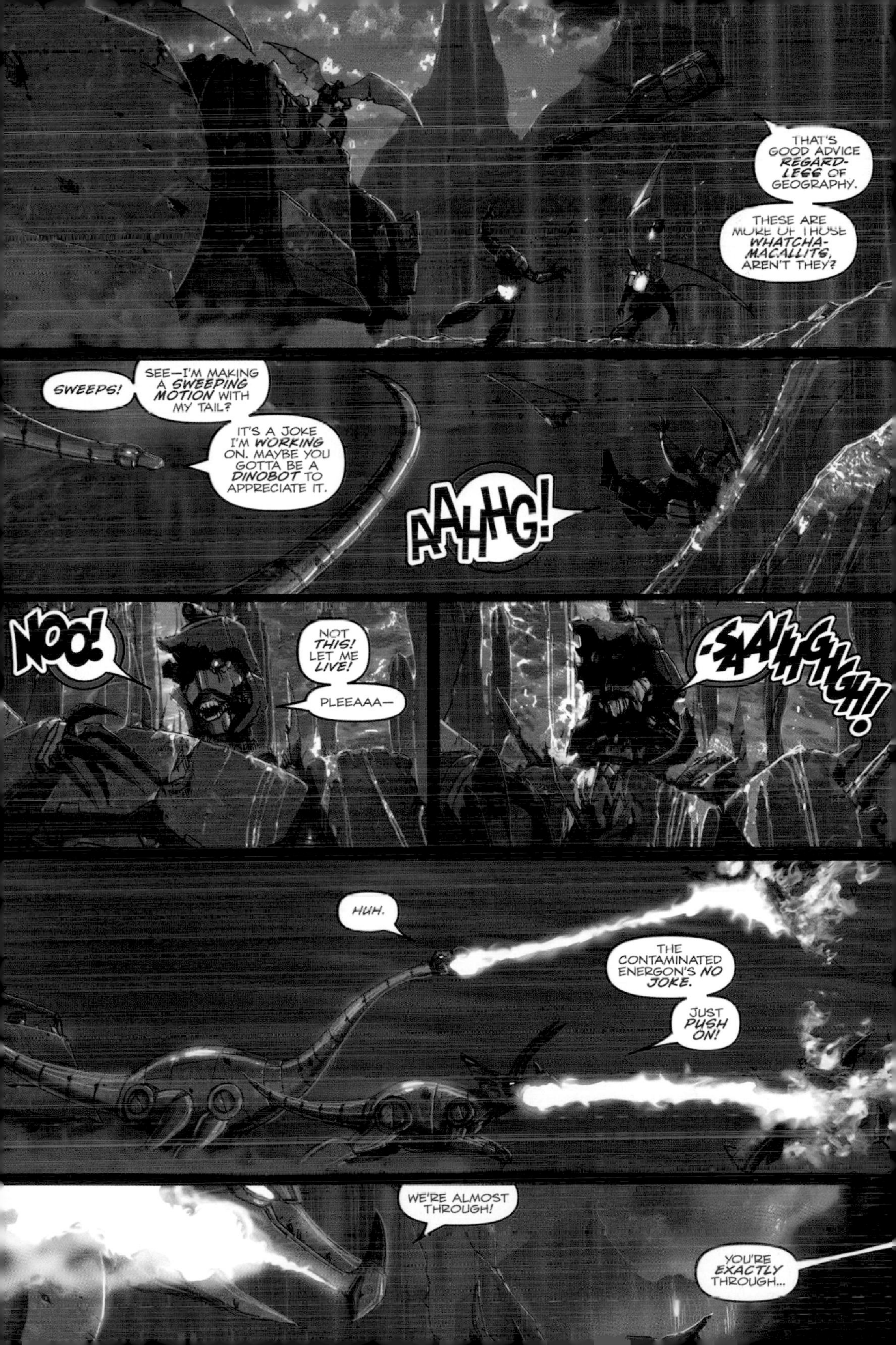
THAT'S GOOD ADVICE REGARDLESS OF GEOGRAPHY.
THESE ARE MORE OF THOSE WHATCHAMACALLITS, AREN'T THEY?
SWEEPS!
SEE—I'M MAKING A SWEEPING MOTION WITH MY TAIL?
IT'S A JOKE I'M WORKING ON. MAYBE YOU GOTTA BE A DINOBOT TO APPRECIATE IT.
AAHHG!
NOO!
NOT THIS! LET ME LIVE!
PLEEAAA—
-SAAHGHGH!!
HUH.
THE CONTAMINATED ENERGON'S NO JOKE.
JUST PUSH ON!
WE'RE ALMOST THROUGH!
YOU'RE EXACTLY THROUGH...

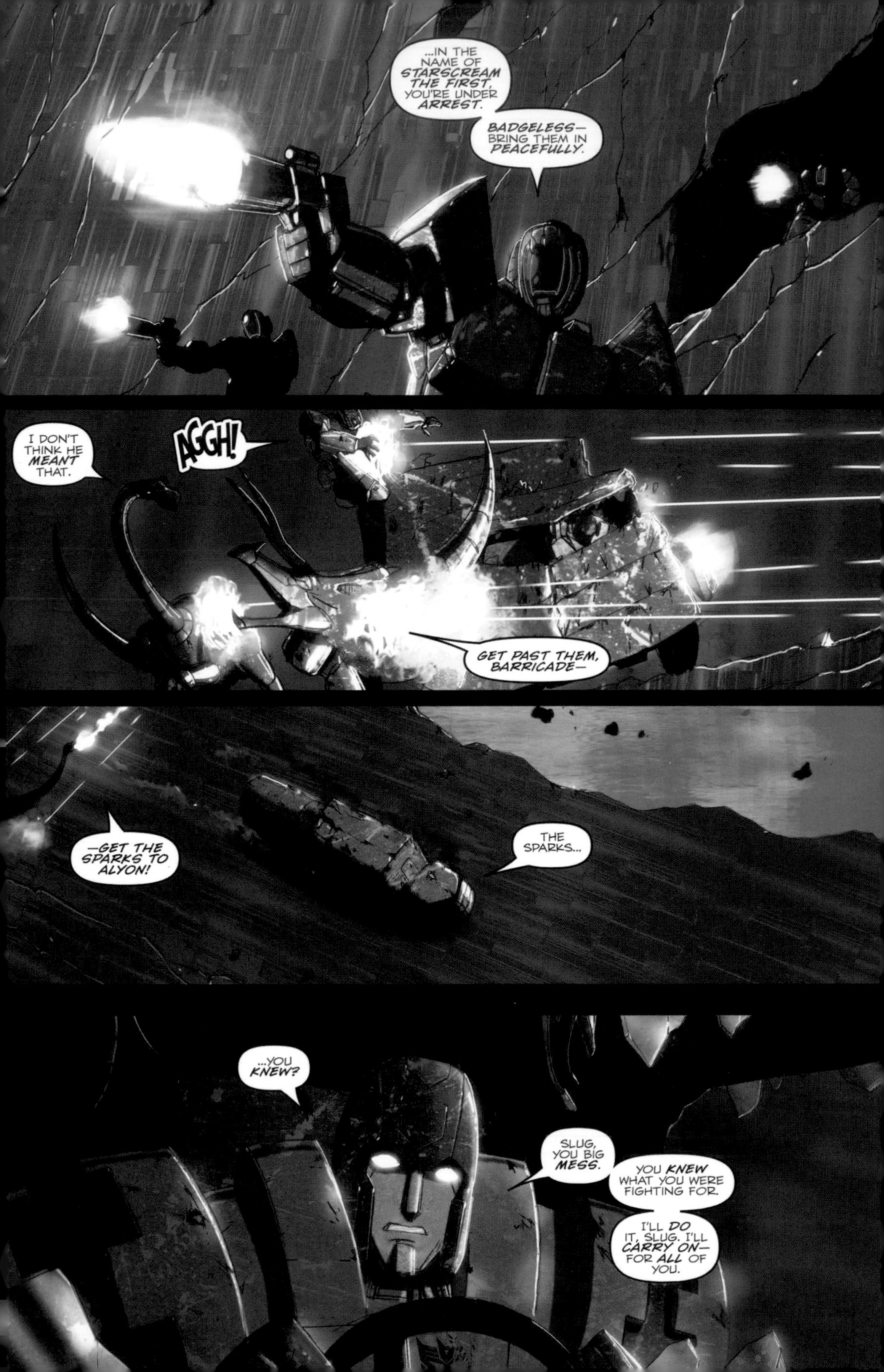
...IN THE NAME OF STARSCREAM THE FIRST, YOU'RE UNDER ARREST.
BADGELESS— BRING THEM IN PEACEFULLY.
I DON'T THINK HE MEANT THAT.
AGGH!
GET PAST THEM, BARRICADE—
—GET THE SPARKS TO ALYON!
THE SPARKS...
...YOU KNEW?
SLUG, YOU BIG MESS.
YOU KNEW WHAT YOU WERE FIGHTING FOR.
I'LL DO IT, SLUG. I'LL CARRY ON— FOR ALL OF YOU.

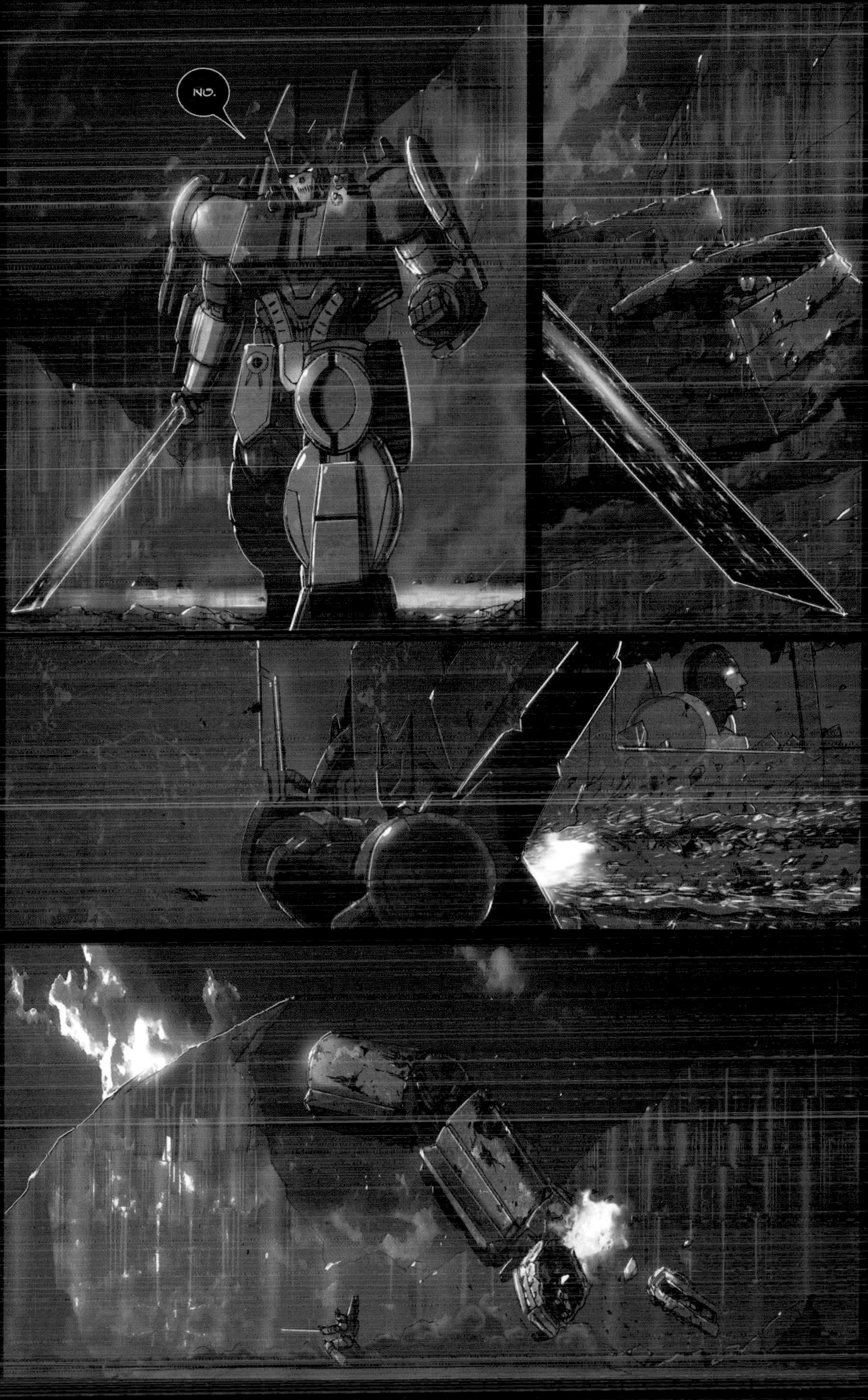
NO.

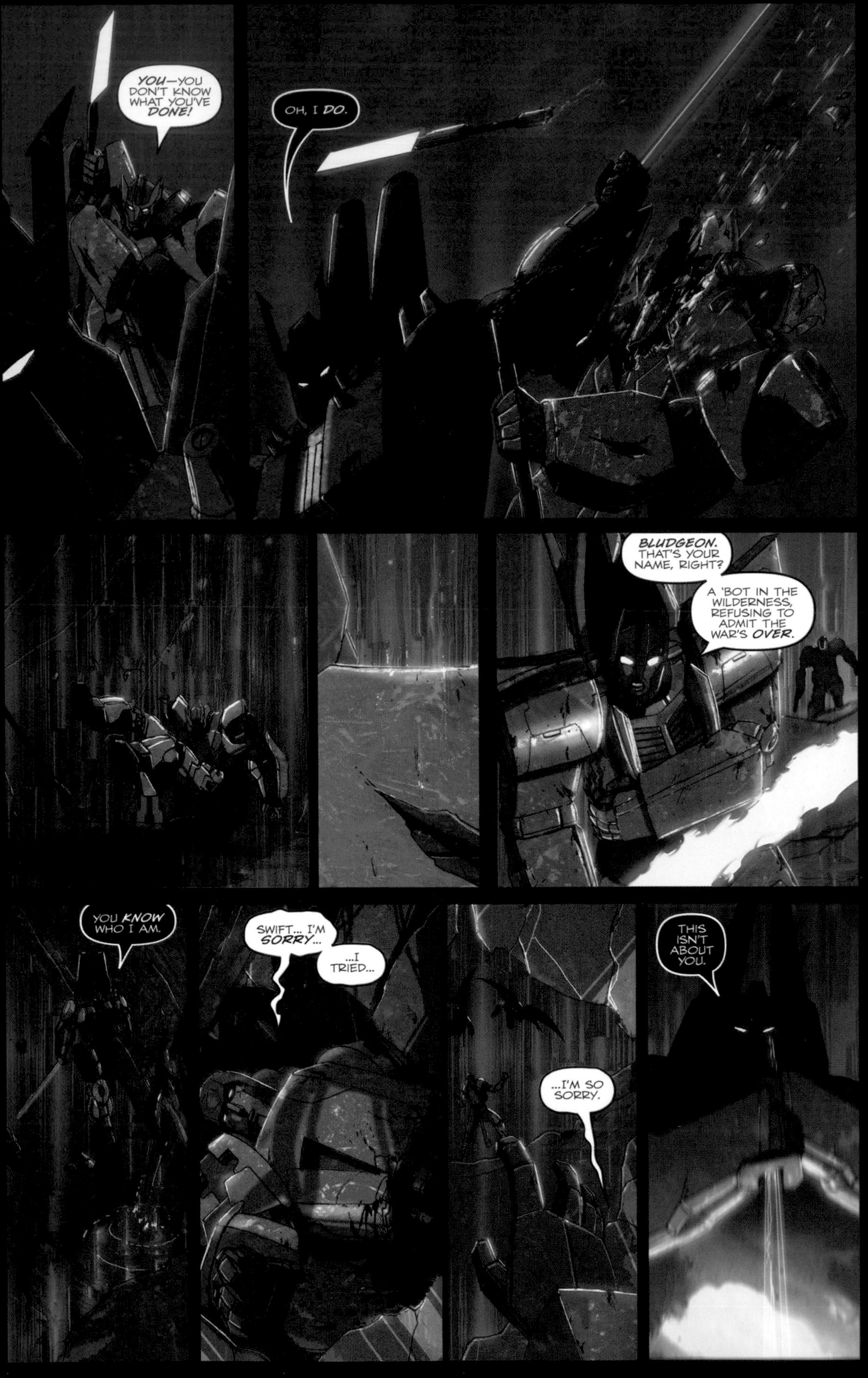

YOU—YOU DON'T KNOW WHAT YOU'VE DONE!
OH, I DO.
BLUDGEON. THAT'S YOUR NAME, RIGHT?
A 'BOT IN THE WILDERNESS, REFUSING TO ADMIT THE WAR'S OVER.
YOU KNOW WHO I AM.
SWIFT... I'M SORRY...
...I TRIED...
...I'M SO SORRY.
THIS ISN'T ABOUT YOU.

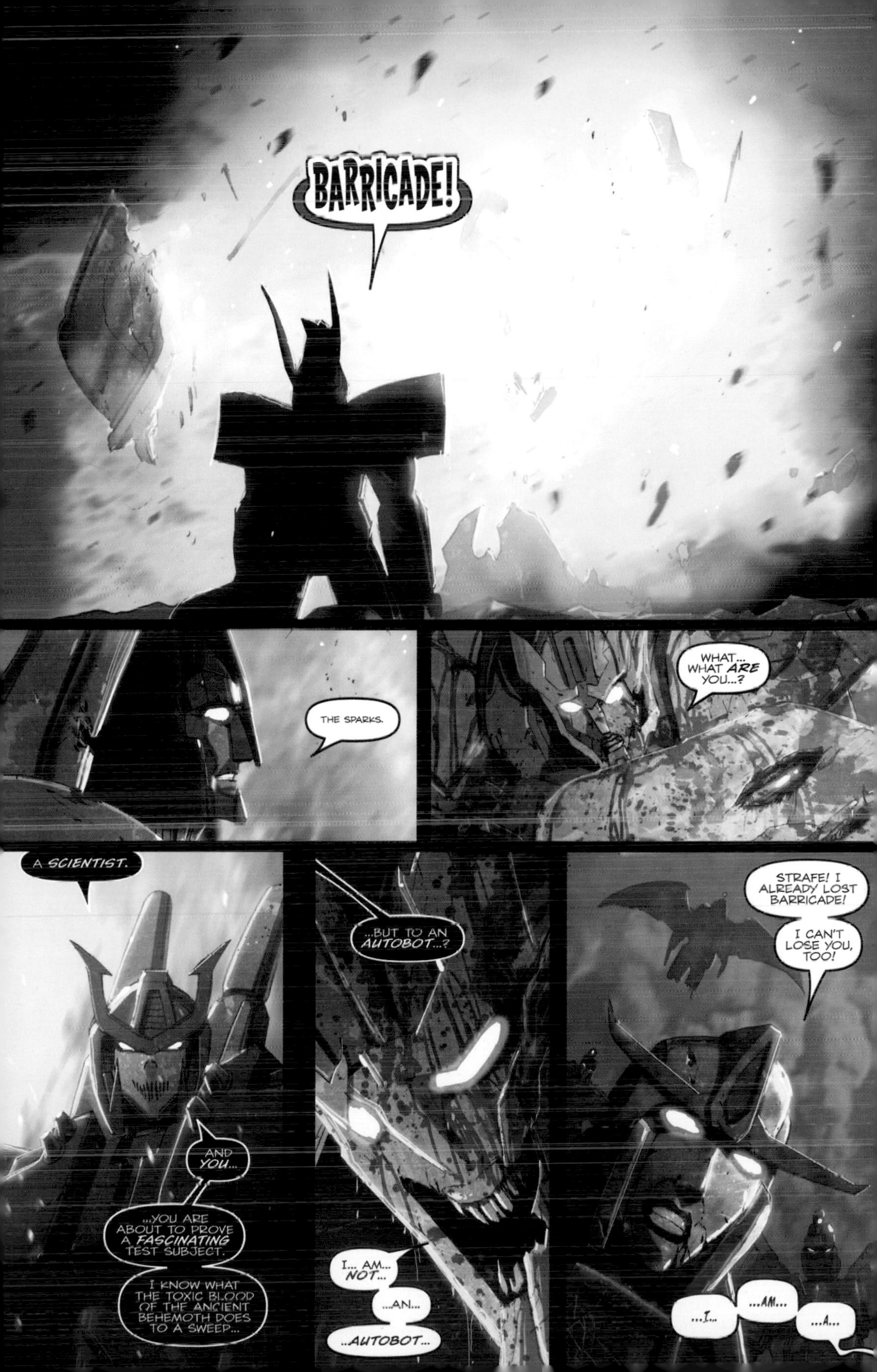
BARRICADE!
THE SPARKS.
WHAT... WHAT ARE YOU...?
A SCIENTIST.
AND YOU...
...YOU ARE ABOUT TO PROVE A FASCINATING TEST SUBJECT.
I KNOW WHAT THE TOXIC BLOOD OF THE ANCIENT BEHEMOTH DOES TO A SWEEP...
...BUT TO AN AUTOBOT...?
I... AM... NOT...
...AN...
..AUTOBOT...
STRAFE! I ALREADY LOST BARRICADE!
I CAN'T LOSE YOU, TOO!
...I...
...AM...
...A...

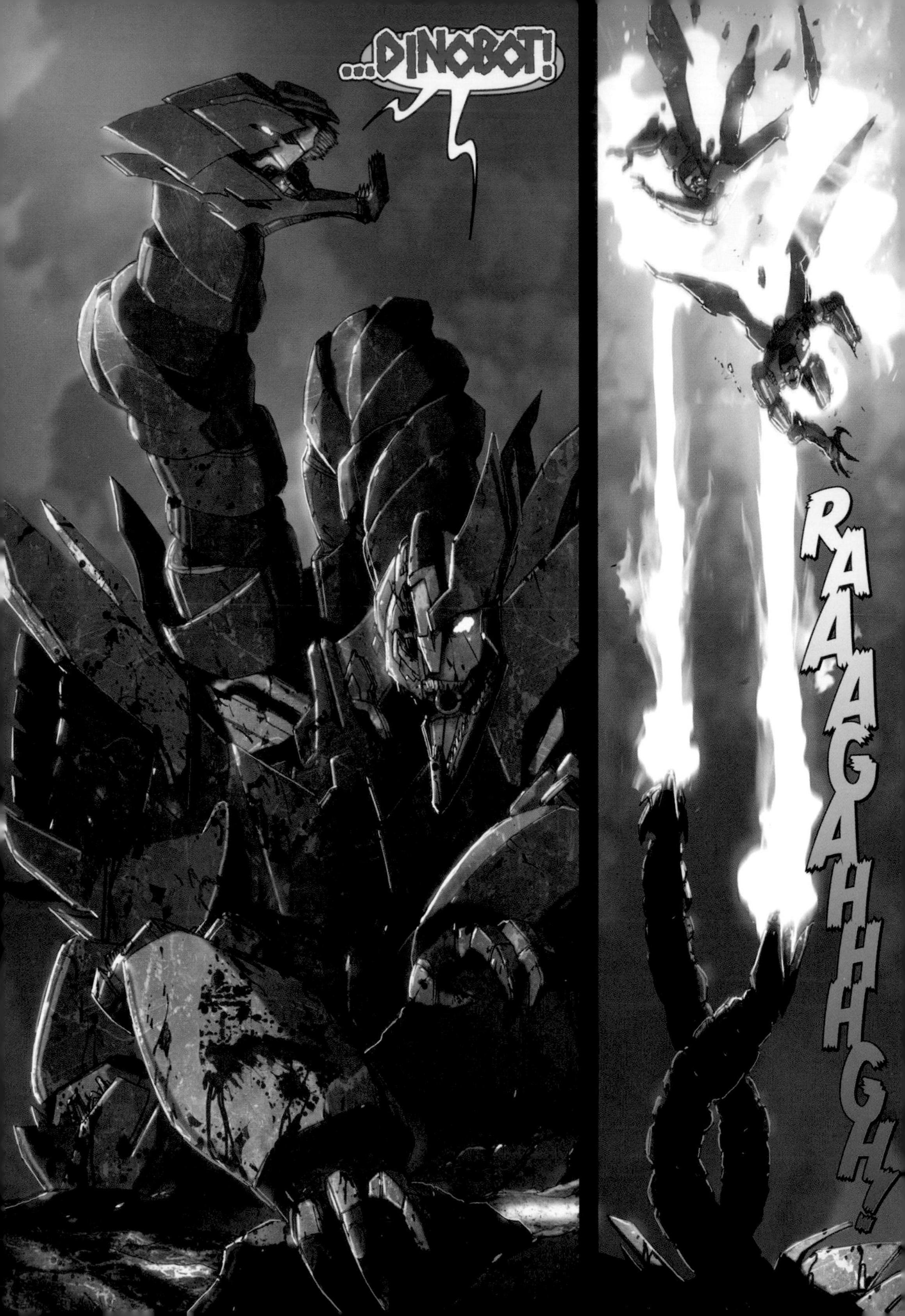
...DINOBOT!
RAAAGAHHHGH!

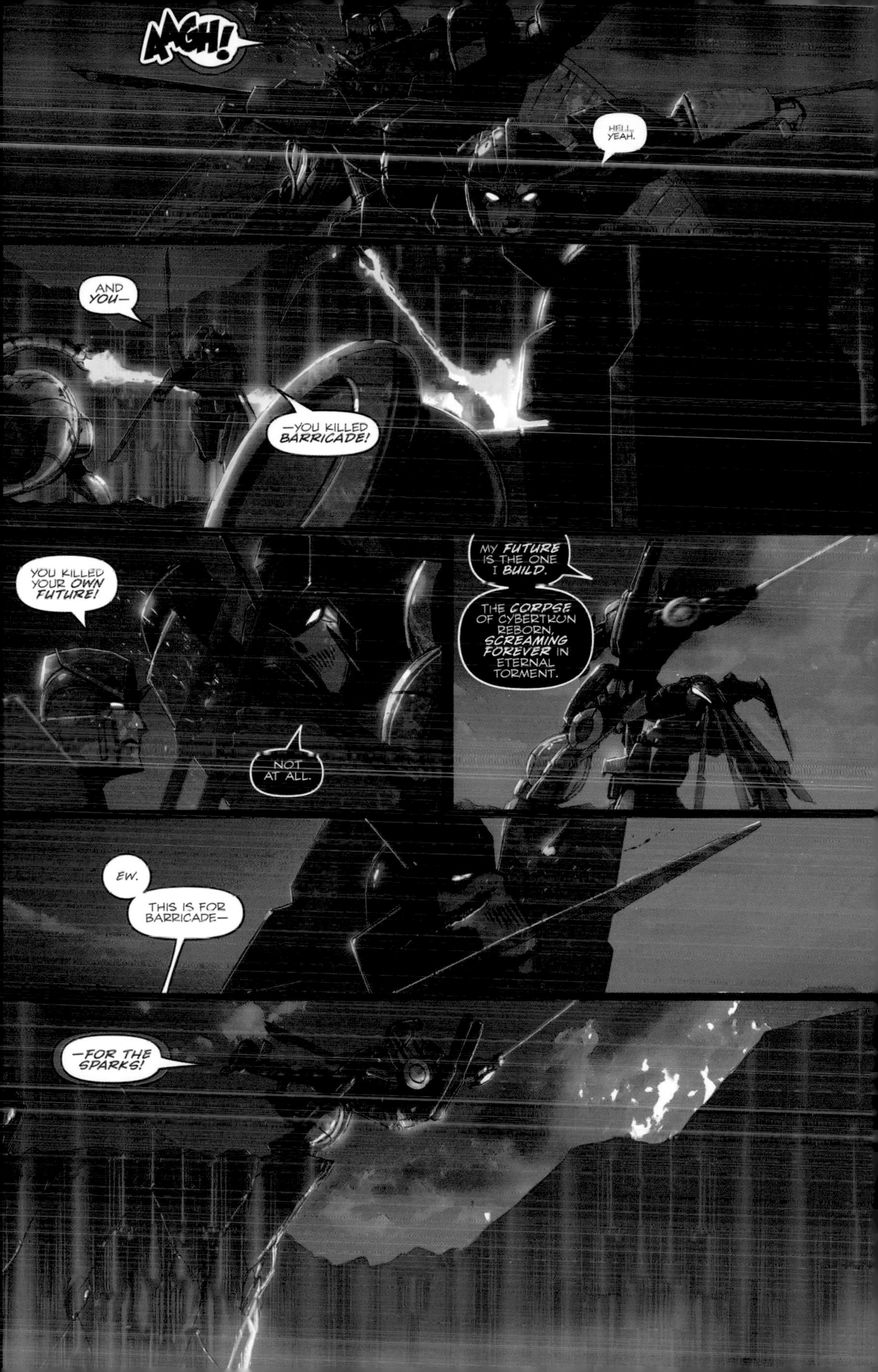
AAGH!
HELL, YEAH.
AND YOU—
—YOU KILLED BARRICADE!
YOU KILLED YOUR OWN FUTURE!
NOT AT ALL.
MY FUTURE IS THE ONE I BUILD.
THE CORPSE OF CYBERTRON REBORN, SCREAMING FOREVER IN ETERNAL TORMENT.
EW.
THIS IS FOR BARRICADE—
—FOR THE SPARKS!

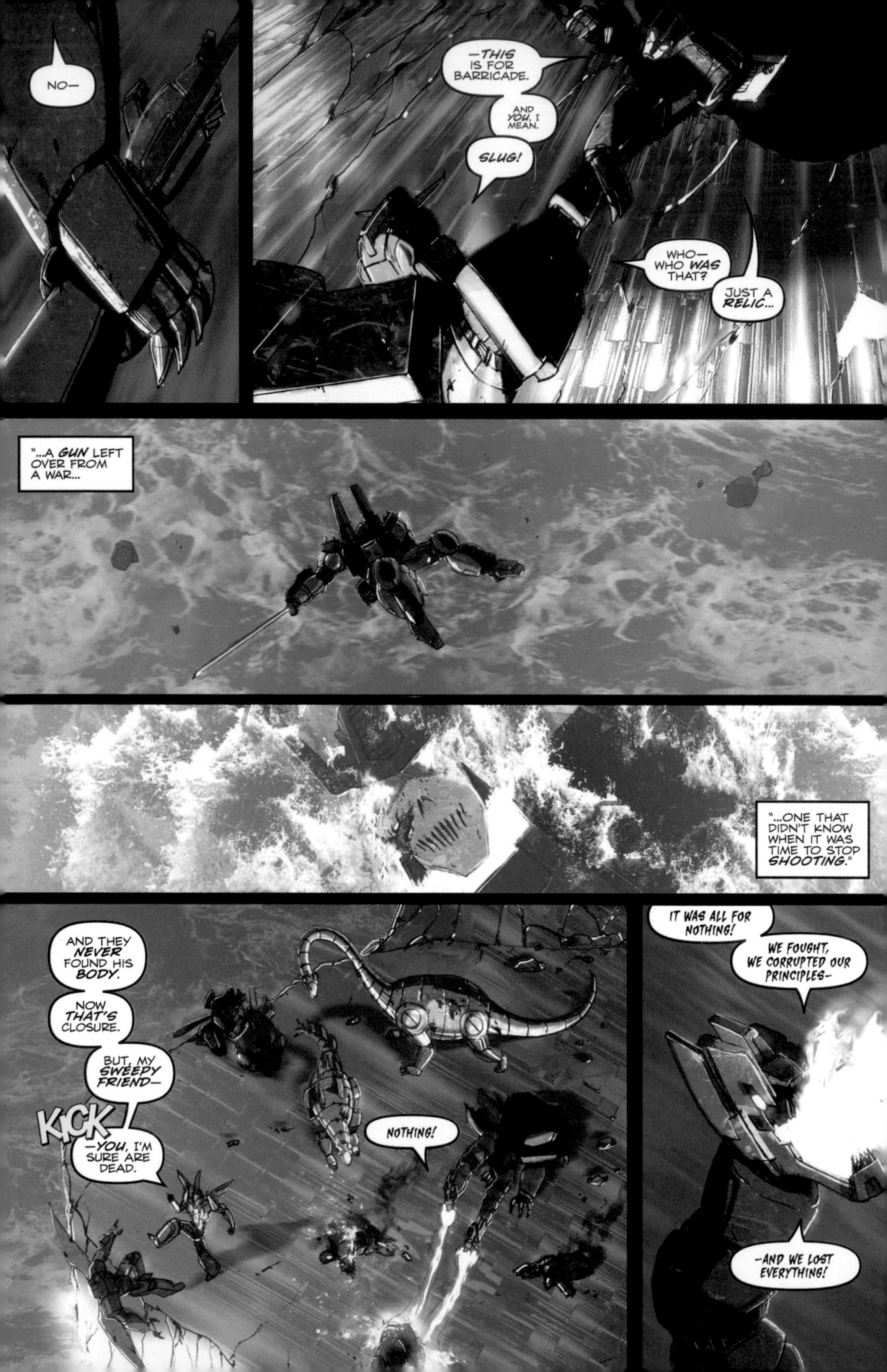
NO—
—THIS IS FOR BARRICADE.
AND YOU, I MEAN.
SLUG!
WHO— WHO WAS THAT?
JUST A RELIC...
"...A GUN LEFT OVER FROM A WAR...
"...ONE THAT DIDN'T KNOW WHEN IT WAS TIME TO STOP SHOOTING."
AND THEY NEVER FOUND HIS BODY.
NOW THAT'S CLOSURE.
BUT, MY SWEEPY FRIEND—
KICK
—YOU, I'M SURE ARE DEAD.
NOTHING!
IT WAS ALL FOR NOTHING!
WE FOUGHT, WE CORRUPTED OUR PRINCIPLES-
-AND WE LOST EVERYTHING!

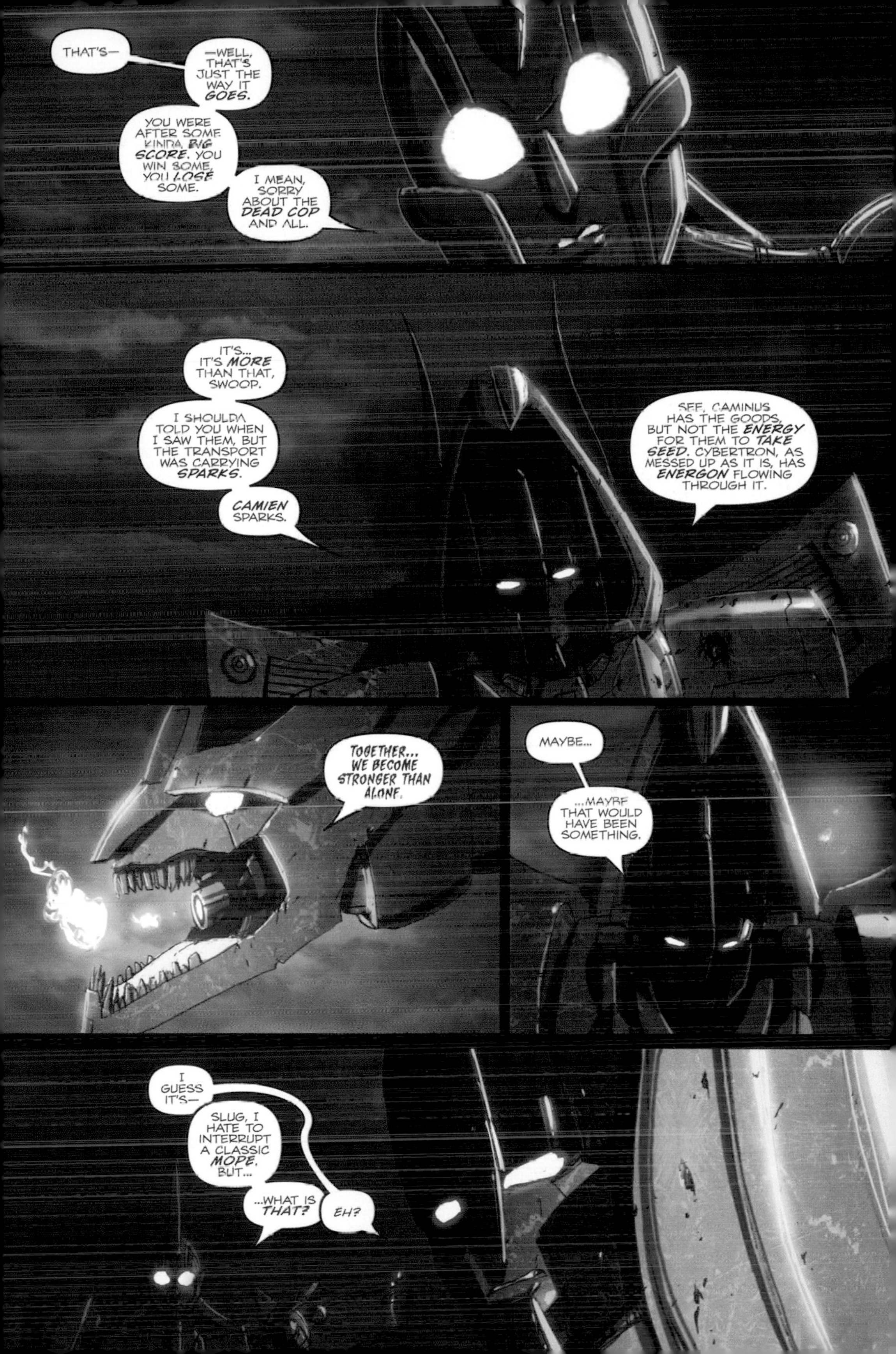
THAT'S—
—WELL, THAT'S JUST THE WAY IT GOES.
YOU WERE AFTER SOME KINDA BIG SCORE. YOU WIN SOME, YOU LOSE SOME.
I MEAN, SORRY ABOUT THE DEAD COP AND ALL.
IT'S... IT'S MORE THAN THAT, SWOOP.
I SHOULDA TOLD YOU WHEN I SAW THEM, BUT THE TRANSPORT WAS CARRYING SPARKS.
CAMIEN SPARKS.
SEE, CAMINUS HAS THE GOODS, BUT NOT THE ENERGY FOR THEM TO TAKE SEED. CYBERTRON, AS MESSED UP AS IT IS, HAS ENERGON FLOWING THROUGH IT.
TOGETHER... WE BECOME STRONGER THAN ALONE.
MAYBE...
...MAYBE THAT WOULD HAVE BEEN SOMETHING.
I GUESS IT'S—
SLUG, I HATE TO INTERRUPT A CLASSIC MOPE, BUT...
...WHAT IS THAT?
EH?

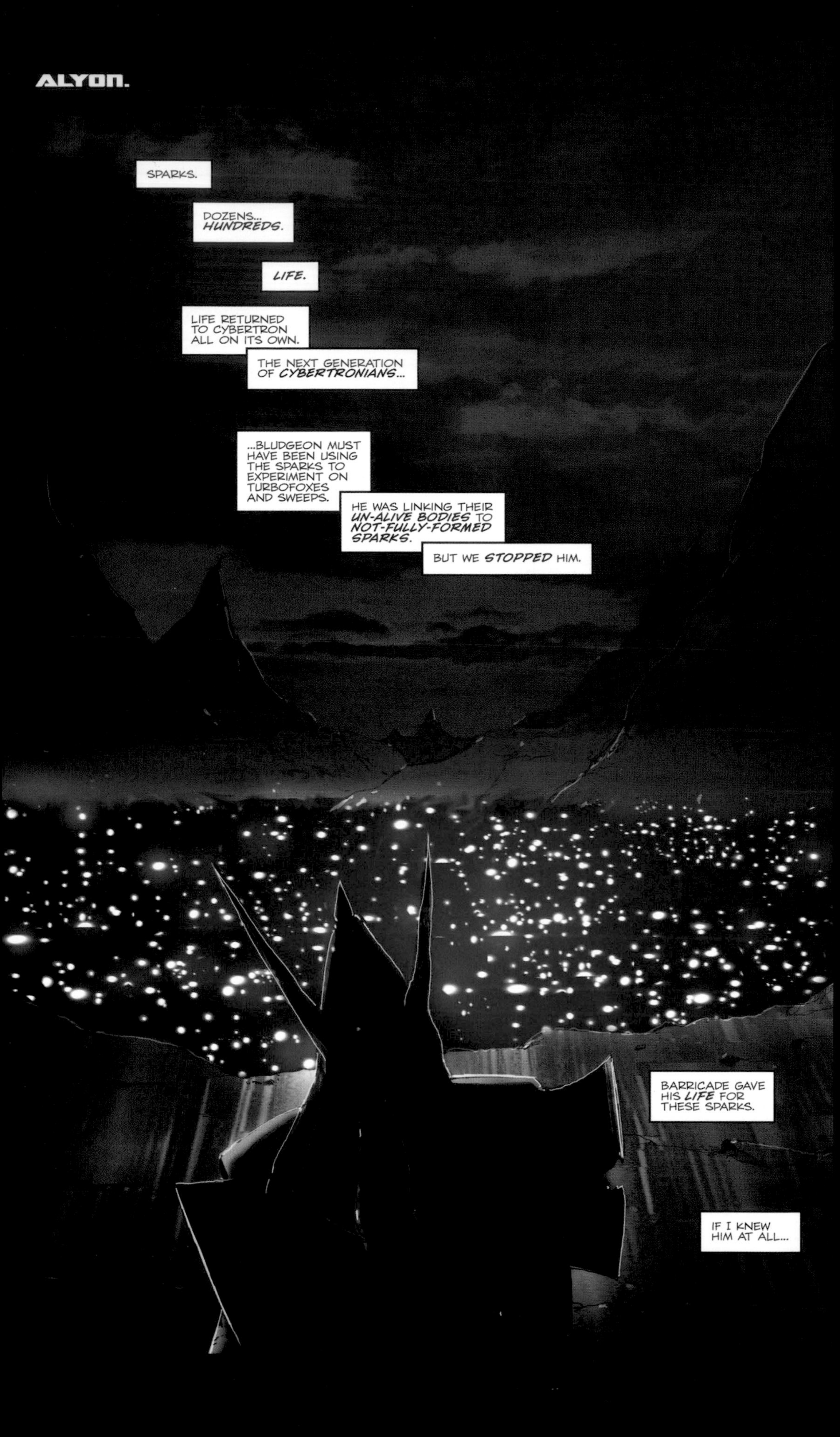
ALYON.
SPARKS.
DOZENS... HUNDREDS.
LIFE.
LIFE RETURNED TO CYBERTRON ALL ON ITS OWN.
THE NEXT GENERATION OF CYBERTRONIANS...
...BLUDGEON MUST HAVE BEEN USING THE SPARKS TO EXPERIMENT ON TURBOFOXES AND SWEEPS.
HE WAS LINKING THEIR UN-ALIVE BODIES TO NOT-FULLY-FORMED SPARKS.
BUT WE STOPPED HIM.
BARRICADE GAVE HIS LIFE FOR THESE SPARKS.
IF I KNEW HIM AT ALL...

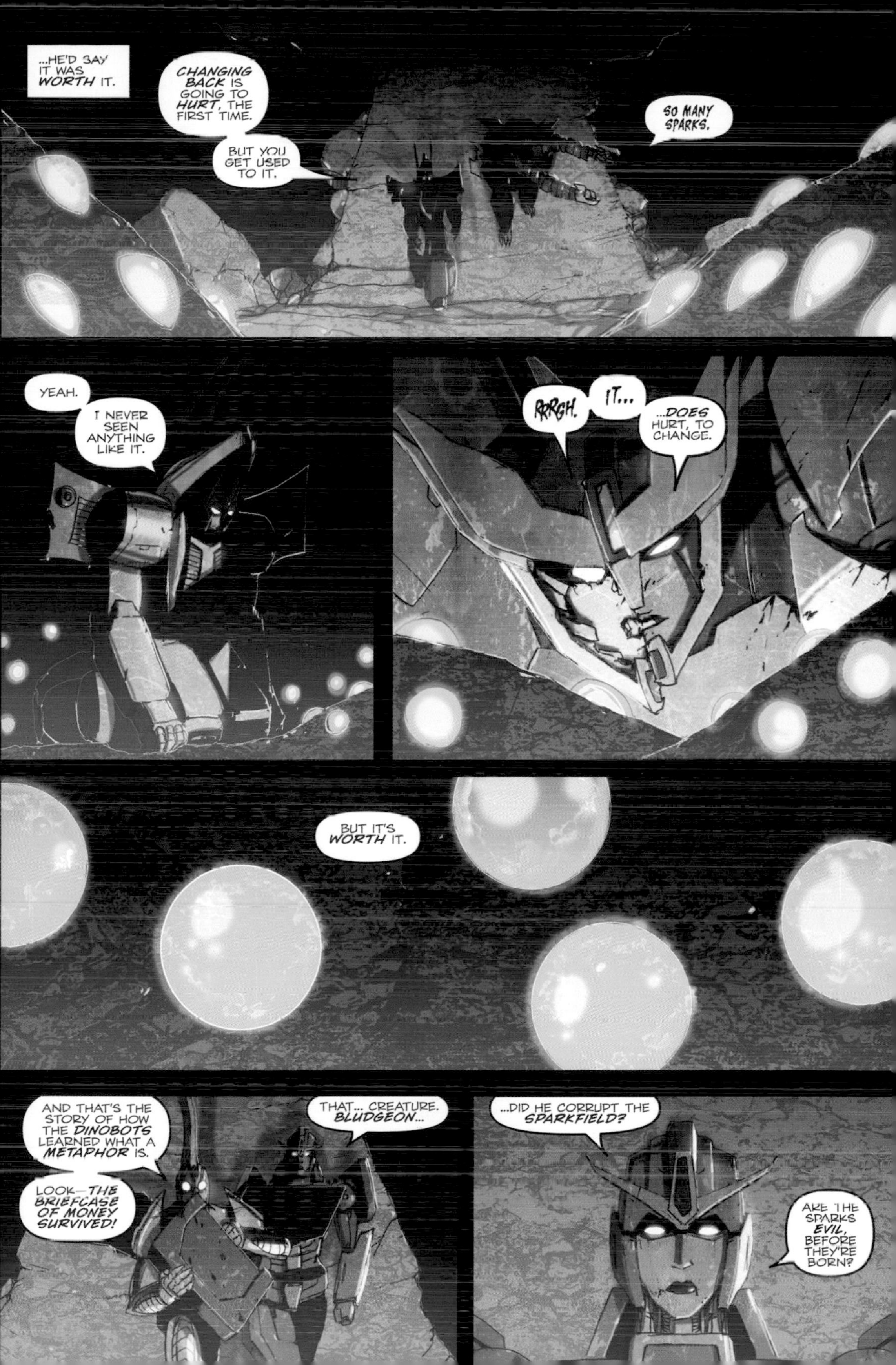

...HE'D SAY IT WAS WORTH IT.
CHANGING BACK IS GOING TO HURT, THE FIRST TIME.
BUT YOU GET USED TO IT.
SO MANY SPARKS.
YEAH.
I NEVER SEEN ANYTHING LIKE IT.
RRRGH.
IT...
...DOES HURT, TO CHANGE.
BUT IT'S WORTH IT.
AND THAT'S THE STORY OF HOW THE DINOBOTS LEARNED WHAT A METAPHOR IS.
LOOK—THE BRIEFCASE OF MONEY SURVIVED!
THAT... CREATURE. BLUDGEON...
...DID HE CORRUPT THE SPARKFIELD?
ARE THE SPARKS EVIL, BEFORE THEY'RE BORN?

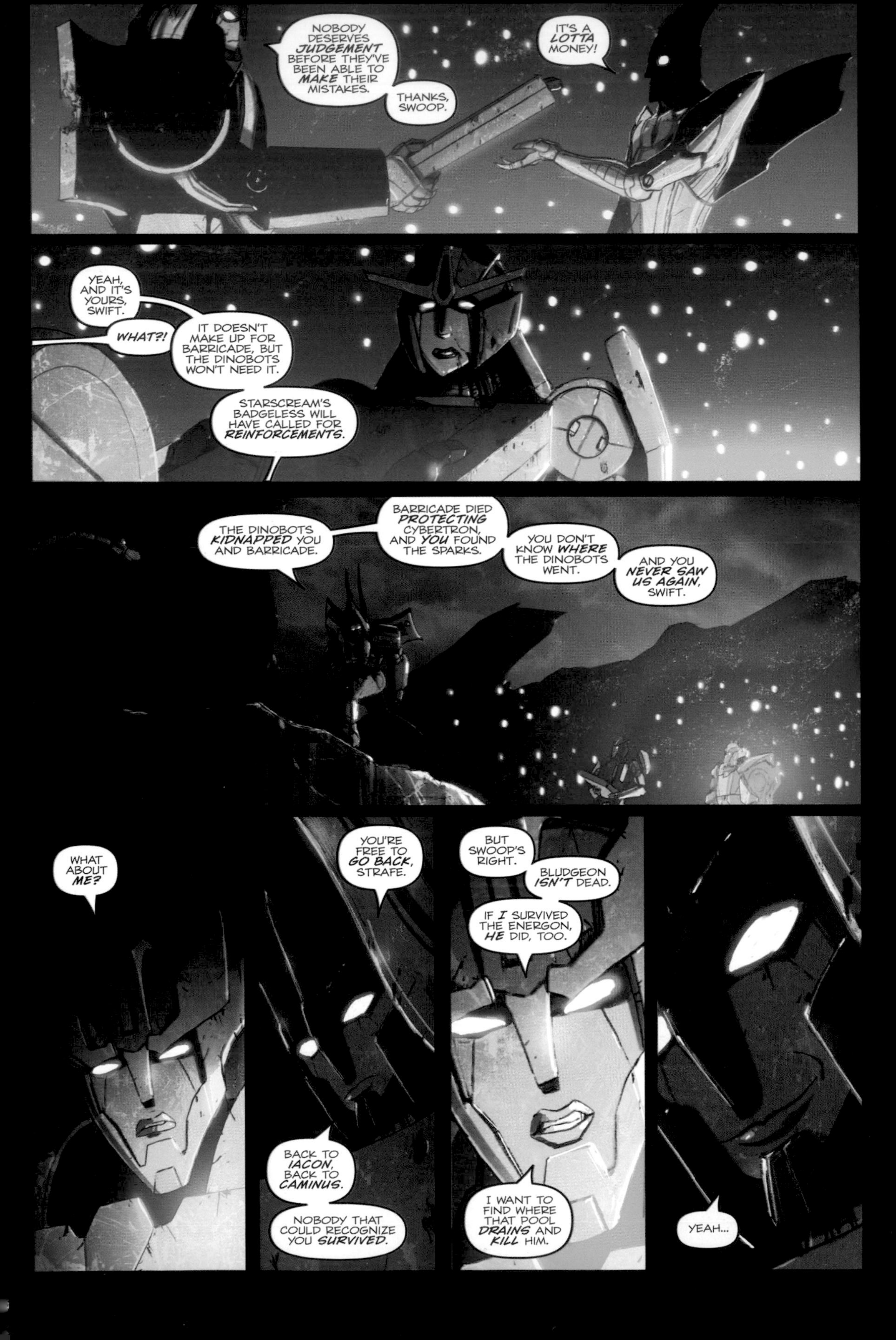
NOBODY DESERVES JUDGEMENT BEFORE THEY'VE BEEN ABLE TO MAKE THEIR MISTAKES.
IT'S A LOTTA MONEY!
THANKS, SWOOP.
YEAH, AND IT'S YOURS, SWIFT.
WHAT?!
IT DOESN'T MAKE UP FOR BARRICADE, BUT THE DINOBOTS WON'T NEED IT.
STARSCREAM'S BADGELESS WILL HAVE CALLED FOR REINFORCEMENTS.
THE DINOBOTS KIDNAPPED YOU AND BARRICADE.
BARRICADE DIED PROTECTING CYBERTRON, AND YOU FOUND THE SPARKS.
YOU DON'T KNOW WHERE THE DINOBOTS WENT.
AND YOU NEVER SAW US AGAIN, SWIFT.
WHAT ABOUT ME?
YOU'RE FREE TO GO BACK, STRAFE.
BACK TO IACON, BACK TO CAMINUS.
NOBODY THAT COULD RECOGNIZE YOU SURVIVED.
BUT SWOOP'S RIGHT.
BLUDGEON ISN'T DEAD.
IF I SURVIVED THE ENERGON, HE DID, TOO.
I WANT TO FIND WHERE THAT POOL DRAINS AND KILL HIM.
YEAH...

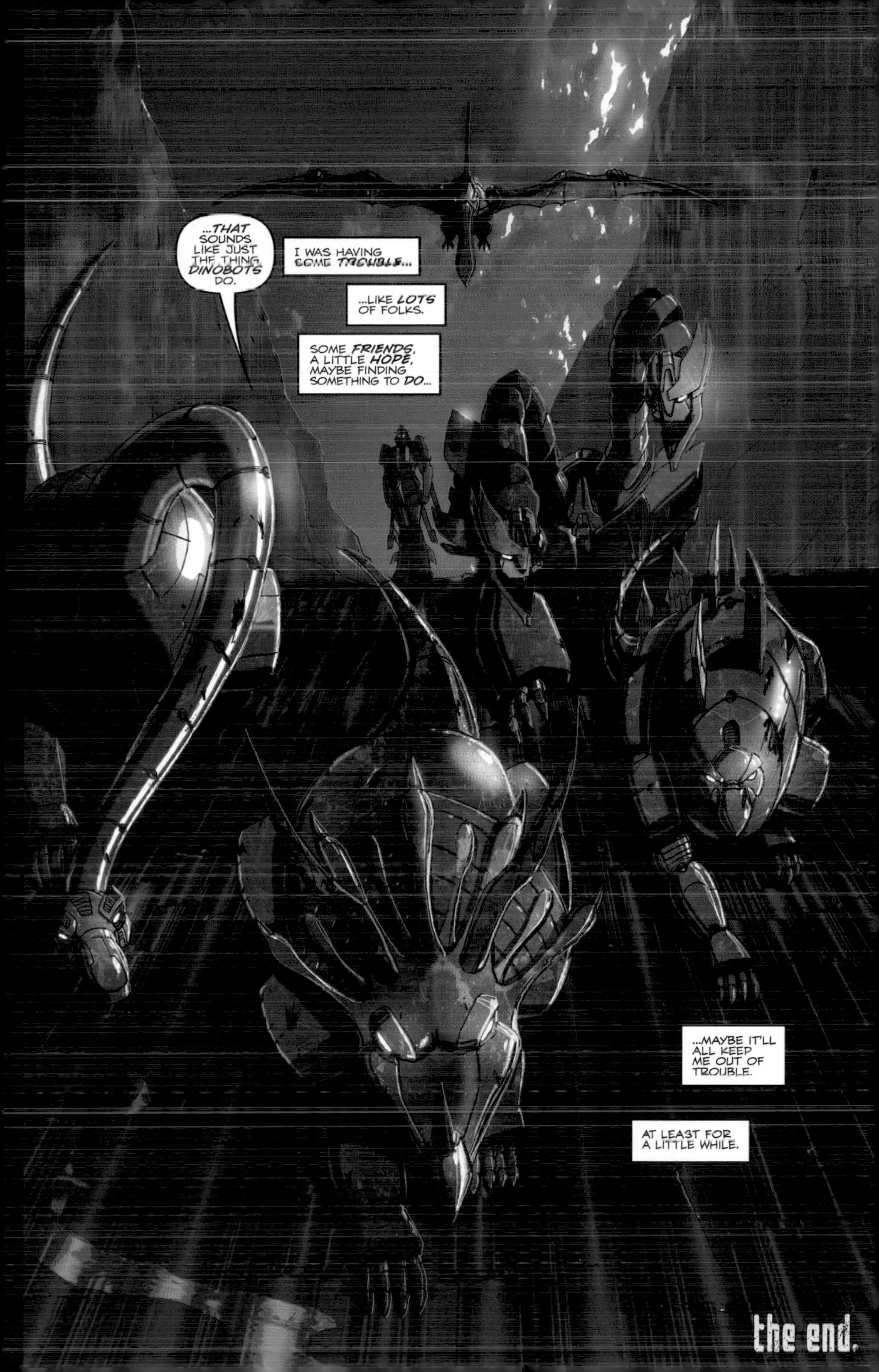
I WAS HAVING SOME TROUBLE...
...THAT SOUNDS LIKE JUST THE THING DINOBOTS DO.
...LIKE LOTS OF FOLKS.
SOME FRIENDS, A LITTLE HOPE, MAYBE FINDING SOMETHING TO DO...
...MAYBE IT'LL ALL KEEP ME OUT OF TROUBLE.
AT LEAST FOR A LITTLE WHILE.
the end.

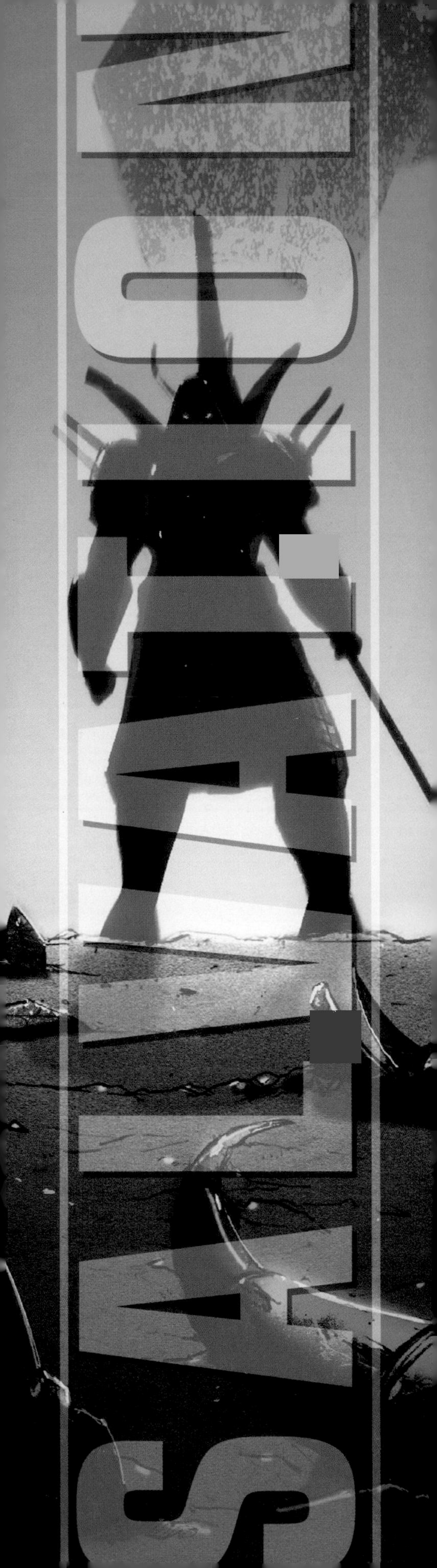
SALVATION

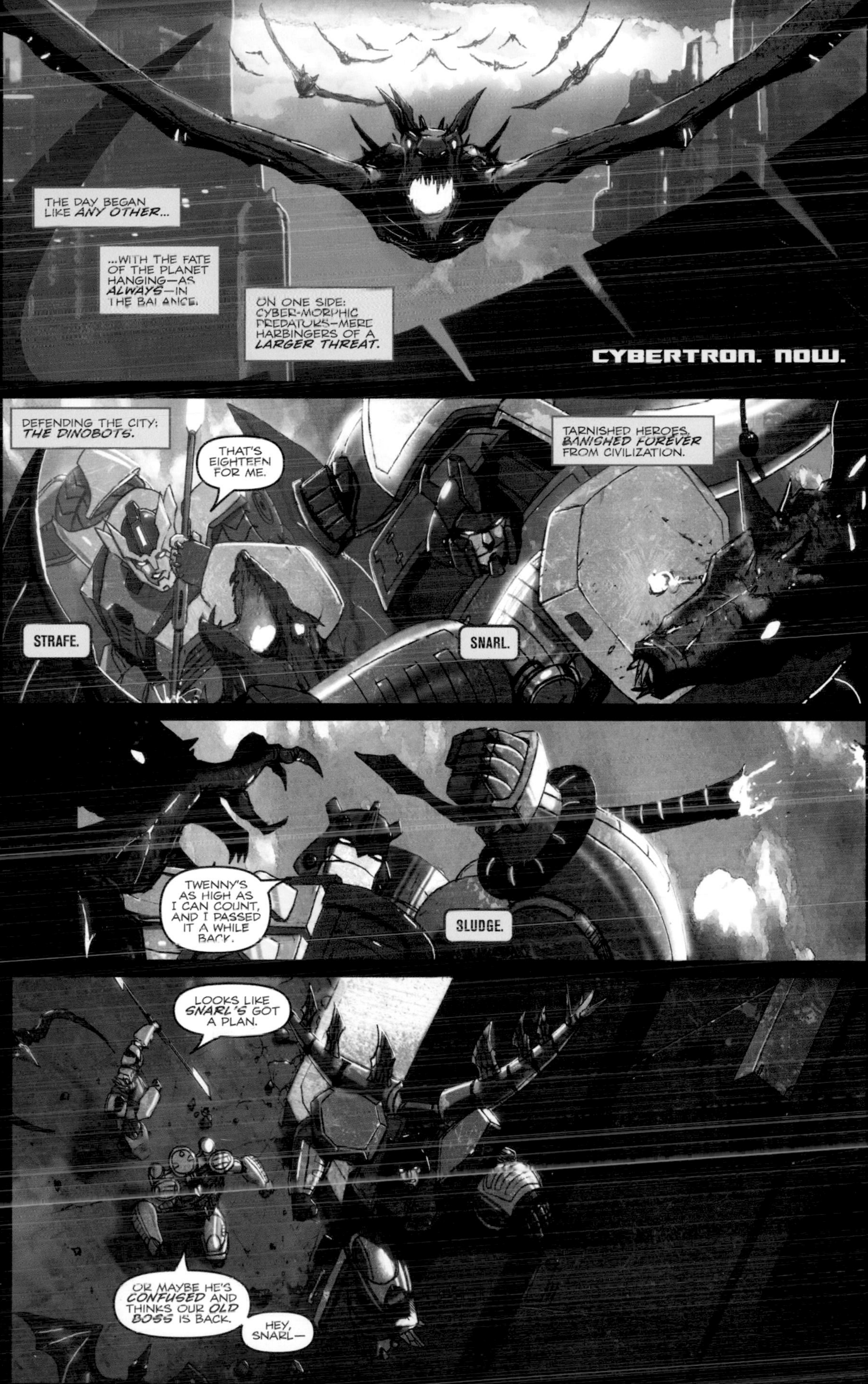
THE DAY BEGAN LIKE ANY OTHER...
...WITH THE FATE OF THE PLANET HANGING—AS ALWAYS—IN THE BALANCE.
ON ONE SIDE: CYBER-MORPHIC PREDATORS—MERE HARBINGERS OF A LARGER THREAT.
CYBERTRON. NOW.
DEFENDING THE CITY: THE DINOBOTS.
THAT'S EIGHTEEN FOR ME.
TARNISHED HEROES, BANISHED FOREVER FROM CIVILIZATION.
STRAFE.
SNARL.
TWENNY'S AS HIGH AS I CAN COUNT, AND I PASSED IT A WHILE BACK.
SLUDGE.
LOOKS LIKE SNARL'S GOT A PLAN.
OR MAYBE HE'S CONFUSED AND THINKS OUR OLD BOSS IS BACK.
HEY, SNARL—

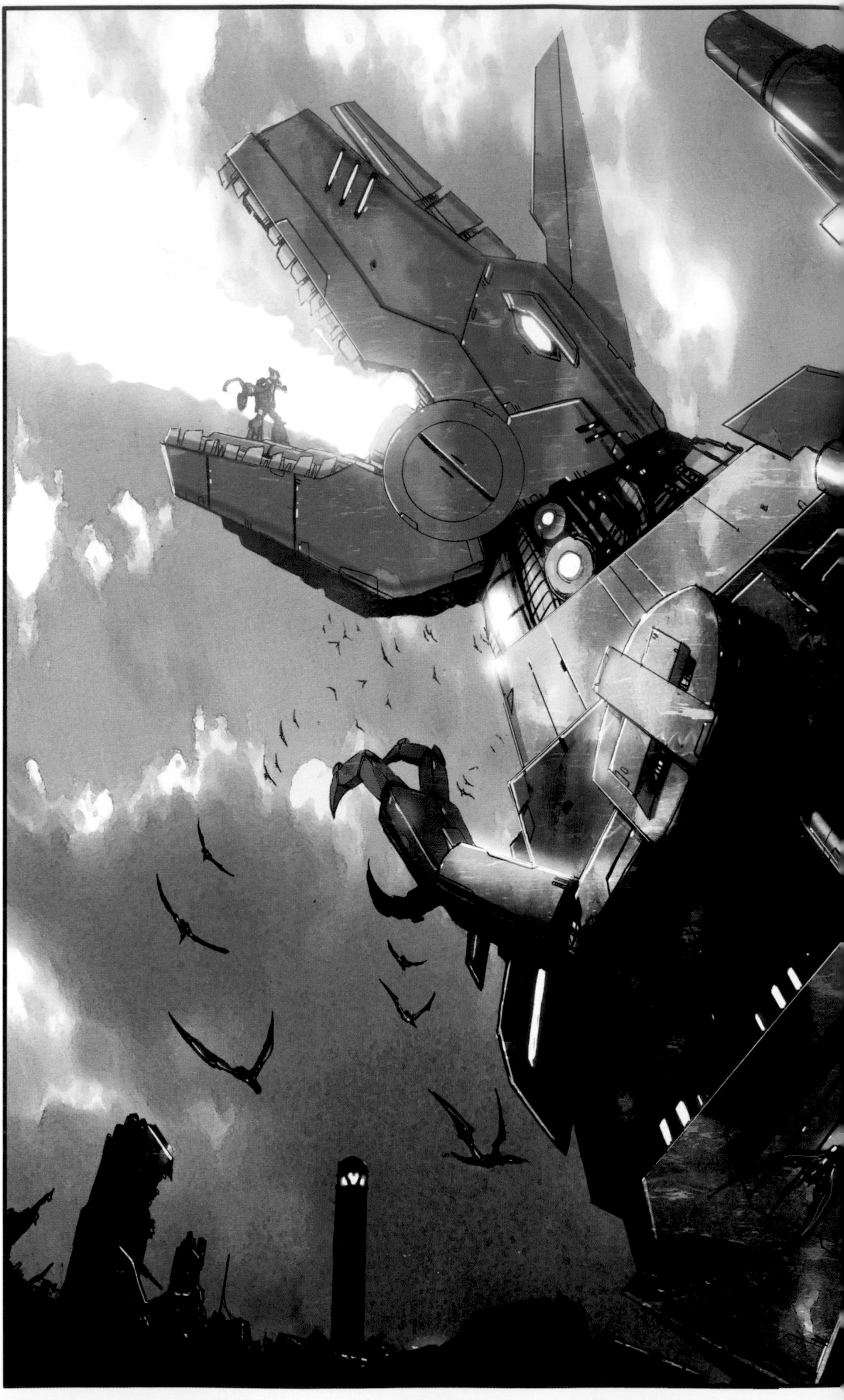

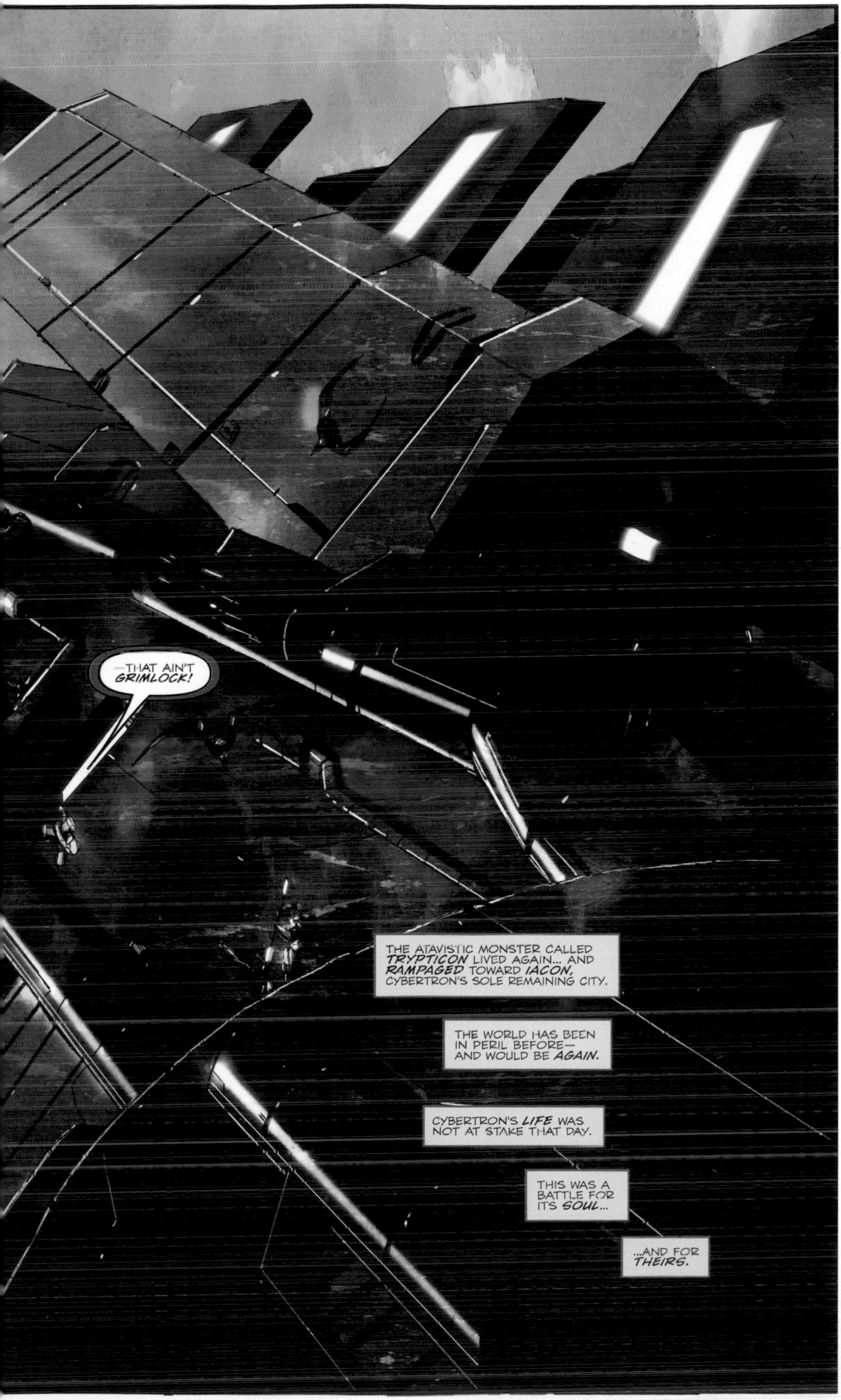
—THAT AIN'T GRIMLOCK!
THE ATAVISTIC MONSTER CALLED TRYPTICON LIVED AGAIN... AND RAMPAGED TOWARD IACON, CYBERTRON'S SOLE REMAINING CITY.
THE WORLD HAS BEEN IN PERIL BEFORE— AND WOULD BE AGAIN.
CYBERTRON'S LIFE WAS NOT AT STAKE THAT DAY.
THIS WAS A BATTLE FOR ITS SOUL...
...AND FOR THEIRS.

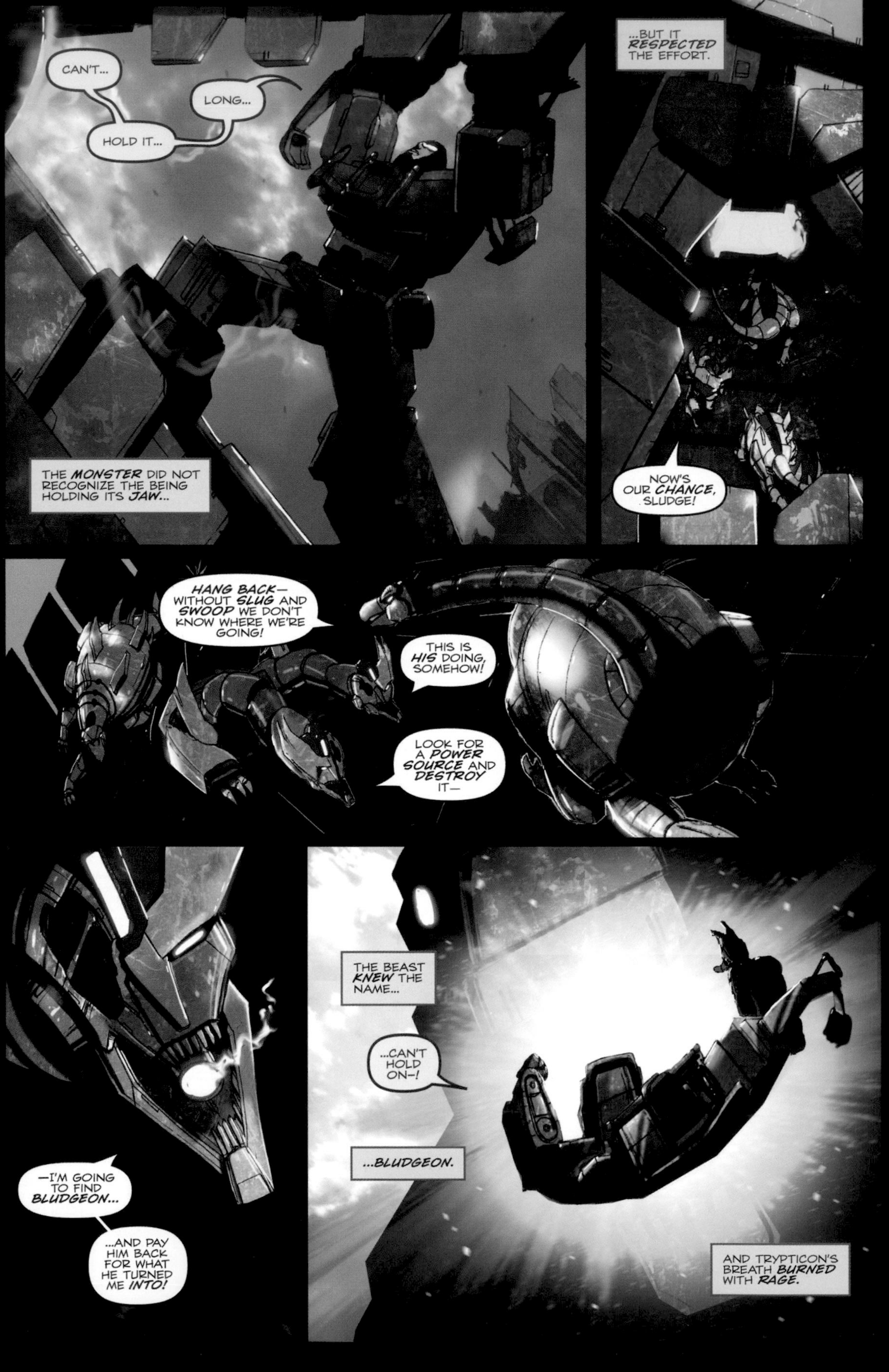
CAN'T...
HOLD IT...
LONG...
THE MONSTER DID NOT RECOGNIZE THE BEING HOLDING ITS JAW...
...BUT IT RESPECTED THE EFFORT.
NOW'S OUR CHANCE, SLUDGE!
HANG BACK—WITHOUT SLUG AND SWOOP WE DON'T KNOW WHERE WE'RE GOING!
THIS IS HIS DOING, SOMEHOW!
LOOK FOR A POWER SOURCE AND DESTROY IT—
—I'M GOING TO FIND BLUDGEON...
...AND PAY HIM BACK FOR WHAT HE TURNED ME INTO!
THE BEAST KNEW THE NAME...
...CAN'T HOLD ON—!
...BLUDGEON.
AND TRYPTICON'S BREATH BURNED WITH RAGE.

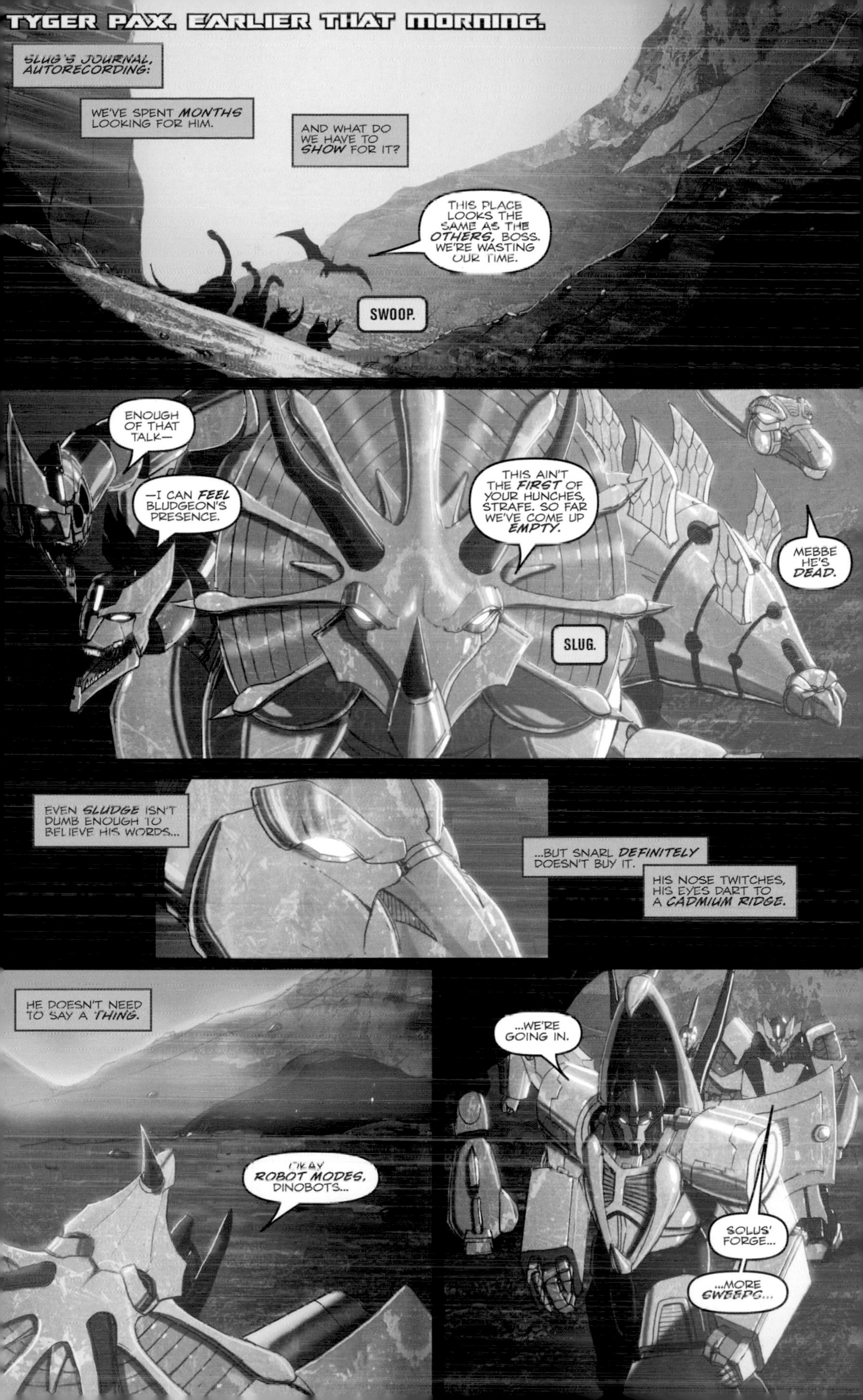
TYGER PAX. EARLIER THAT MORNING.
SLUG'S JOURNAL, AUTORECORDING:
WE'VE SPENT MONTHS LOOKING FOR HIM.
AND WHAT DO WE HAVE TO SHOW FOR IT?
THIS PLACE LOOKS THE SAME AS THE OTHERS, BOSS. WE'RE WASTING OUR TIME.
SWOOP.
ENOUGH OF THAT TALK—
—I CAN FEEL BLUDGEON'S PRESENCE.
THIS AIN'T THE FIRST OF YOUR HUNCHES, STRAFE. SO FAR WE'VE COME UP EMPTY.
SLUG.
MEBBE HE'S DEAD.
EVEN SLUDGE ISN'T DUMB ENOUGH TO BELIEVE HIS WORDS...
...BUT SNARL DEFINITELY DOESN'T BUY IT.
HIS NOSE TWITCHES, HIS EYES DART TO A CADMIUM RIDGE.
HE DOESN'T NEED TO SAY A THING.
OKAY ROBOT MODES, DINOBOTS...
...WE'RE GOING IN.
SOLUS' FORGE...
...MORE SWEEPS...

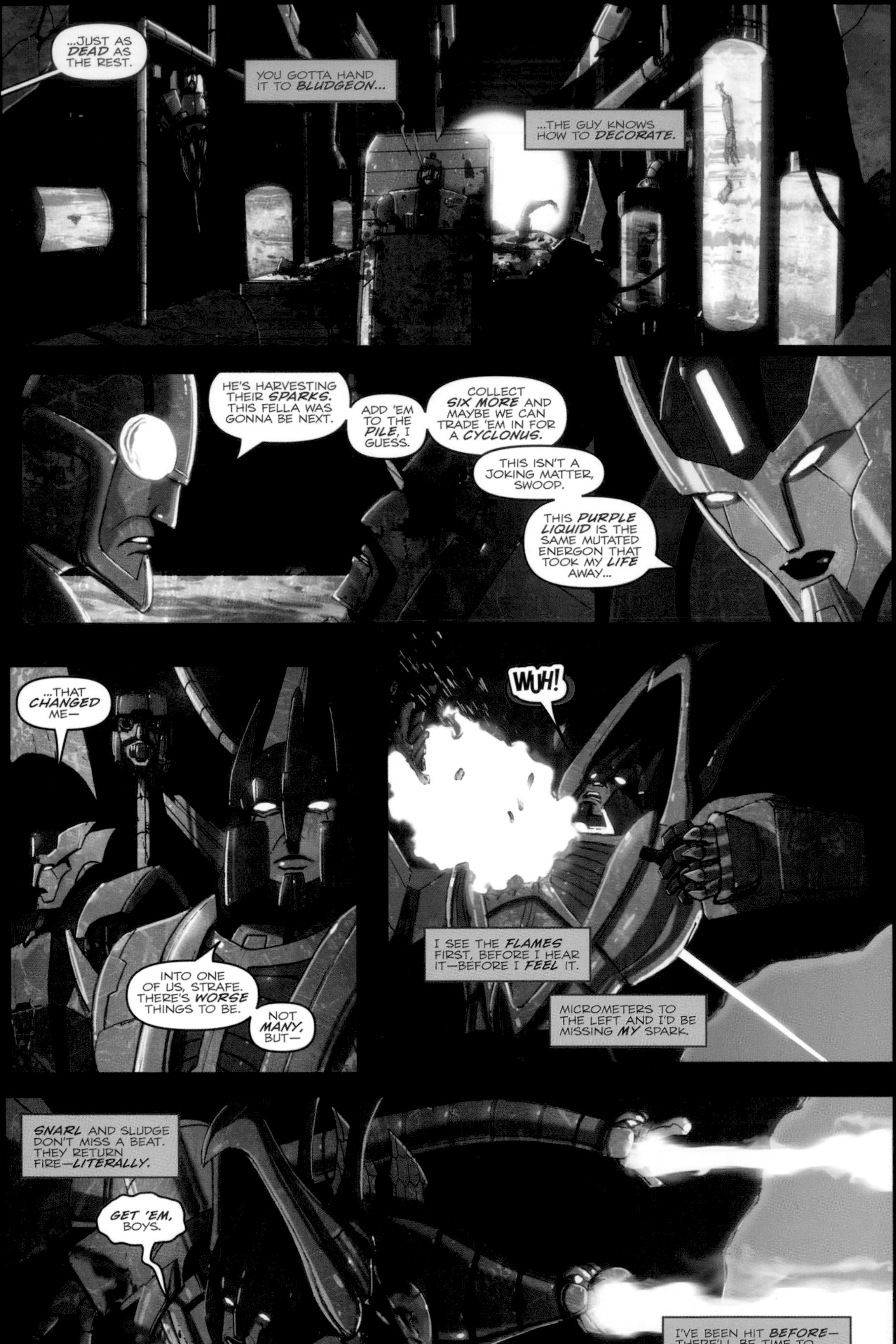
...JUST AS DEAD AS THE REST.
YOU GOTTA HAND IT TO BLUDGEON...
...THE GUY KNOWS HOW TO DECORATE.
HE'S HARVESTING THEIR SPARKS. THIS FELLA WAS GONNA BE NEXT.
ADD 'EM TO THE PILE, I GUESS.
COLLECT SIX MORE AND MAYBE WE CAN TRADE 'EM IN FOR A CYCLONUS.
THIS ISN'T A JOKING MATTER, SWOOP.
THIS PURPLE LIQUID IS THE SAME MUTATED ENERGON THAT TOOK MY LIFE AWAY...
...THAT CHANGED ME—
INTO ONE OF US, STRAFE. THERE'S WORSE THINGS TO BE.
NOT MANY, BUT—
WUH!
I SEE THE FLAMES FIRST, BEFORE I HEAR IT—BEFORE I FEEL IT.
MICROMETERS TO THE LEFT AND I'D BE MISSING MY SPARK.
SNARL AND SLUDGE DON'T MISS A BEAT. THEY RETURN FIRE—LITERALLY.
GET 'EM, BOYS.
I'VE BEEN HIT BEFORE—THERE'LL BE TIME TO TAKE STOCK LATER.

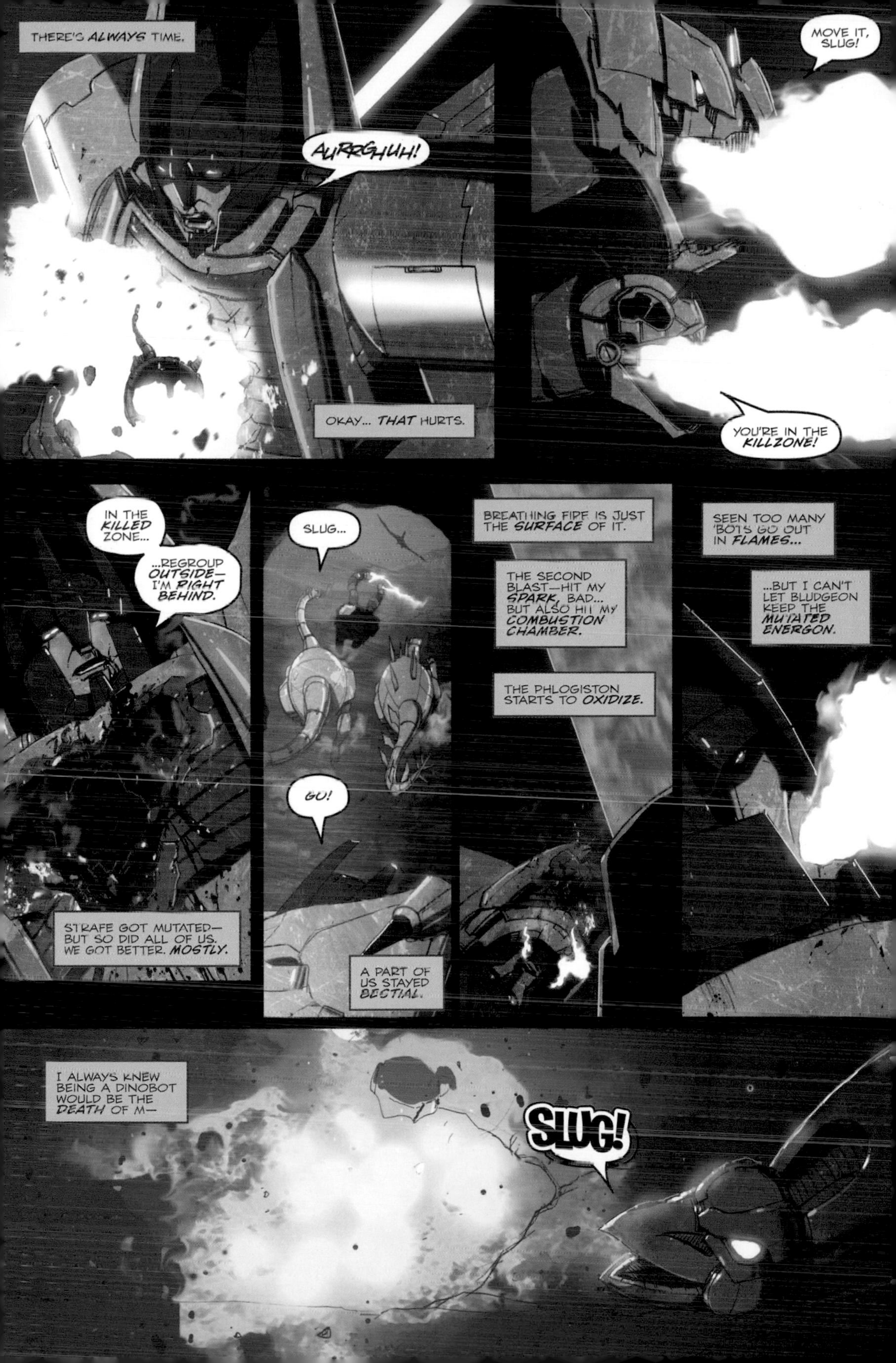
THERE'S ALWAYS TIME.
AURRGHUH!
OKAY... THAT HURTS.
MOVE IT, SLUG!
YOU'RE IN THE KILLZONE!
IN THE KILLED ZONE...
...REGROUP OUTSIDE— I'M RIGHT BEHIND.
STRAFE GOT MUTATED— BUT SO DID ALL OF US. WE GOT BETTER. MOSTLY.
SLUG...
GO!
A PART OF US STAYED BESTIAL.
BREATHING FIRE IS JUST THE SURFACE OF IT.
THE SECOND BLAST—HIT MY SPARK, BAD... BUT ALSO HIT MY COMBUSTION CHAMBER.
THE PHLOGISTON STARTS TO OXIDIZE.
SEEN TOO MANY 'BOTS GO OUT IN FLAMES...
...BUT I CAN'T LET BLUDGEON KEEP THE MUTATED ENERGON.
I ALWAYS KNEW BEING A DINOBOT WOULD BE THE DEATH OF M—
SLUG!

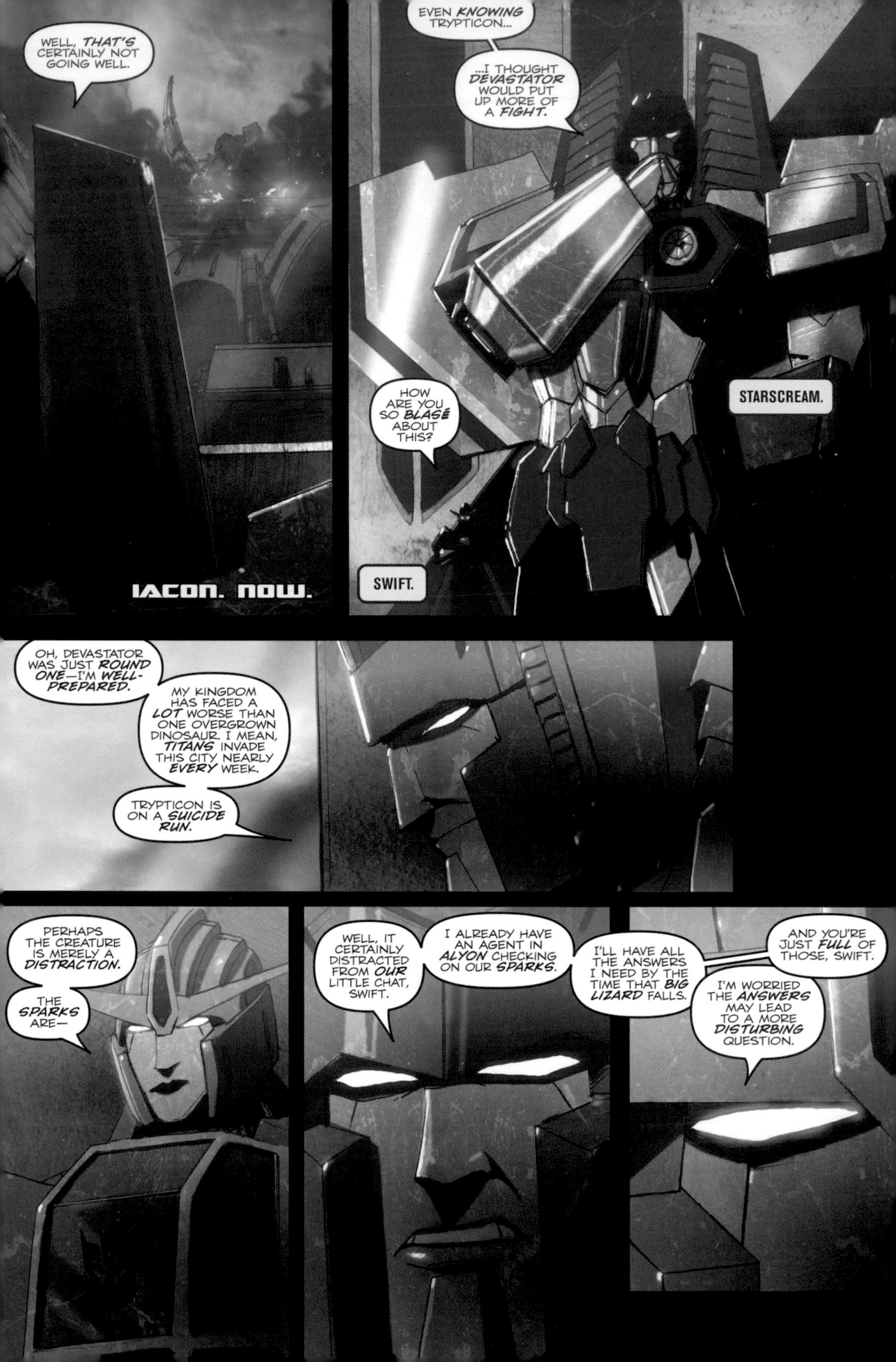
WELL, THAT'S CERTAINLY NOT GOING WELL.
IACON. NOW.
EVEN KNOWING TRYPTICON...
...I THOUGHT DEVASTATOR WOULD PUT UP MORE OF A FIGHT.
STARSCREAM.
HOW ARE YOU SO BLASÉ ABOUT THIS?
SWIFT.
OH, DEVASTATOR WAS JUST ROUND ONE—I'M WELL-PREPARED.
MY KINGDOM HAS FACED A LOT WORSE THAN ONE OVERGROWN DINOSAUR. I MEAN, TITANS INVADE THIS CITY NEARLY EVERY WEEK.
TRYPTICON IS ON A SUICIDE RUN.
PERHAPS THE CREATURE IS MERELY A DISTRACTION.
THE SPARKS ARE—
WELL, IT CERTAINLY DISTRACTED FROM OUR LITTLE CHAT, SWIFT.
I ALREADY HAVE AN AGENT IN ALYON CHECKING ON OUR SPARKS.
I'LL HAVE ALL THE ANSWERS I NEED BY THE TIME THAT BIG LIZARD FALLS.
AND YOU'RE JUST FULL OF THOSE, SWIFT.
I'M WORRIED THE ANSWERS MAY LEAD TO A MORE DISTURBING QUESTION.

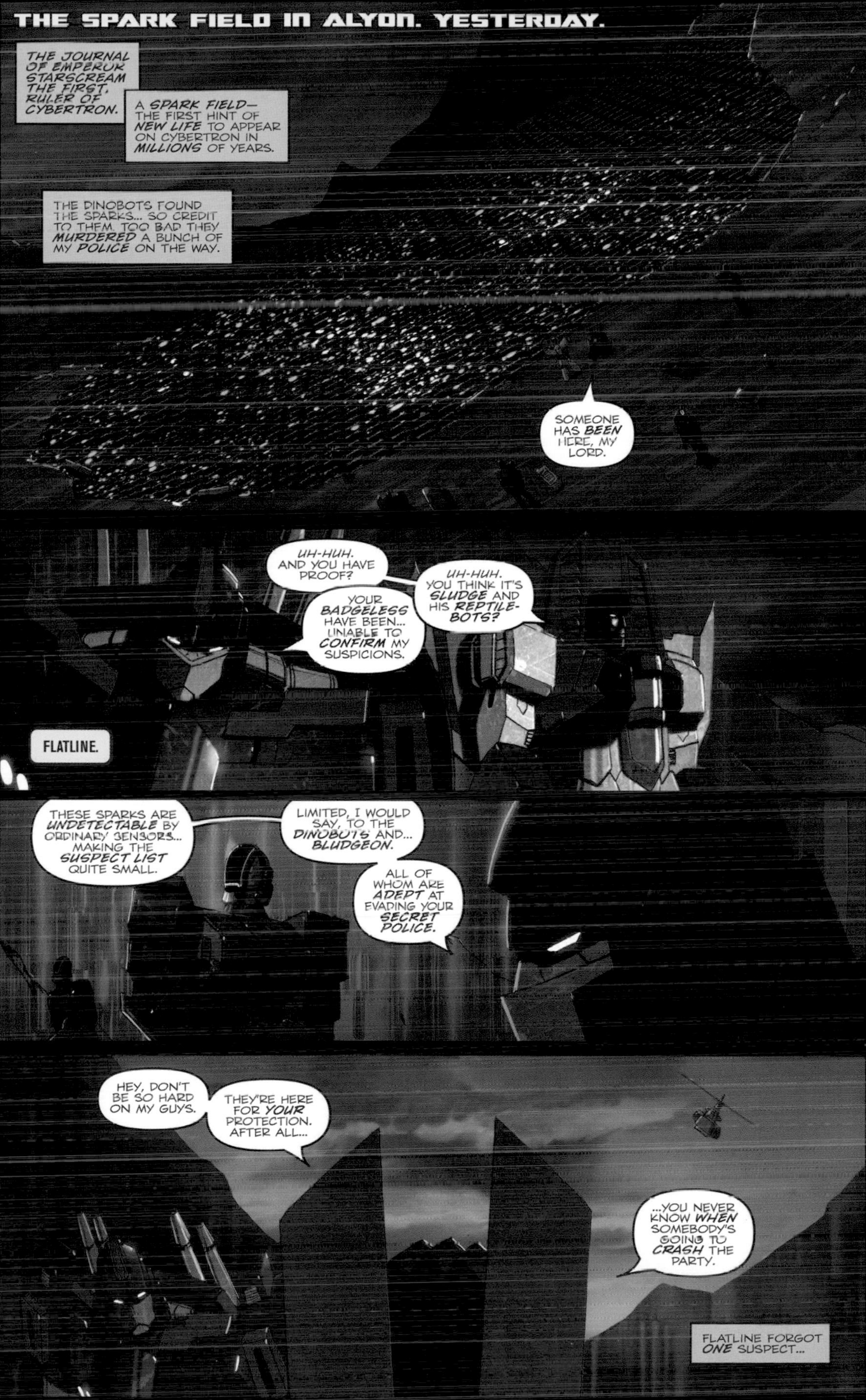
THE SPARK FIELD IN ALYON. YESTERDAY.
THE JOURNAL OF EMPEROR STARSCREAM THE FIRST, RULER OF CYBERTRON.
A SPARK FIELD— THE FIRST HINT OF NEW LIFE TO APPEAR ON CYBERTRON IN MILLIONS OF YEARS.
THE DINOBOTS FOUND THE SPARKS... SO CREDIT TO THEM. TOO BAD THEY MURDERED A BUNCH OF MY POLICE ON THE WAY.
SOMEONE HAS BEEN HERE, MY LORD.
UH-HUH. AND YOU HAVE PROOF?
YOUR BADGELESS HAVE BEEN... UNABLE TO CONFIRM MY SUSPICIONS.
UH-HUH. YOU THINK IT'S SLUDGE AND HIS REPTILE-BOTS?
FLATLINE.
THESE SPARKS ARE UNDETECTABLE BY ORDINARY SENSORS... MAKING THE SUSPECT LIST QUITE SMALL.
LIMITED, I WOULD SAY, TO THE DINOBOTS AND... BLUDGEON.
ALL OF WHOM ARE ADEPT AT EVADING YOUR SECRET POLICE.
HEY, DON'T BE SO HARD ON MY GUYS.
THEY'RE HERE FOR YOUR PROTECTION. AFTER ALL...
...YOU NEVER KNOW WHEN SOMEBODY'S GOING TO CRASH THE PARTY.
FLATLINE FORGOT ONE SUSPECT...

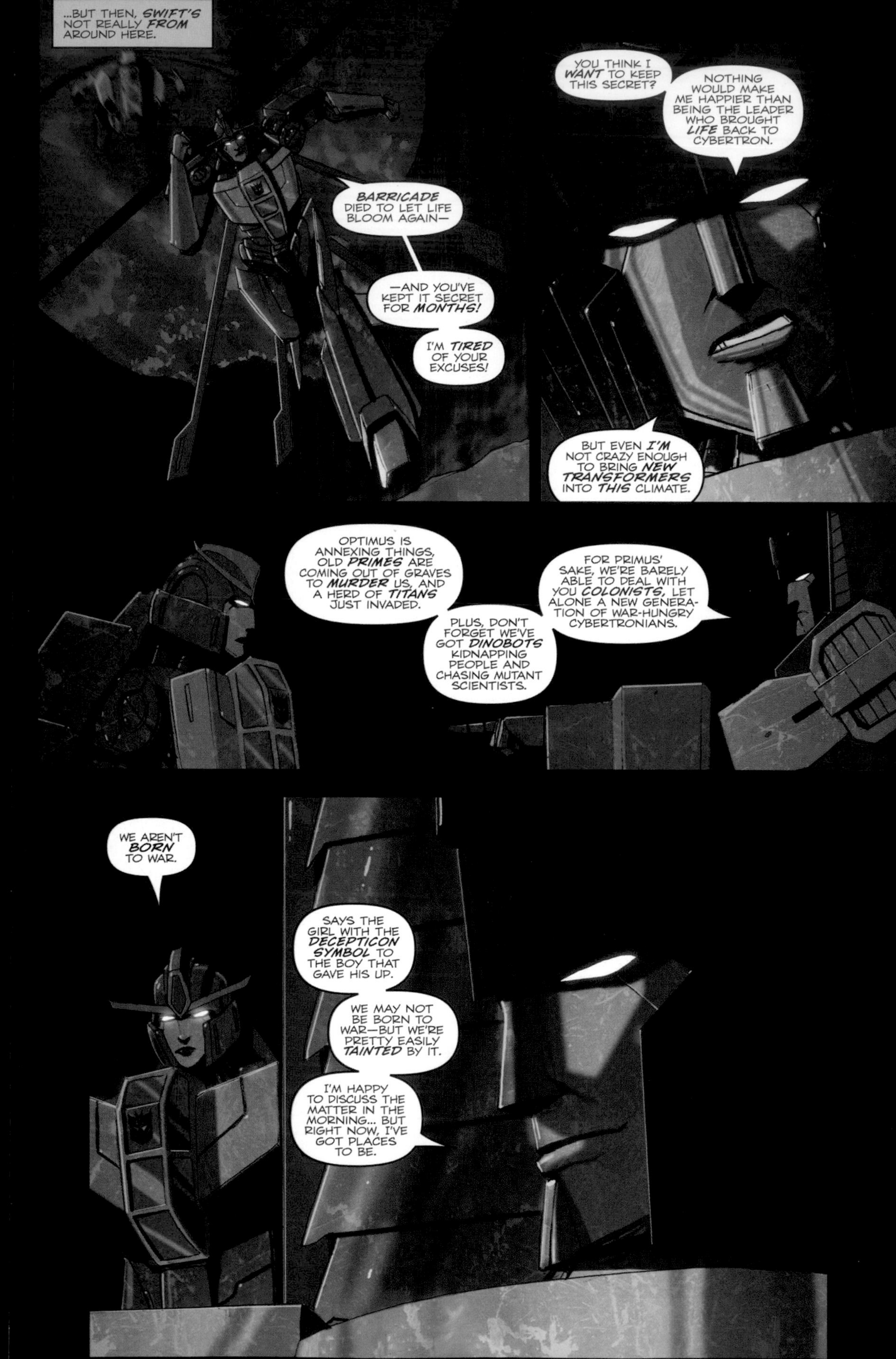

...BUT THEN, SWIFT'S NOT REALLY FROM AROUND HERE.
BARRICADE DIED TO LET LIFE BLOOM AGAIN—
—AND YOU'VE KEPT IT SECRET FOR MONTHS!
I'M TIRED OF YOUR EXCUSES!
YOU THINK I WANT TO KEEP THIS SECRET?
NOTHING WOULD MAKE ME HAPPIER THAN BEING THE LEADER WHO BROUGHT LIFE BACK TO CYBERTRON.
BUT EVEN I'M NOT CRAZY ENOUGH TO BRING NEW TRANSFORMERS INTO THIS CLIMATE.
OPTIMUS IS ANNEXING THINGS, OLD PRIMES ARE COMING OUT OF GRAVES TO MURDER US, AND A HERD OF TITANS JUST INVADED.
PLUS, DON'T FORGET WE'VE GOT DINOBOTS KIDNAPPING PEOPLE AND CHASING MUTANT SCIENTISTS.
FOR PRIMUS' SAKE, WE'RE BARELY ABLE TO DEAL WITH YOU COLONISTS, LET ALONE A NEW GENERATION OF WAR-HUNGRY CYBERTRONIANS.
WE AREN'T BORN TO WAR.
SAYS THE GIRL WITH THE DECEPTICON SYMBOL TO THE BOY THAT GAVE HIS UP.
WE MAY NOT BE BORN TO WAR—BUT WE'RE PRETTY EASILY TAINTED BY IT.
I'M HAPPY TO DISCUSS THE MATTER IN THE MORNING... BUT RIGHT NOW, I'VE GOT PLACES TO BE.

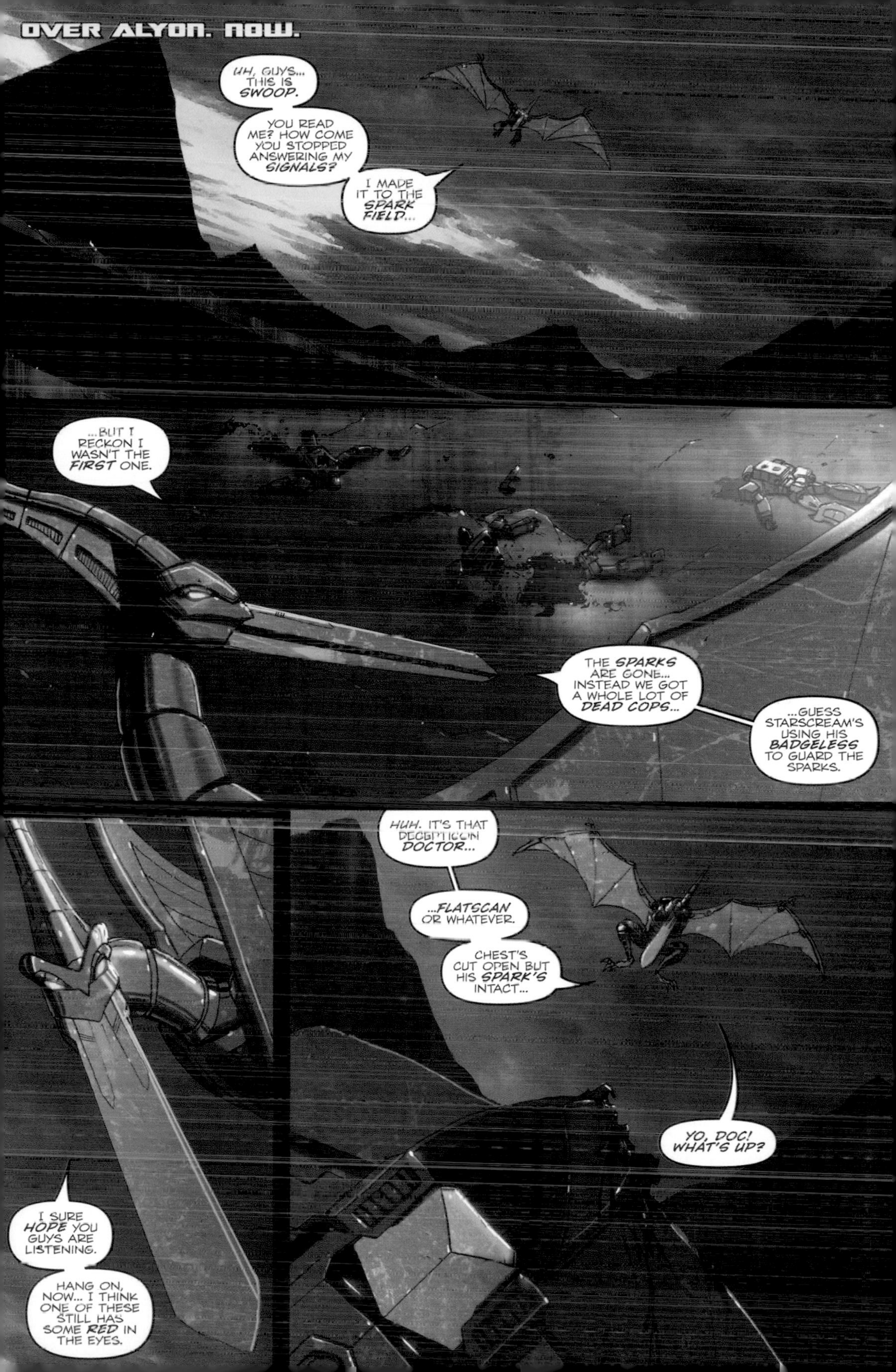
OVER ALYON. NOW.
UH, GUYS... THIS IS SWOOP.
YOU READ ME? HOW COME YOU STOPPED ANSWERING MY SIGNALS?
I MADE IT TO THE SPARK FIELD...
...BUT I RECKON I WASN'T THE FIRST ONE.
THE SPARKS ARE GONE... INSTEAD WE GOT A WHOLE LOT OF DEAD COPS...
...GUESS STARSCREAM'S USING HIS BADGELESS TO GUARD THE SPARKS.
I SURE HOPE YOU GUYS ARE LISTENING.
HANG ON, NOW... I THINK ONE OF THESE STILL HAS SOME RED IN THE EYES.
HUH. IT'S THAT DECEPTICON DOCTOR...
...FLATSCAN OR WHATEVER.
CHEST'S CUT OPEN BUT HIS SPARK'S INTACT...
YO, DOC! WHAT'S UP?

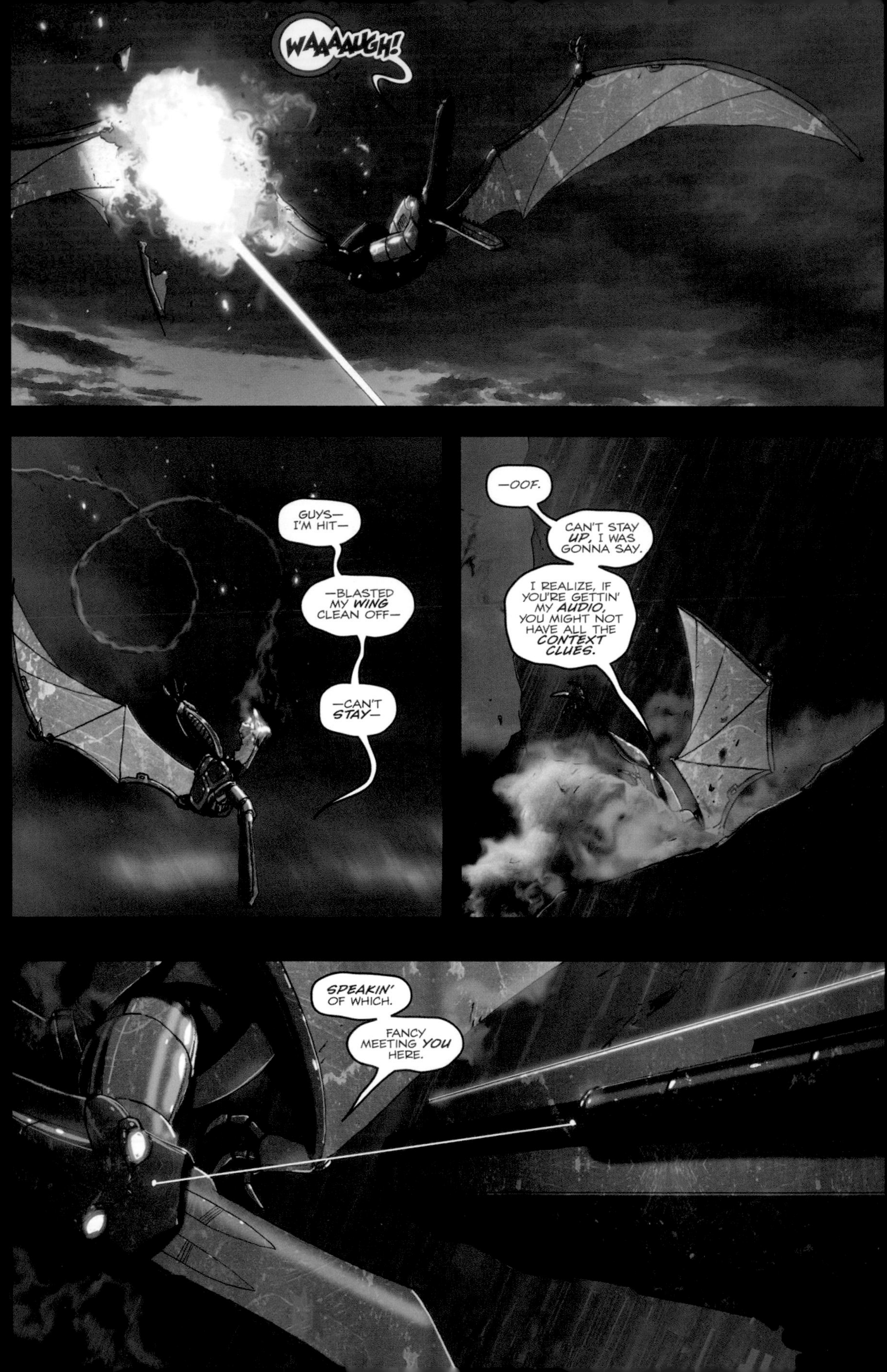
WAAAAUGH!
GUYS— I'M HIT—
—BLASTED MY WING CLEAN OFF—
—CAN'T STAY—
—OOF.
CAN'T STAY UP, I WAS GONNA SAY.
I REALIZE, IF YOU'RE GETTIN' MY AUDIO, YOU MIGHT NOT HAVE ALL THE CONTEXT CLUES.
SPEAKIN' OF WHICH.
FANCY MEETING YOU HERE.

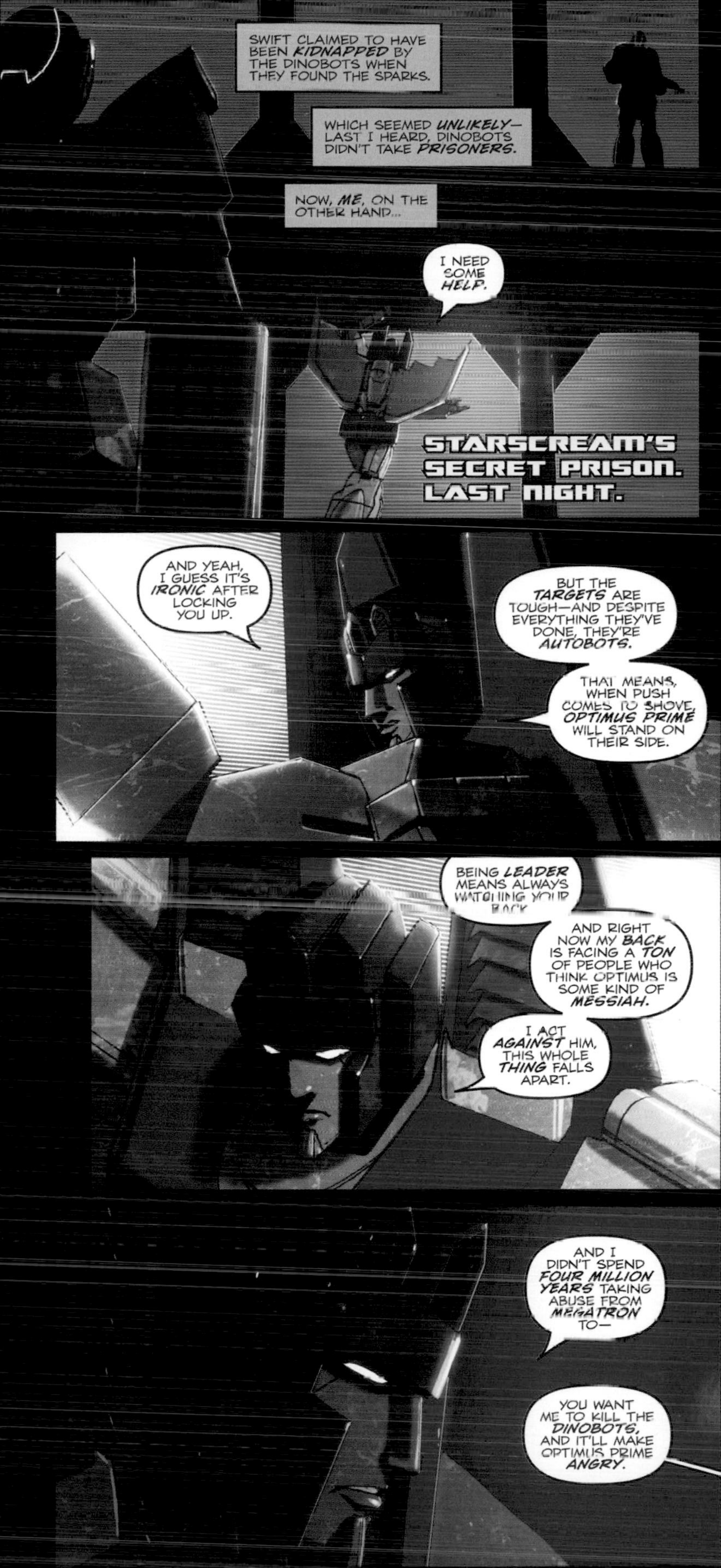
SWIFT CLAIMED TO HAVE BEEN KIDNAPPED BY THE DINOBOTS WHEN THEY FOUND THE SPARKS.
WHICH SEEMED UNLIKELY—LAST I HEARD, DINOBOTS DIDN'T TAKE PRISONERS.
NOW, ME, ON THE OTHER HAND...
I NEED SOME HELP.
STARSCREAM'S SECRET PRISON. LAST NIGHT.
AND YEAH, I GUESS IT'S IRONIC AFTER LOCKING YOU UP.
BUT THE TARGETS ARE TOUGH—AND DESPITE EVERYTHING THEY'VE DONE, THEY'RE AUTOBOTS.
THAT MEANS, WHEN PUSH COMES TO SHOVE, OPTIMUS PRIME WILL STAND ON THEIR SIDE.
BEING LEADER MEANS ALWAYS WATCHING YOUR BACK.
AND RIGHT NOW MY BACK IS FACING A TON OF PEOPLE WHO THINK OPTIMUS IS SOME KIND OF MESSIAH.
I ACT AGAINST HIM, THIS WHOLE THING FALLS APART.
AND I DIDN'T SPEND FOUR MILLION YEARS TAKING ABUSE FROM MEGATRON TO—
YOU WANT ME TO KILL THE DINOBOTS, AND IT'LL MAKE OPTIMUS PRIME ANGRY.

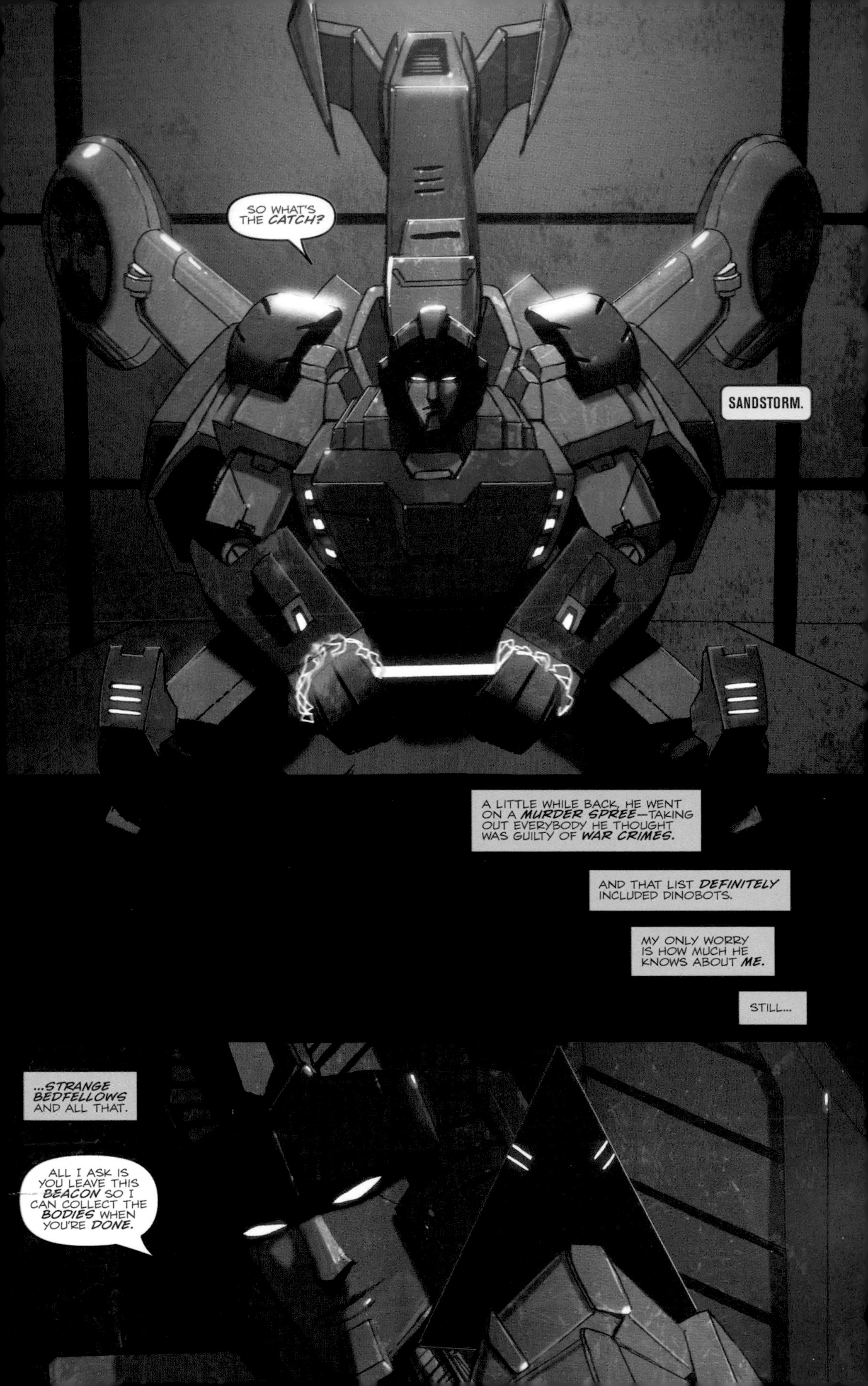
SO WHAT'S THE CATCH?
SANDSTORM.
A LITTLE WHILE BACK, HE WENT ON A MURDER SPREE—TAKING OUT EVERYBODY HE THOUGHT WAS GUILTY OF WAR CRIMES.
AND THAT LIST DEFINITELY INCLUDED DINOBOTS.
MY ONLY WORRY IS HOW MUCH HE KNOWS ABOUT ME.
STILL...
...STRANGE BEDFELLOWS AND ALL THAT.
ALL I ASK IS YOU LEAVE THIS BEACON SO I CAN COLLECT THE BODIES WHEN YOU'RE DONE.

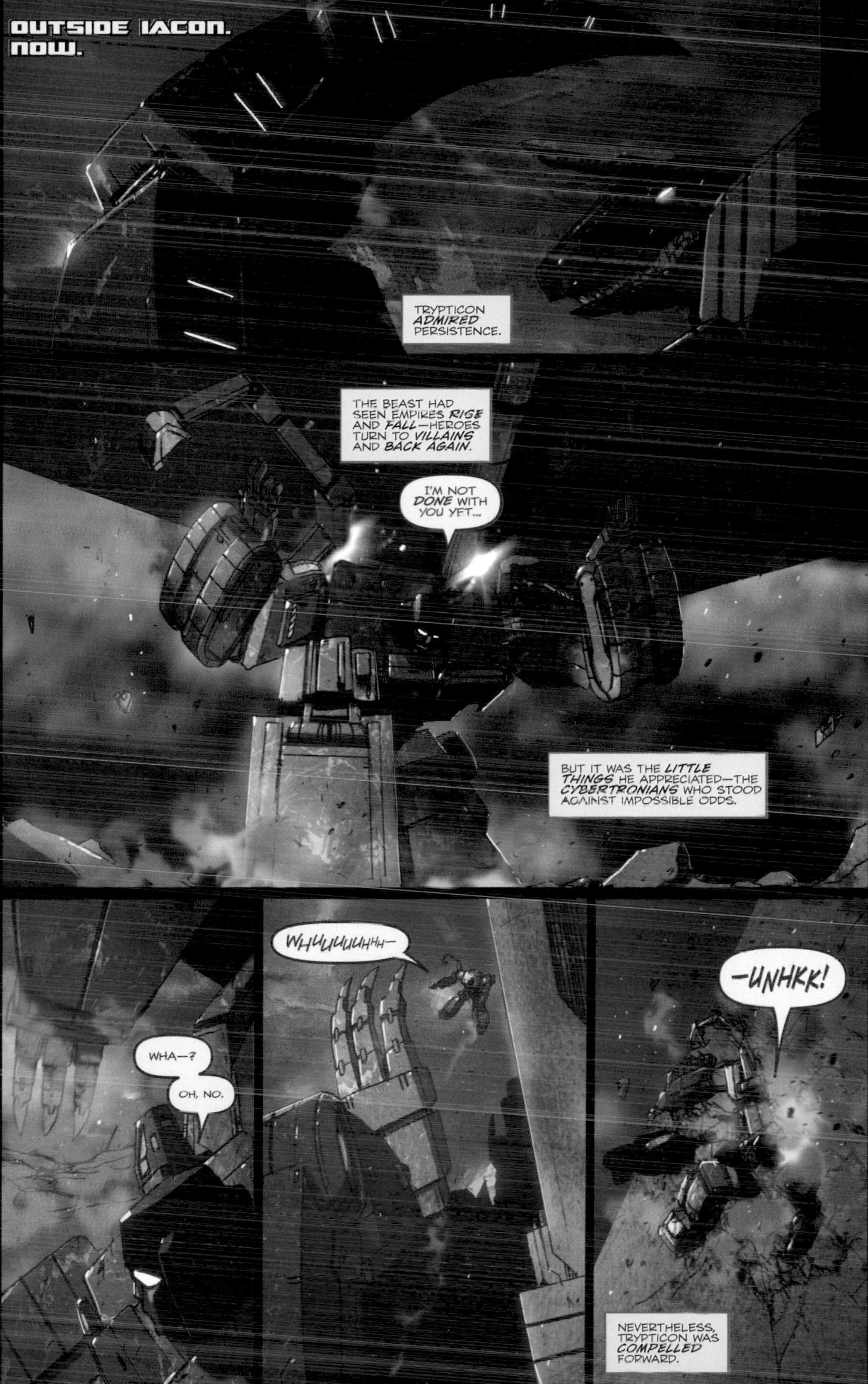
OUTSIDE IACON.
NOW.
TRYPTICON ADMIRED PERSISTENCE.
THE BEAST HAD SEEN EMPIRES RISE AND FALL—HEROES TURN TO VILLAINS AND BACK AGAIN.
I'M NOT DONE WITH YOU YET...
BUT IT WAS THE LITTLE THINGS HE APPRECIATED—THE CYBERTRONIANS WHO STOOD AGAINST IMPOSSIBLE ODDS.
WHA—?
OH, NO.
WHUUUUUHH—
—UNHKK!
NEVERTHELESS, TRYPTICON WAS COMPELLED FORWARD.

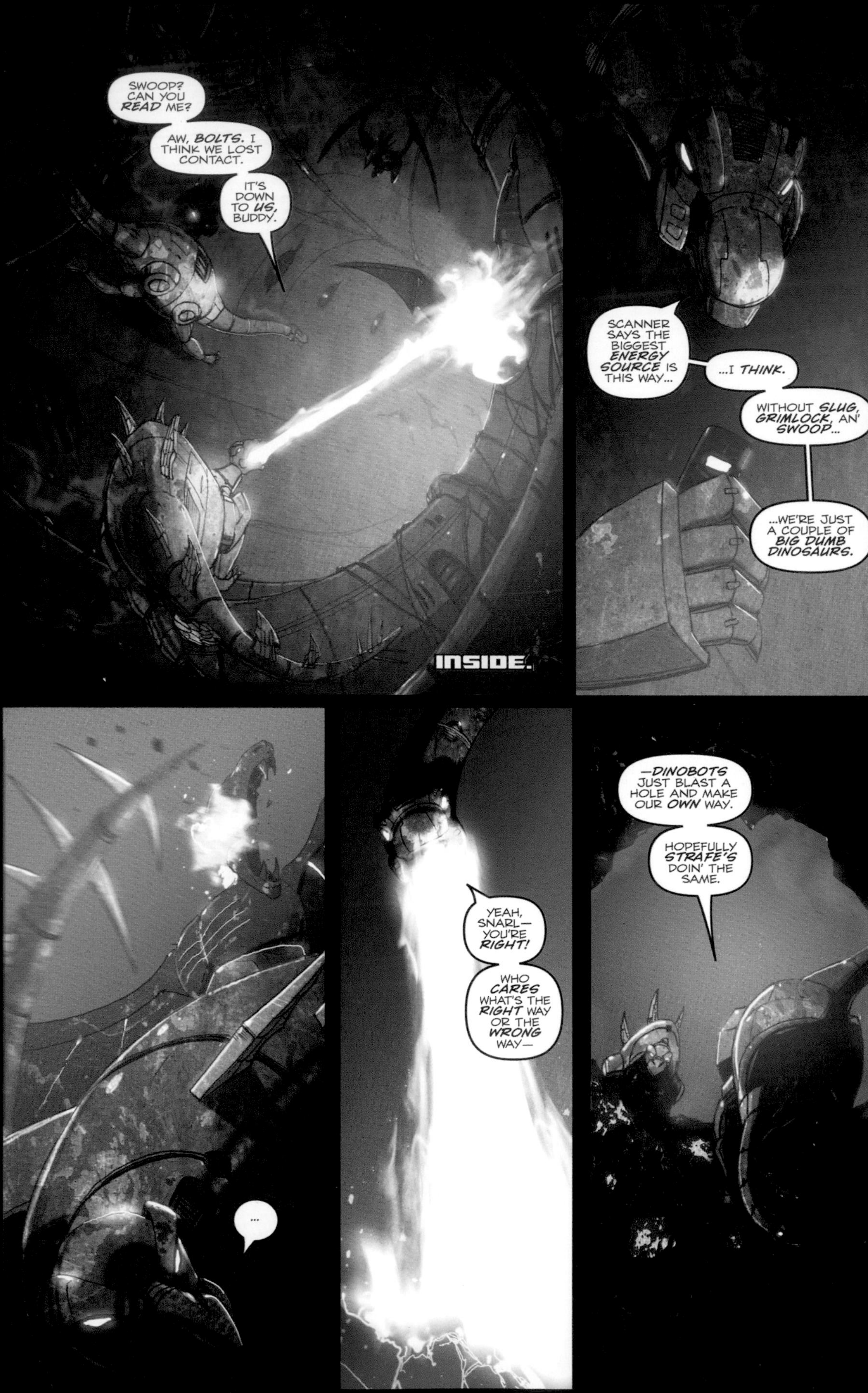
SWOOP? CAN YOU READ ME?
AW, BOLTS. I THINK WE LOST CONTACT.
IT'S DOWN TO US, BUDDY.
INSIDE.
SCANNER SAYS THE BIGGEST ENERGY SOURCE IS THIS WAY...
...I THINK.
WITHOUT SLUG, GRIMLOCK, AN' SWOOP...
...WE'RE JUST A COUPLE OF BIG DUMB DINOSAURS.
...
YEAH, SNARL— YOU'RE RIGHT!
WHO CARES WHAT'S THE RIGHT WAY OR THE WRONG WAY—
—DINOBOTS JUST BLAST A HOLE AND MAKE OUR OWN WAY.
HOPEFULLY STRAFE'S DOIN' THE SAME.

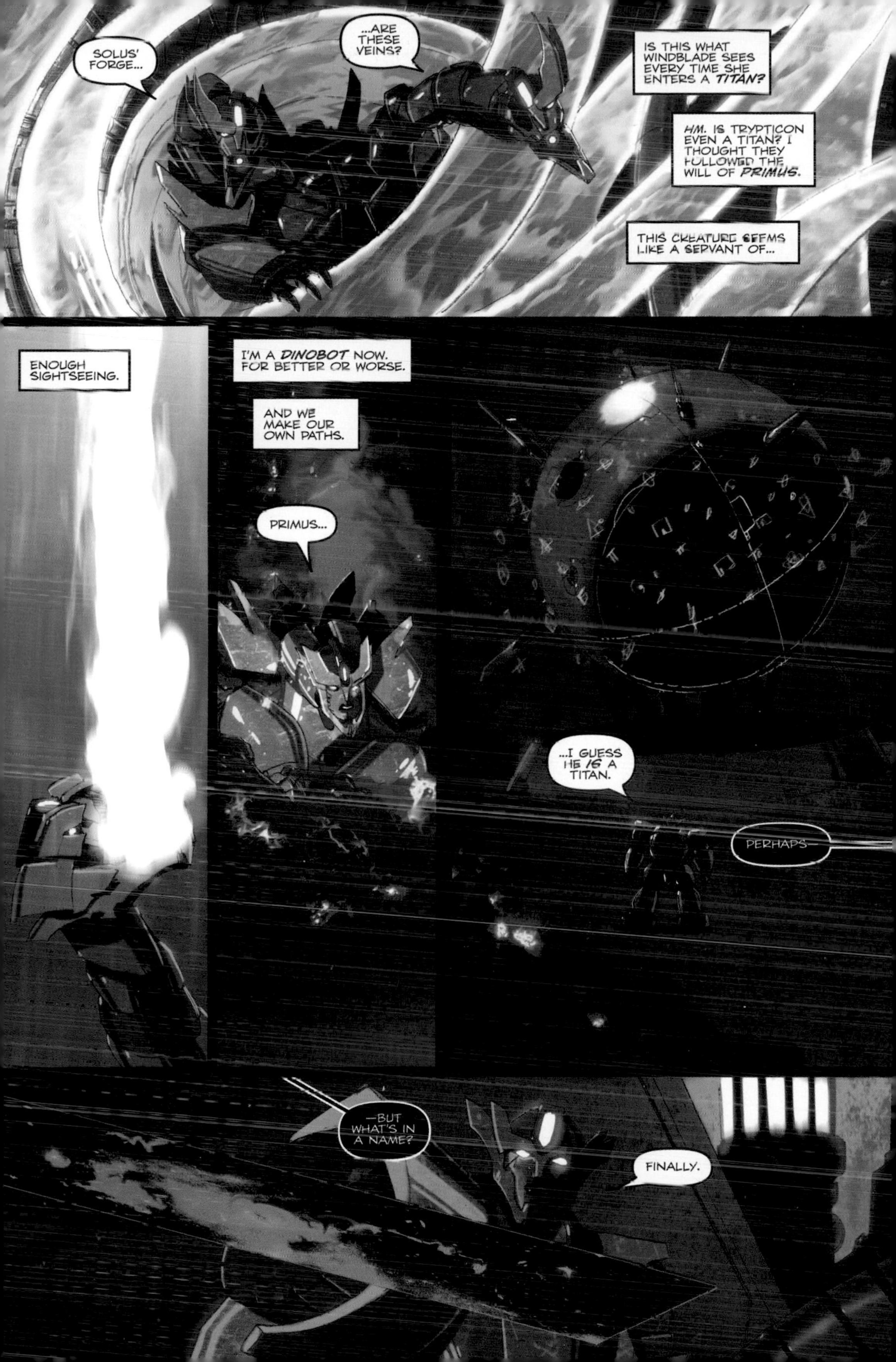
SOLUS' FORGE...
...ARE THESE VEINS?
IS THIS WHAT WINDBLADE SEES EVERY TIME SHE ENTERS A TITAN?
HM. IS TRYPTICON EVEN A TITAN? I THOUGHT THEY FOLLOWED THE WILL OF PRIMUS.
THIS CREATURE SEEMS LIKE A SERVANT OF...
ENOUGH SIGHTSEEING.
I'M A DINOBOT NOW. FOR BETTER OR WORSE.
AND WE MAKE OUR OWN PATHS.
PRIMUS...
...I GUESS HE IS A TITAN.
PERHAPS—
—BUT WHAT'S IN A NAME?
FINALLY.

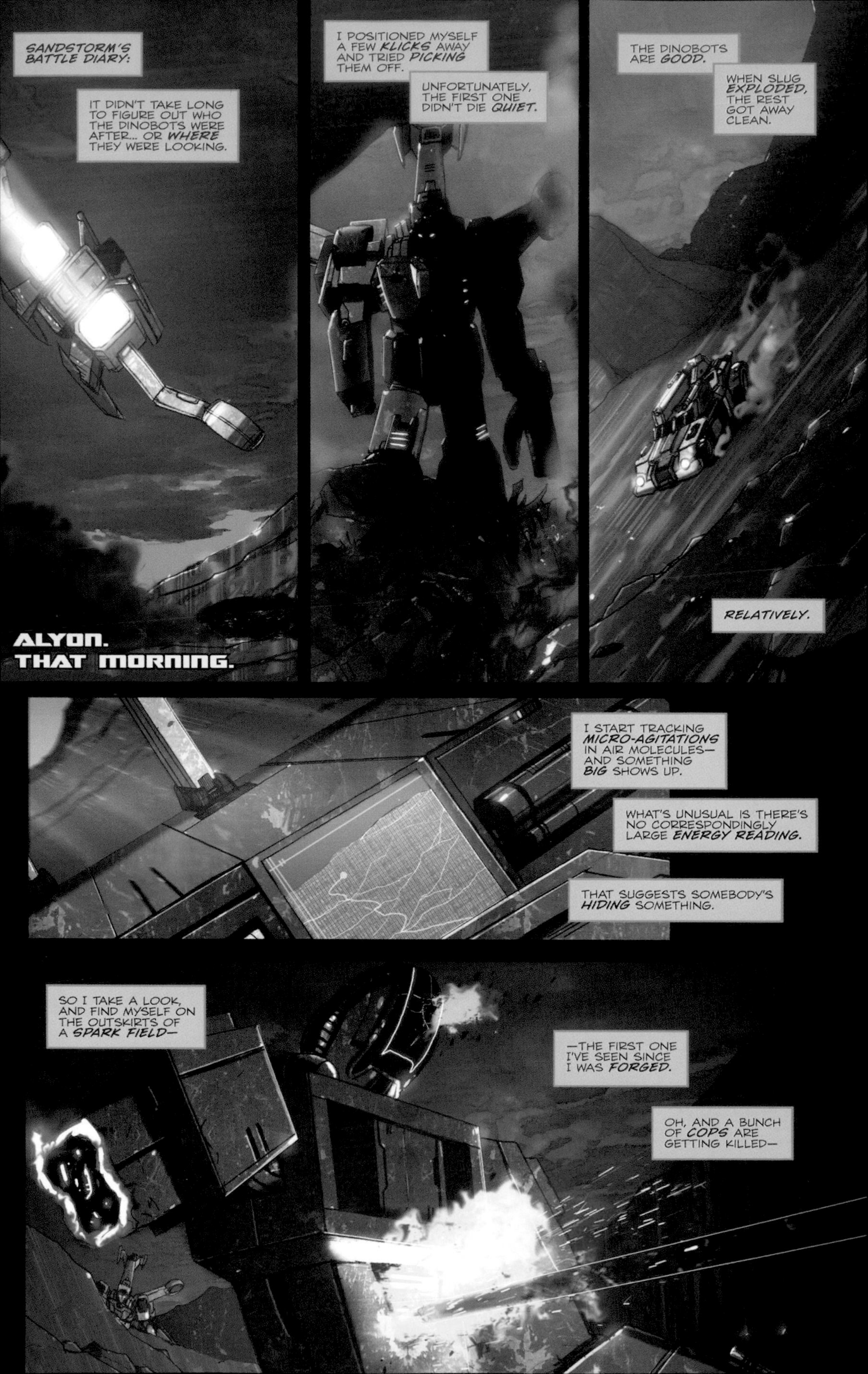
SANDSTORM'S BATTLE DIARY:
IT DIDN'T TAKE LONG TO FIGURE OUT WHO THE DINOBOTS WERE AFTER... OR WHERE THEY WERE LOOKING.
ALYON. THAT MORNING.
I POSITIONED MYSELF A FEW KLICKS AWAY AND TRIED PICKING THEM OFF.
UNFORTUNATELY, THE FIRST ONE DIDN'T DIE QUIET.
THE DINOBOTS ARE GOOD.
WHEN SLUG EXPLODED, THE REST GOT AWAY CLEAN.
RELATIVELY.
I START TRACKING MICRO-AGITATIONS IN AIR MOLECULES—AND SOMETHING BIG SHOWS UP.
WHAT'S UNUSUAL IS THERE'S NO CORRESPONDINGLY LARGE ENERGY READING.
THAT SUGGESTS SOMEBODY'S HIDING SOMETHING.
SO I TAKE A LOOK, AND FIND MYSELF ON THE OUTSKIRTS OF A SPARK FIELD—
—THE FIRST ONE I'VE SEEN SINCE I WAS FORGED.
OH, AND A BUNCH OF COPS ARE GETTING KILLED—

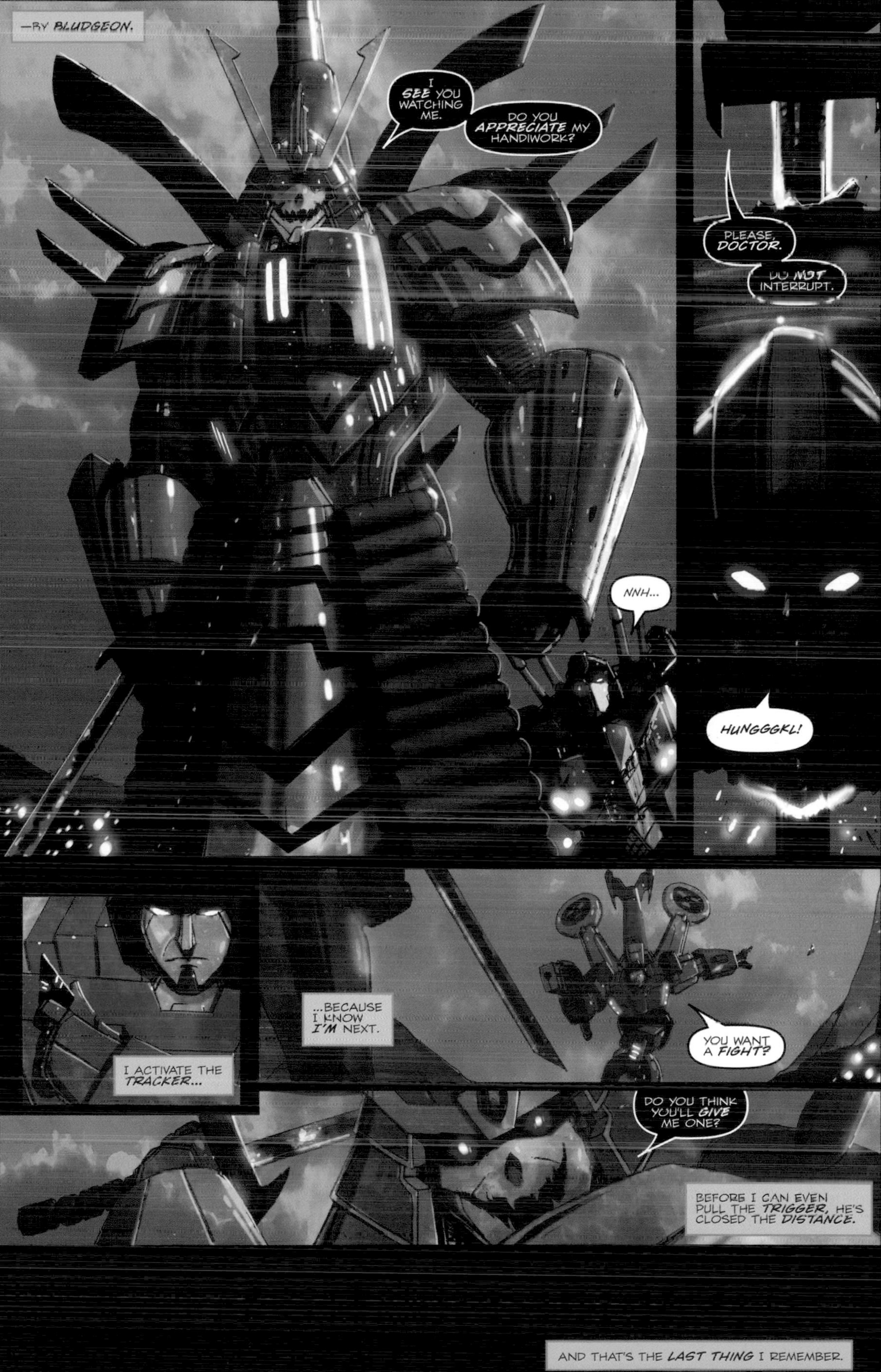
—BY BLUDGEON.
I SEE YOU WATCHING ME.
DO YOU APPRECIATE MY HANDIWORK?
PLEASE, DOCTOR.
DO NOT INTERRUPT.
NNH...
HUNGGGKL!
I ACTIVATE THE TRACKER...
...BECAUSE I KNOW I'M NEXT.
YOU WANT A FIGHT?
DO YOU THINK YOU'LL GIVE ME ONE?
BEFORE I CAN EVEN PULL THE TRIGGER, HE'S CLOSED THE DISTANCE.
AND THAT'S THE LAST THING I REMEMBER.

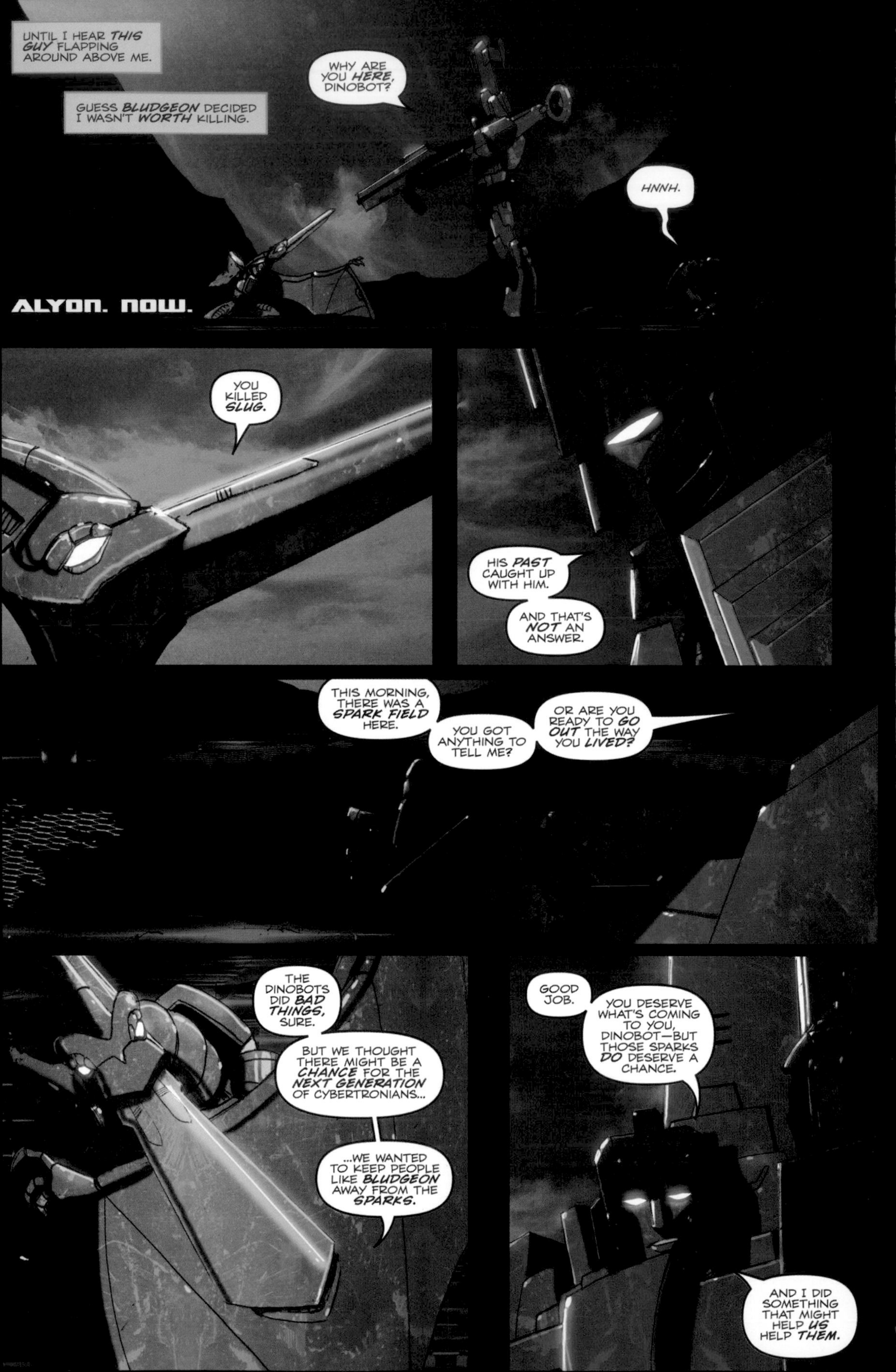
UNTIL I HEAR THIS GUY FLAPPING AROUND ABOVE ME.
GUESS BLUDGEON DECIDED I WASN'T WORTH KILLING.
WHY ARE YOU HERE, DINOBOT?
HNNH.
ALYON. NOW.
YOU KILLED SLUG.
HIS PAST CAUGHT UP WITH HIM.
AND THAT'S NOT AN ANSWER.
THIS MORNING, THERE WAS A SPARK FIELD HERE.
YOU GOT ANYTHING TO TELL ME?
OR ARE YOU READY TO GO OUT THE WAY YOU LIVED?
THE DINOBOTS DID BAD THINGS, SURE.
BUT WE THOUGHT THERE MIGHT BE A CHANCE FOR THE NEXT GENERATION OF CYBERTRONIANS...
...WE WANTED TO KEEP PEOPLE LIKE BLUDGEON AWAY FROM THE SPARKS.
GOOD JOB.
YOU DESERVE WHAT'S COMING TO YOU, DINOBOT—BUT THOSE SPARKS DO DESERVE A CHANCE.
AND I DID SOMETHING THAT MIGHT HELP US HELP THEM.

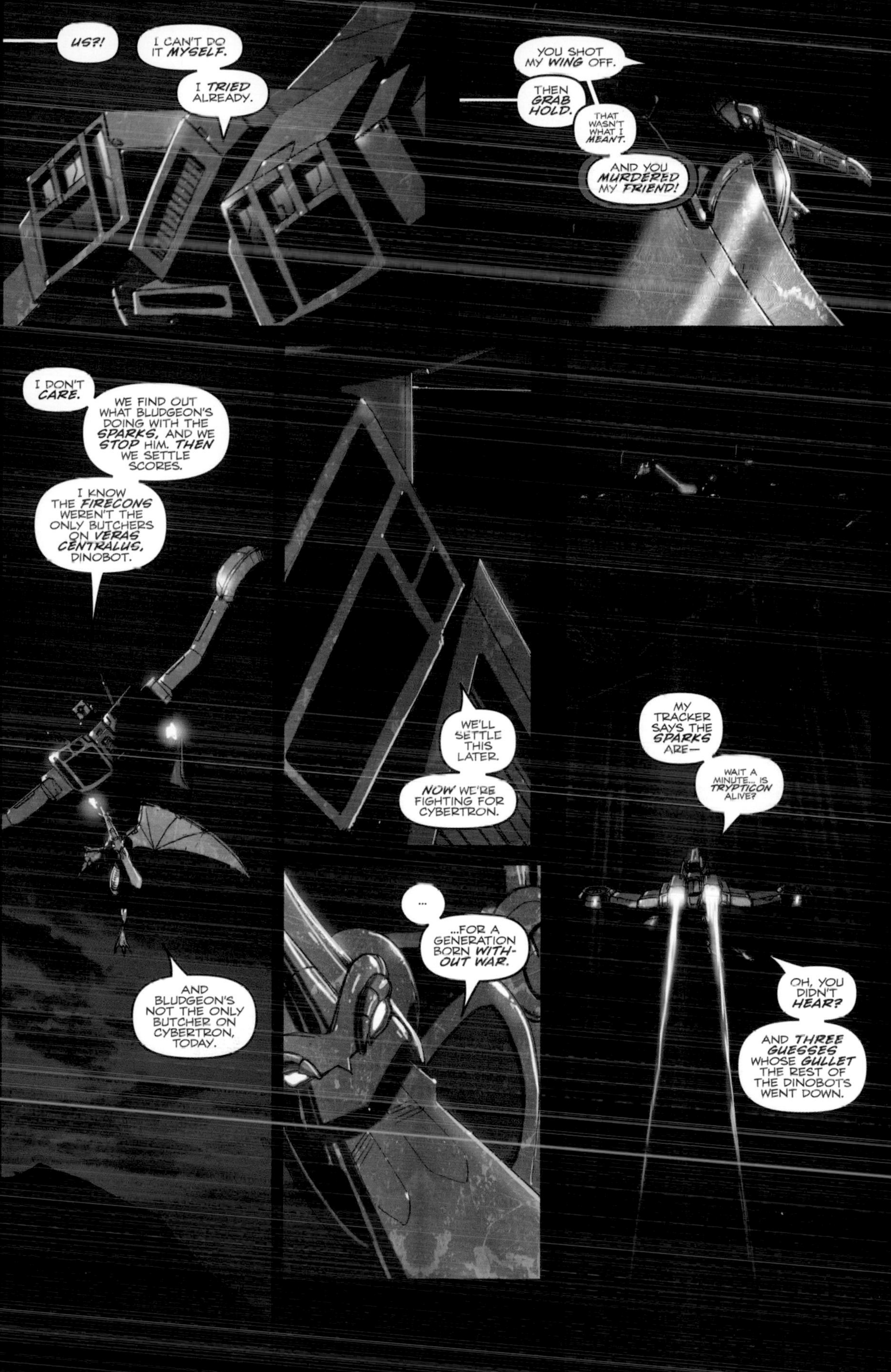
US?!
I CAN'T DO IT MYSELF.
I TRIED ALREADY.
YOU SHOT MY WING OFF.
THEN GRAB HOLD.
THAT WASN'T WHAT I MEANT.
AND YOU MURDERED MY FRIEND!
I DON'T CARE.
WE FIND OUT WHAT BLUDGEON'S DOING WITH THE SPARKS, AND WE STOP HIM. THEN WE SETTLE SCORES.
I KNOW THE FIRECONS WEREN'T THE ONLY BUTCHERS ON VERAS CENTRALUS, DINOBOT.
WE'LL SETTLE THIS LATER.
NOW WE'RE FIGHTING FOR CYBERTRON.
MY TRACKER SAYS THE SPARKS ARE—
WAIT A MINUTE... IS TRYPTICON ALIVE?
AND BLUDGEON'S NOT THE ONLY BUTCHER ON CYBERTRON, TODAY.
...
...FOR A GENERATION BORN WITH-OUT WAR.
OH, YOU DIDN'T HEAR?
AND THREE GUESSES WHOSE GULLET THE REST OF THE DINOBOTS WENT DOWN.

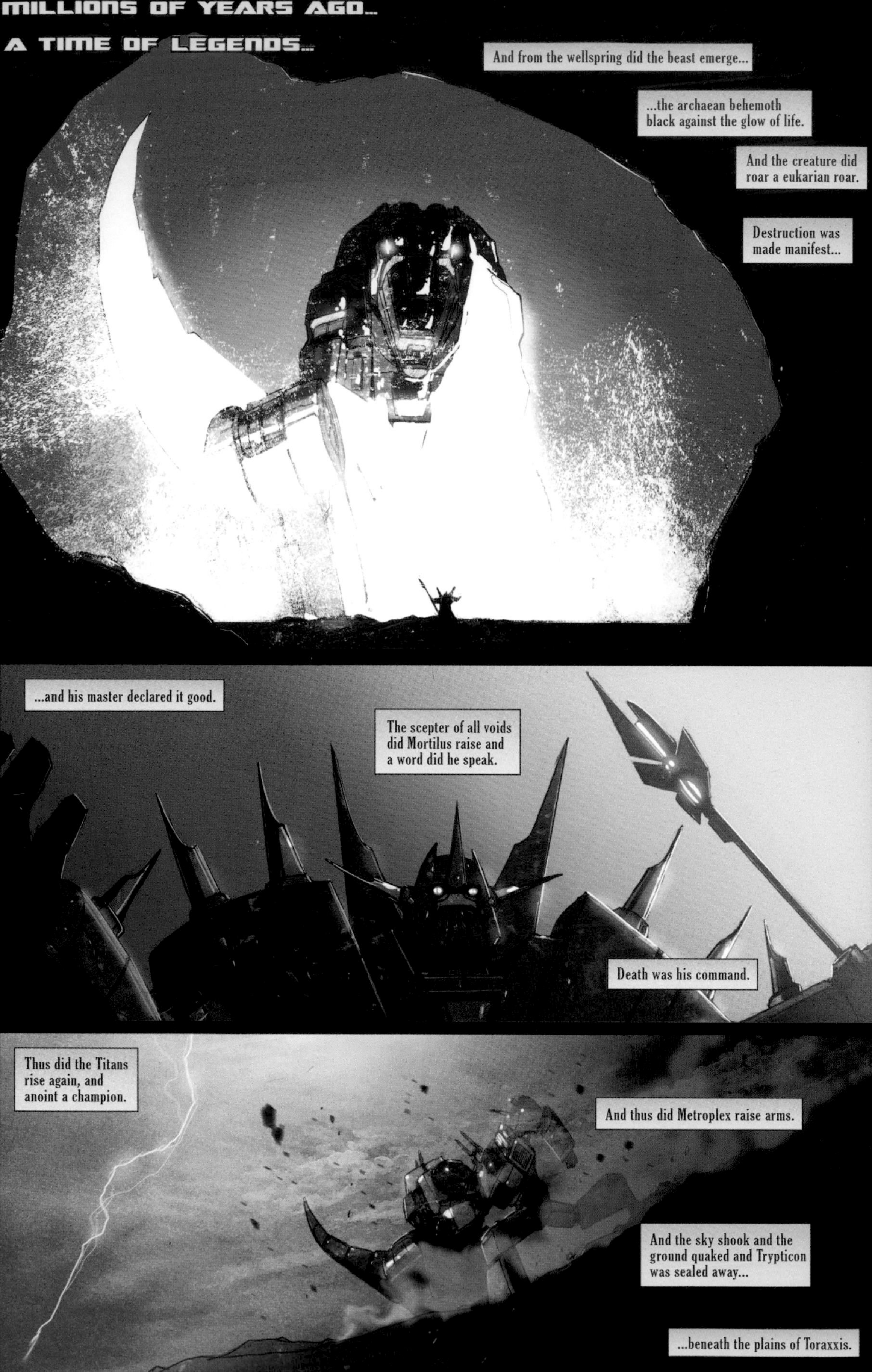
MILLIONS OF YEARS AGO...
A TIME OF LEGENDS...
And from the wellspring did the beast emerge...
...the archaean behemoth black against the glow of life.
And the creature did roar a eukarian roar.
Destruction was made manifest...
...and his master declared it good.
The scepter of all voids did Mortilus raise and a word did he speak.
Death was his command.
Thus did the Titans rise again, and anoint a champion.
And thus did Metroplex raise arms.
And the sky shook and the ground quaked and Trypticon was sealed away...
...beneath the plains of Toraxxis.

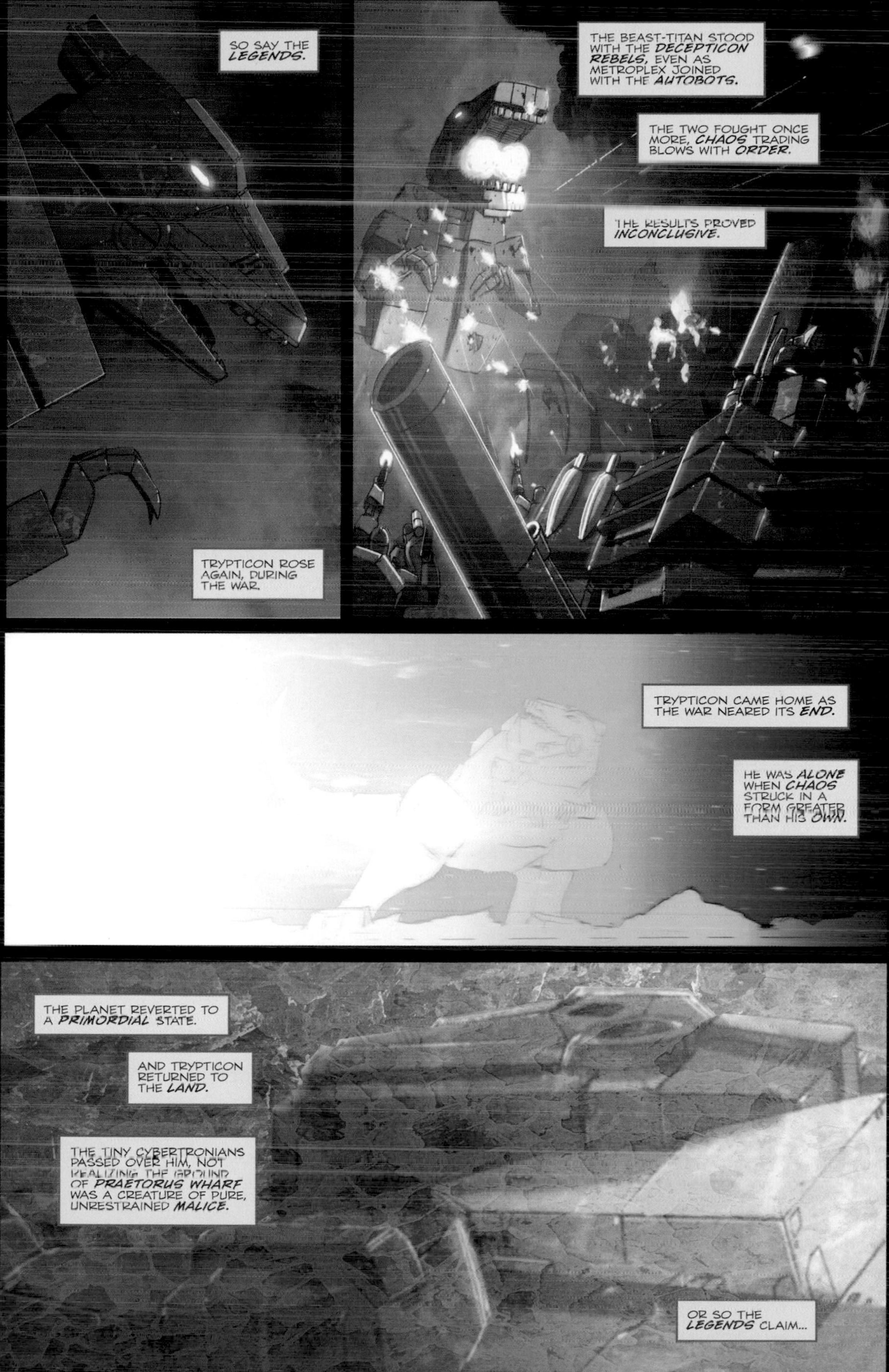
SO SAY THE LEGENDS.
TRYPTICON ROSE AGAIN, DURING THE WAR.
THE BEAST-TITAN STOOD WITH THE DECEPTICON REBELS, EVEN AS METROPLEX JOINED WITH THE AUTOBOTS.
THE TWO FOUGHT ONCE MORE, CHAOS TRADING BLOWS WITH ORDER.
THE RESULTS PROVED INCONCLUSIVE.
TRYPTICON CAME HOME AS THE WAR NEARED ITS END.
HE WAS ALONE WHEN CHAOS STRUCK IN A FORM GREATER THAN HIS OWN.
THE PLANET REVERTED TO A PRIMORDIAL STATE.
AND TRYPTICON RETURNED TO THE LAND.
THE TINY CYBERTRONIANS PASSED OVER HIM, NOT REALIZING THE GROUND OF PRAETORUS WHARF WAS A CREATURE OF PURE, UNRESTRAINED MALICE.
OR SO THE LEGENDS CLAIM...

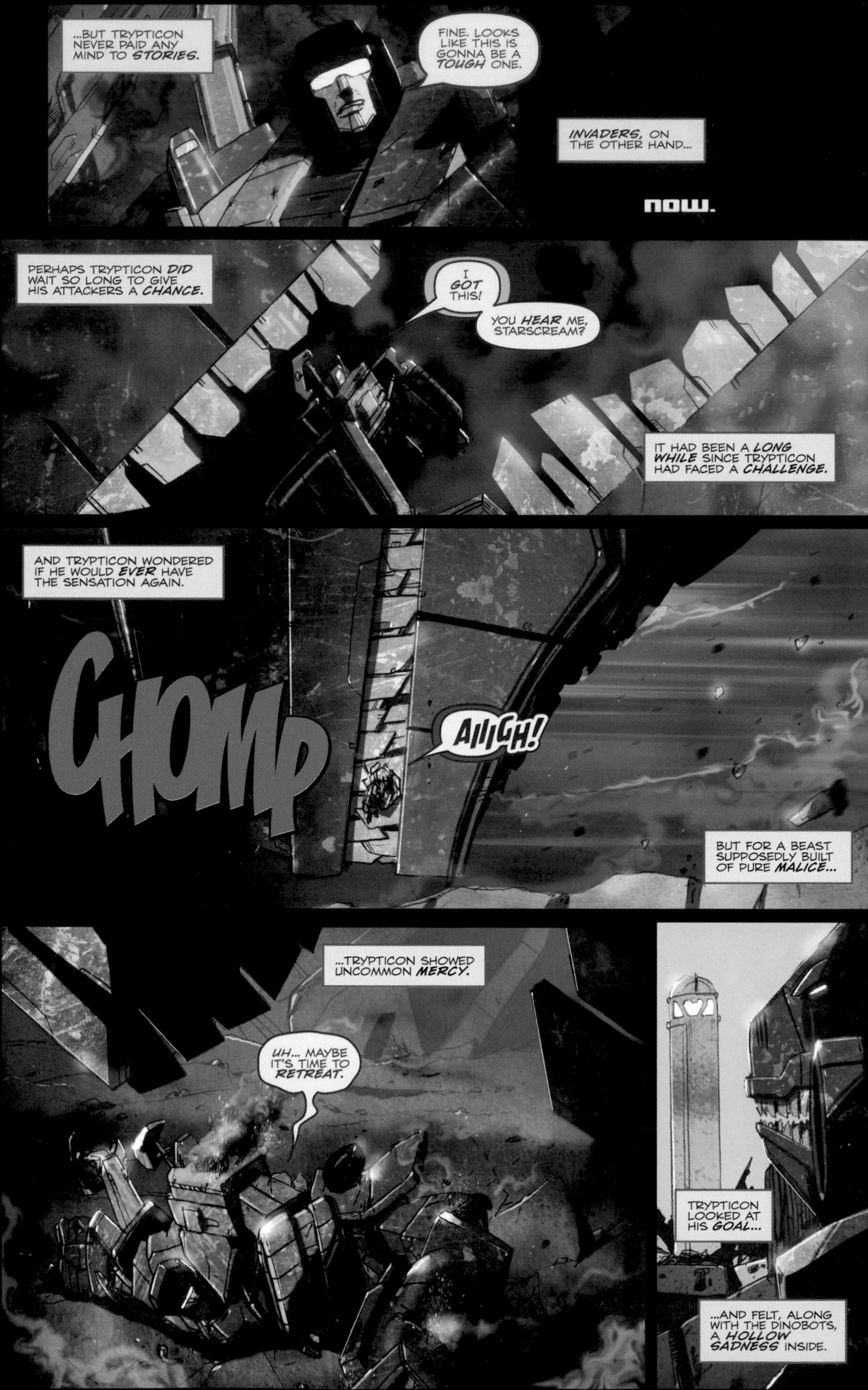
...BUT TRYPTICON NEVER PAID ANY MIND TO STORIES.
FINE. LOOKS LIKE THIS IS GONNA BE A TOUGH ONE.
INVADERS, ON THE OTHER HAND...
NOW.
PERHAPS TRYPTICON DID WAIT SO LONG TO GIVE HIS ATTACKERS A CHANCE.
I GOT THIS!
YOU HEAR ME, STARSCREAM?
IT HAD BEEN A LONG WHILE SINCE TRYPTICON HAD FACED A CHALLENGE.
AND TRYPTICON WONDERED IF HE WOULD EVER HAVE THE SENSATION AGAIN.
CHOMP
AIIIGH!
BUT FOR A BEAST SUPPOSEDLY BUILT OF PURE MALICE...
...TRYPTICON SHOWED UNCOMMON MERCY.
UH... MAYBE IT'S TIME TO RETREAT.
TRYPTICON LOOKED AT HIS GOAL...
...AND FELT, ALONG WITH THE DINOBOTS, A HOLLOW SADNESS INSIDE.

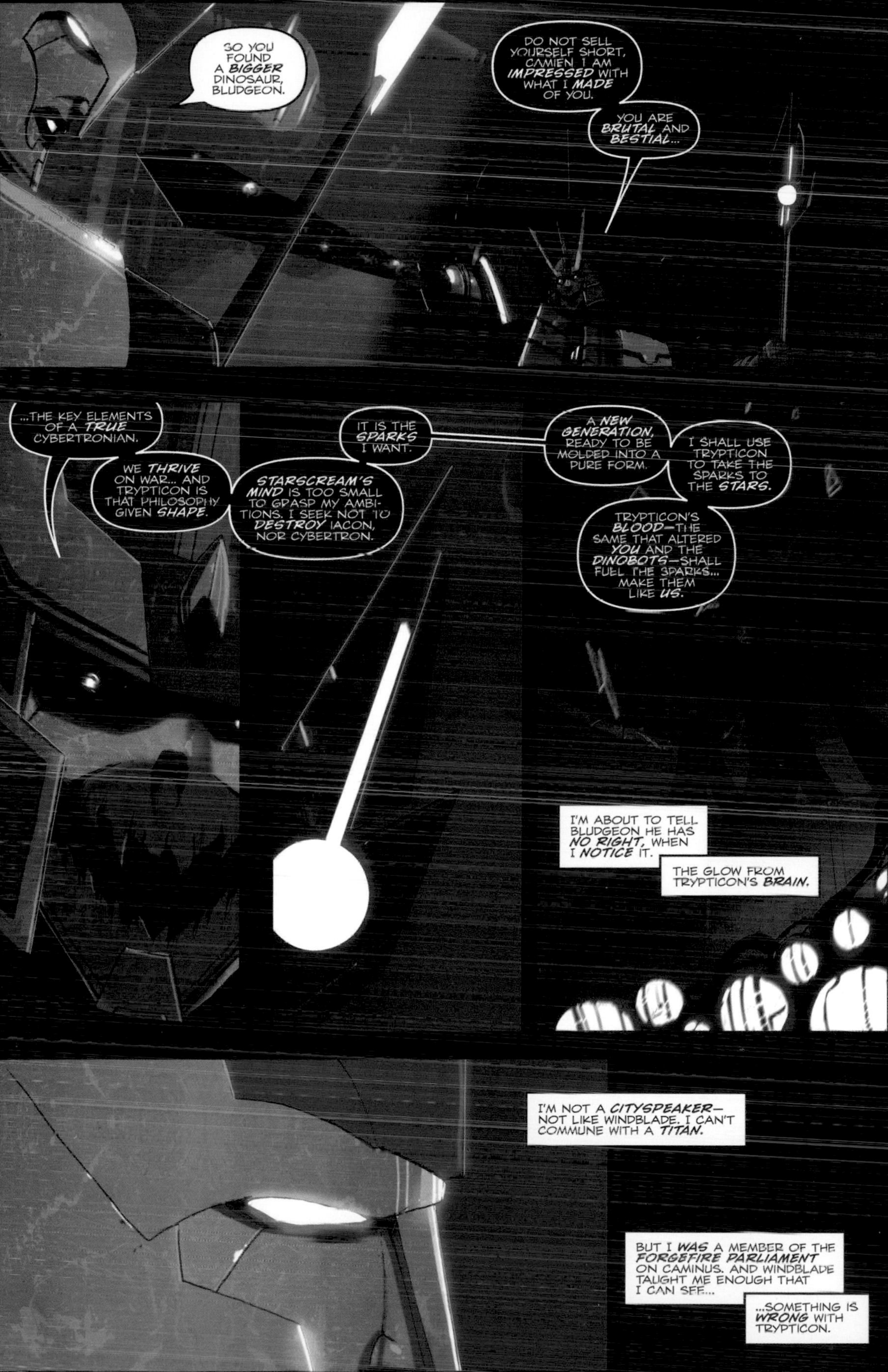
SO YOU FOUND A BIGGER DINOSAUR, BLUDGEON.
DO NOT SELL YOURSELF SHORT, CAMIEN. I AM IMPRESSED WITH WHAT I MADE OF YOU.
YOU ARE BRUTAL AND BESTIAL...
...THE KEY ELEMENTS OF A TRUE CYBERTRONIAN.
WE THRIVE ON WAR... AND TRYPTICON IS THAT PHILOSOPHY GIVEN SHAPE.
STARSCREAM'S MIND IS TOO SMALL TO GRASP MY AMBITIONS. I SEEK NOT TO DESTROY IACON, NOR CYBERTRON.
IT IS THE SPARKS I WANT.
A NEW GENERATION, READY TO BE MOLDED INTO A PURE FORM.
I SHALL USE TRYPTICON TO TAKE THE SPARKS TO THE STARS.
TRYPTICON'S BLOOD—THE SAME THAT ALTERED YOU AND THE DINOBOTS—SHALL FUEL THE SPARKS... MAKE THEM LIKE US.
I'M ABOUT TO TELL BLUDGEON HE HAS NO RIGHT, WHEN I NOTICE IT.
THE GLOW FROM TRYPTICON'S BRAIN.
I'M NOT A CITYSPEAKER—NOT LIKE WINDBLADE. I CAN'T COMMUNE WITH A TITAN.
BUT I WAS A MEMBER OF THE FORGEFIRE PARLIAMENT ON CAMINUS. AND WINDBLADE TAUGHT ME ENOUGH THAT I CAN SEE...
...SOMETHING IS WRONG WITH TRYPTICON.

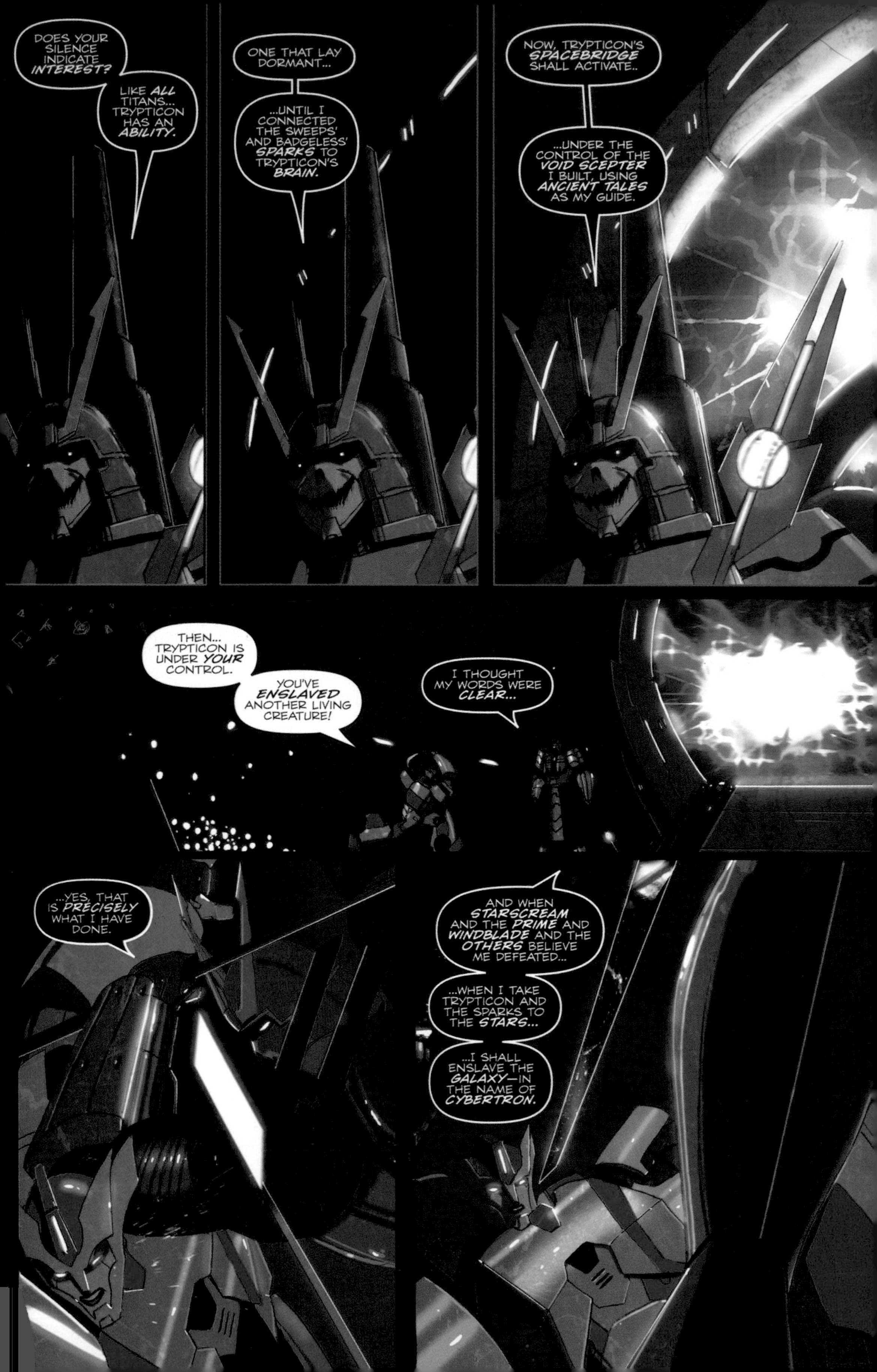
DOES YOUR SILENCE INDICATE INTEREST?
LIKE ALL TITANS... TRYPTICON HAS AN ABILITY.
ONE THAT LAY DORMANT...
...UNTIL I CONNECTED THE SWEEPS' AND BADGELESS' SPARKS TO TRYPTICON'S BRAIN.
NOW, TRYPTICON'S SPACEBRIDGE SHALL ACTIVATE..
...UNDER THE CONTROL OF THE VOID SCEPTER I BUILT, USING ANCIENT TALES AS MY GUIDE.
THEN... TRYPTICON IS UNDER YOUR CONTROL.
YOU'VE ENSLAVED ANOTHER LIVING CREATURE!
I THOUGHT MY WORDS WERE CLEAR...
...YES, THAT IS PRECISELY WHAT I HAVE DONE.
AND WHEN STARSCREAM AND THE PRIME AND WINDBLADE AND THE OTHERS BELIEVE ME DEFEATED...
...WHEN I TAKE TRYPTICON AND THE SPARKS TO THE STARS...
...I SHALL ENSLAVE THE GALAXY—IN THE NAME OF CYBERTRON.

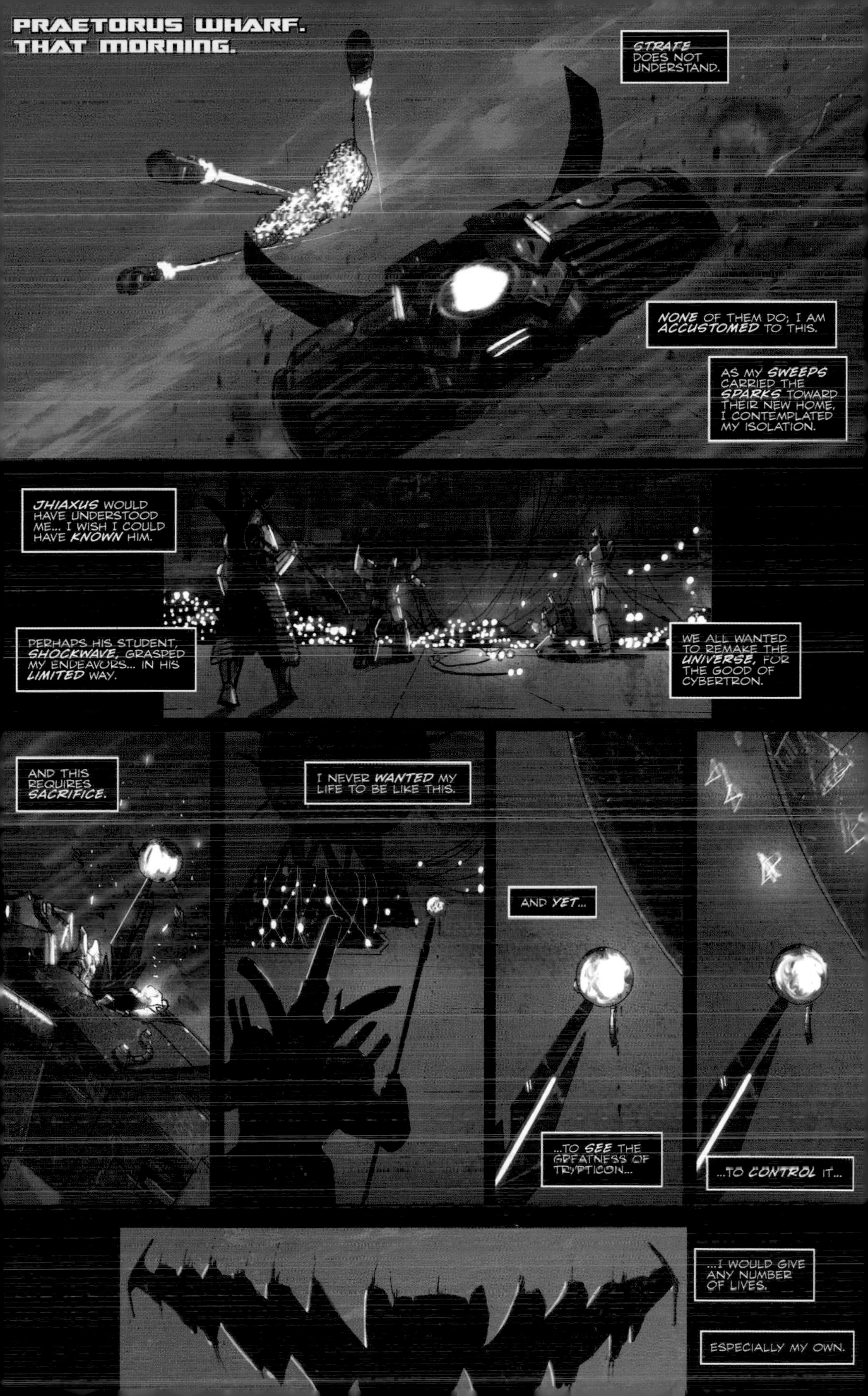
PRAETORUS WHARF.
THAT MORNING.
STRAFE DOES NOT UNDERSTAND.
NONE OF THEM DO; I AM ACCUSTOMED TO THIS.
AS MY SWEEPS CARRIED THE SPARKS TOWARD THEIR NEW HOME, I CONTEMPLATED MY ISOLATION.
JHIAXUS WOULD HAVE UNDERSTOOD ME... I WISH I COULD HAVE KNOWN HIM.
PERHAPS HIS STUDENT, SHOCKWAVE, GRASPED MY ENDEAVORS... IN HIS LIMITED WAY.
WE ALL WANTED TO REMAKE THE UNIVERSE, FOR THE GOOD OF CYBERTRON.
AND THIS REQUIRES SACRIFICE.
I NEVER WANTED MY LIFE TO BE LIKE THIS.
AND YET...
...TO SEE THE GREATNESS OF TRYPTICON...
...TO CONTROL IT...
...I WOULD GIVE ANY NUMBER OF LIVES.
ESPECIALLY MY OWN.

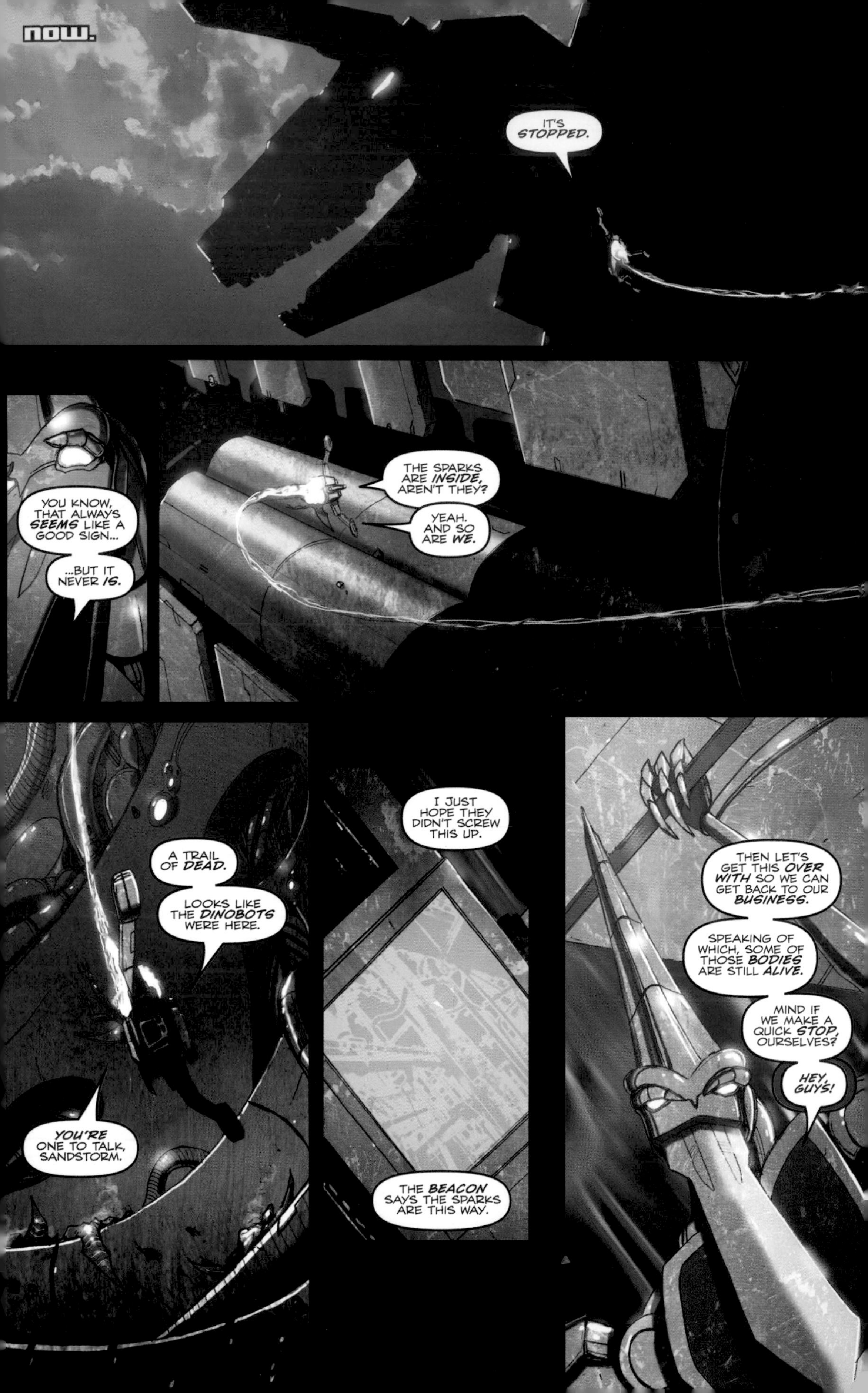
NOW.
IT'S STOPPED.
YOU KNOW, THAT ALWAYS SEEMS LIKE A GOOD SIGN...
...BUT IT NEVER IS.
THE SPARKS ARE INSIDE, AREN'T THEY?
YEAH. AND SO ARE WE.
A TRAIL OF DEAD.
LOOKS LIKE THE DINOBOTS WERE HERE.
YOU'RE ONE TO TALK, SANDSTORM.
I JUST HOPE THEY DIDN'T SCREW THIS UP.
THE BEACON SAYS THE SPARKS ARE THIS WAY.
THEN LET'S GET THIS OVER WITH SO WE CAN GET BACK TO OUR BUSINESS.
SPEAKING OF WHICH, SOME OF THOSE BODIES ARE STILL ALIVE.
MIND IF WE MAKE A QUICK STOP, OURSELVES?
HEY, GUYS!

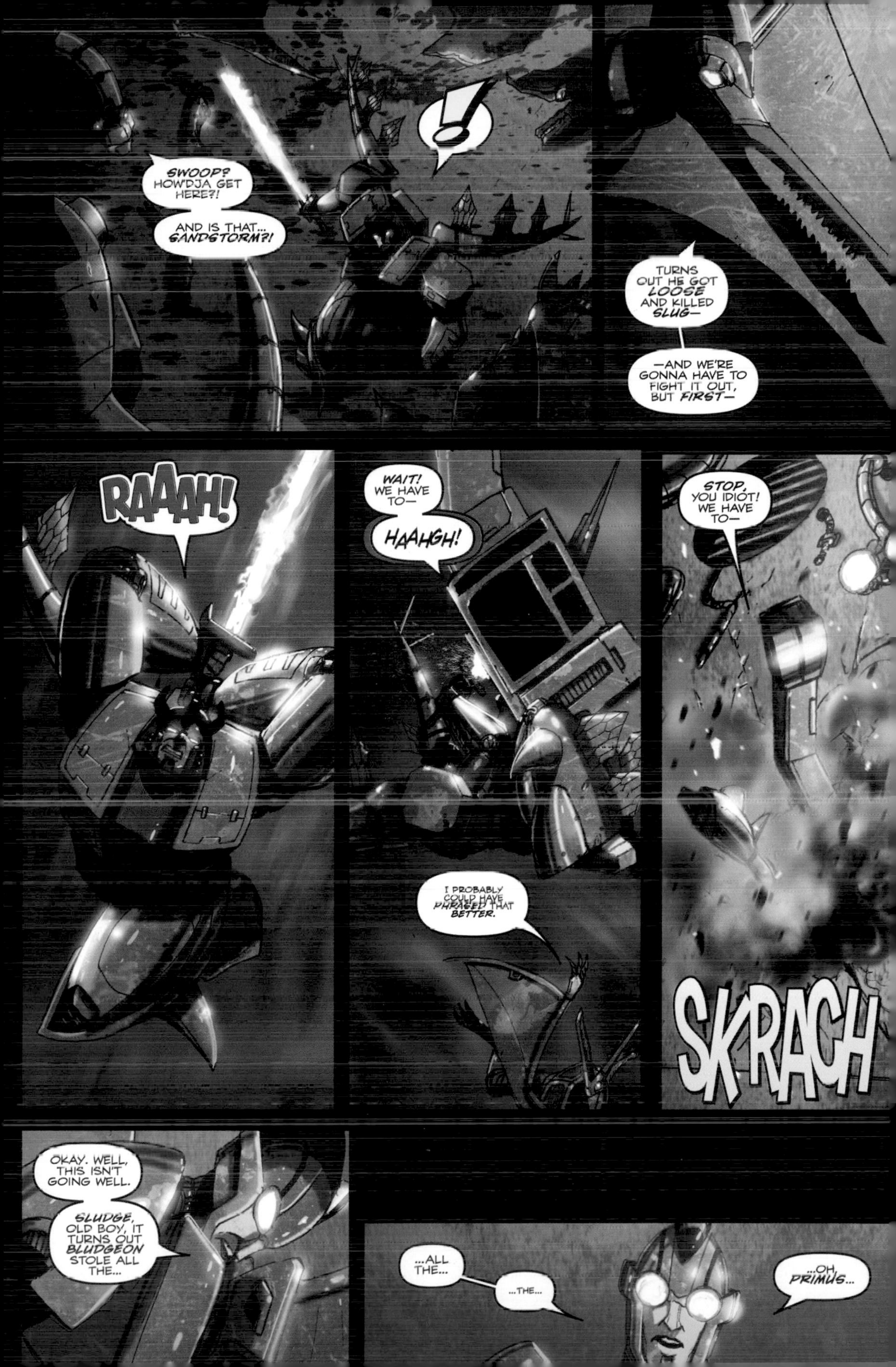
SWOOP? HOW'DJA GET HERE?!
AND IS THAT... SANDSTORM?!
!
TURNS OUT HE GOT LOOSE AND KILLED SLUG—
—AND WE'RE GONNA HAVE TO FIGHT IT OUT, BUT FIRST—
RAAAH!
WAIT! WE HAVE TO—
HAAHGH!
I PROBABLY COULD HAVE PHRASED THAT BETTER.
STOP, YOU IDIOT! WE HAVE TO—
SKRACH
OKAY. WELL, THIS ISN'T GOING WELL.
SLUDGE, OLD BOY, IT TURNS OUT BLUDGEON STOLE ALL THE...
...ALL THE...
...THE...
...OH, PRIMUS...

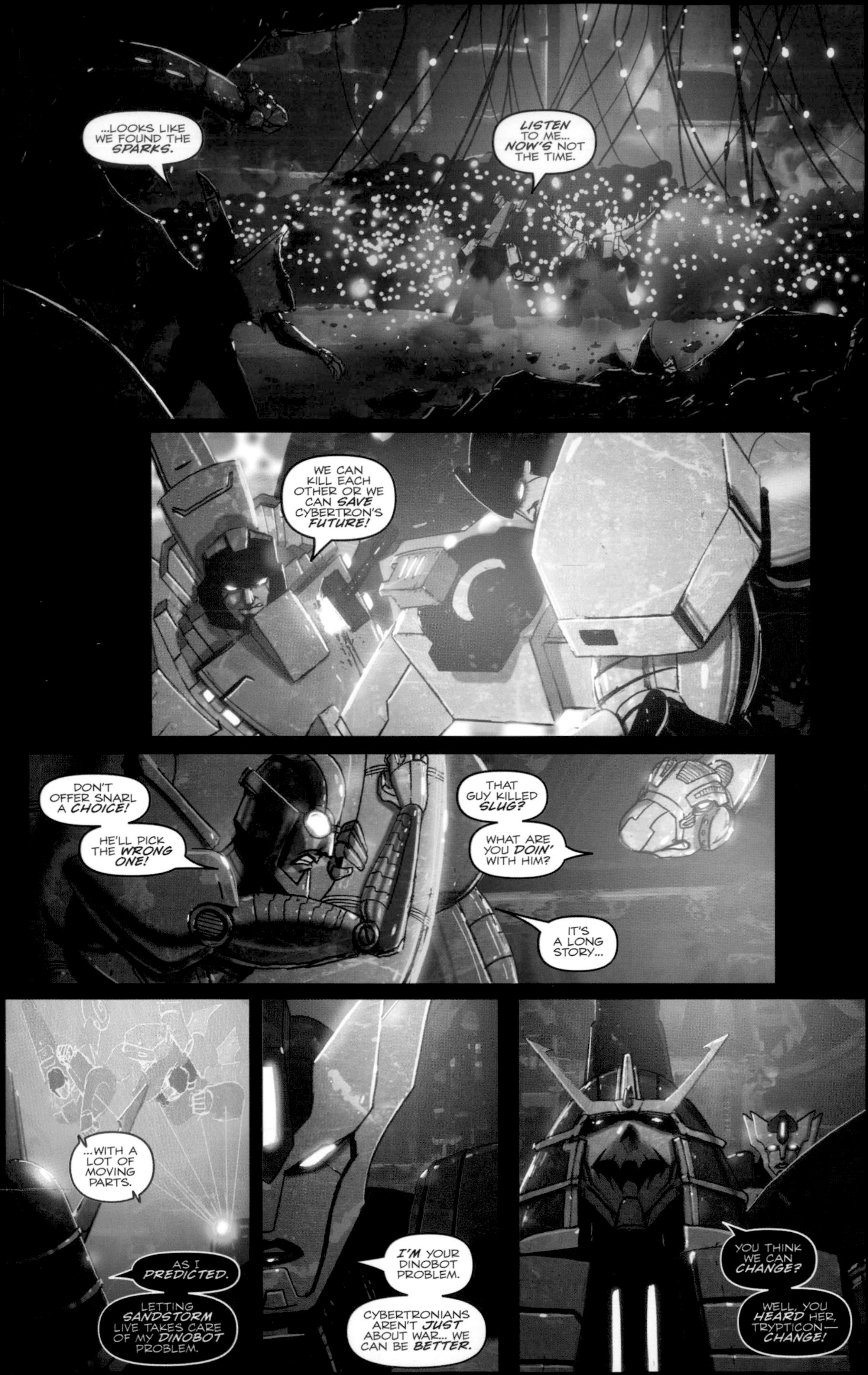
...LOOKS LIKE WE FOUND THE SPARKS.
LISTEN TO ME... NOW'S NOT THE TIME.
WE CAN KILL EACH OTHER OR WE CAN SAVE CYBERTRON'S FUTURE!
DON'T OFFER SNARL A CHOICE!
HE'LL PICK THE WRONG ONE!
THAT GUY KILLED SLUG?
WHAT ARE YOU DOIN' WITH HIM?
IT'S A LONG STORY...
...WITH A LOT OF MOVING PARTS.
AS I PREDICTED.
LETTING SANDSTORM LIVE TAKES CARE OF MY DINOBOT PROBLEM.
I'M YOUR DINOBOT PROBLEM.
CYBERTRONIANS AREN'T JUST ABOUT WAR... WE CAN BE BETTER.
YOU THINK WE CAN CHANGE?
WELL, YOU HEARD HER, TRYPTICON—CHANGE!

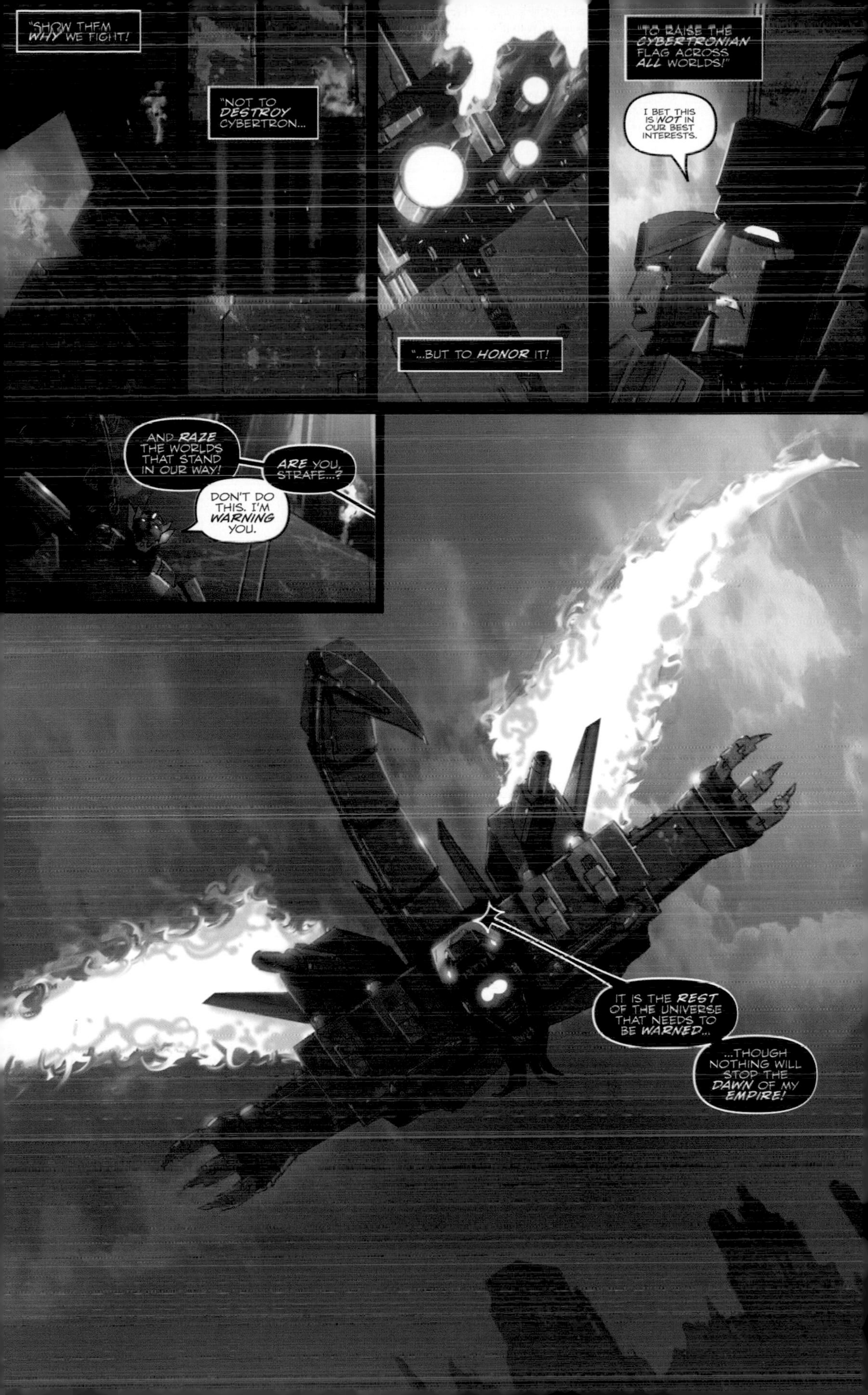
"SHOW THEM WHY WE FIGHT!
"NOT TO DESTROY CYBERTRON...
"...BUT TO HONOR IT!
"TO RAISE THE CYBERTRONIAN FLAG ACROSS ALL WORLDS!"
I BET THIS IS NOT IN OUR BEST INTERESTS.
AND RAZE THE WORLDS THAT STAND IN OUR WAY!
ARE YOU, STRAFE...?
DON'T DO THIS. I'M WARNING YOU.
IT IS THE REST OF THE UNIVERSE THAT NEEDS TO BE WARNED...
...THOUGH NOTHING WILL STOP THE DAWN OF MY EMPIRE!

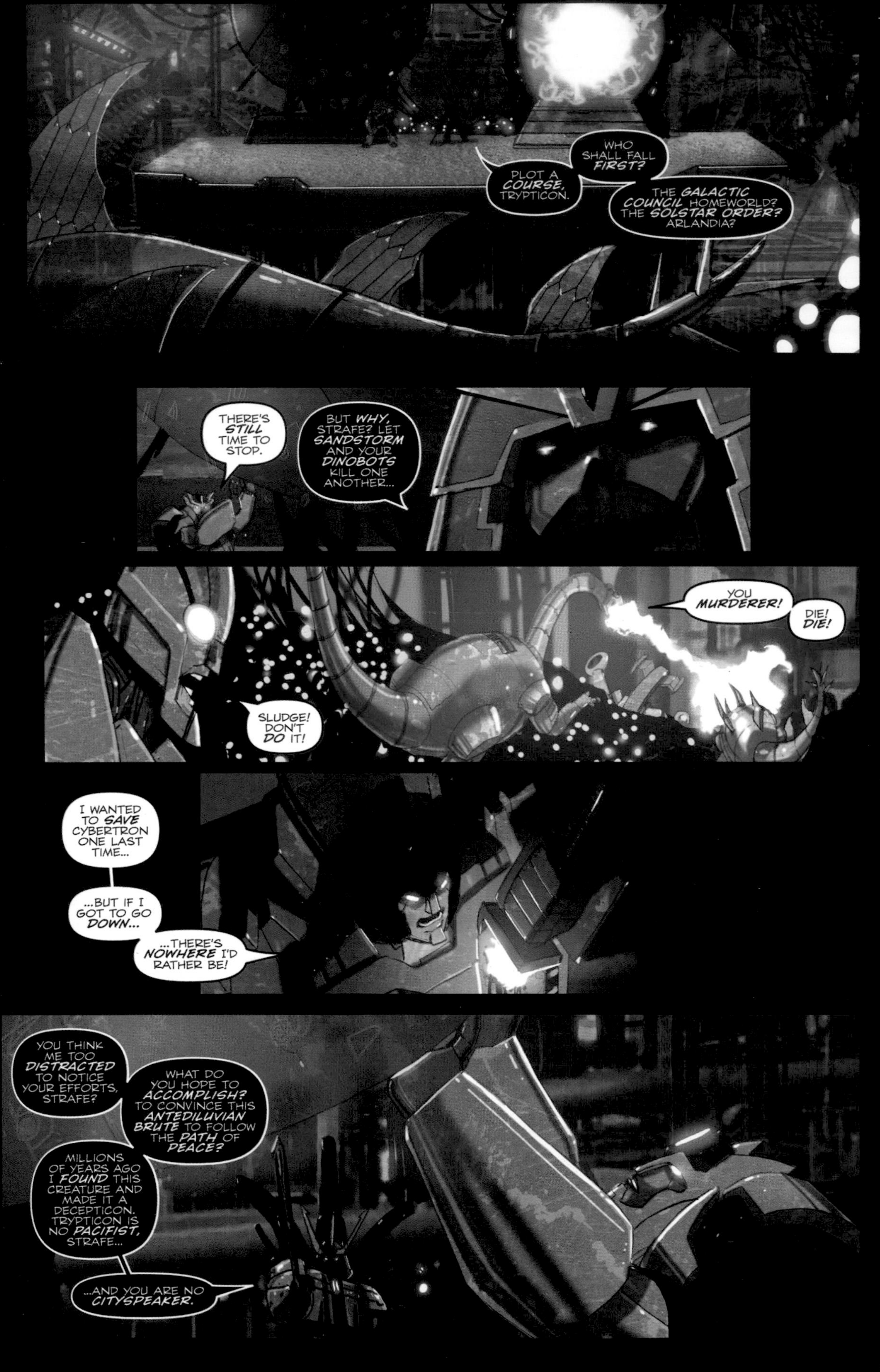
PLOT A COURSE, TRYPTICON.
WHO SHALL FALL FIRST?
THE GALACTIC COUNCIL HOMEWORLD? THE SOLSTAR ORDER? ARLANDIA?
THERE'S STILL TIME TO STOP.
BUT WHY, STRAFE? LET SANDSTORM AND YOUR DINOBOTS KILL ONE ANOTHER...
YOU MURDERER!
DIE! DIE!
SLUDGE! DON'T DO IT!
I WANTED TO SAVE CYBERTRON ONE LAST TIME...
...BUT IF I GOT TO GO DOWN...
...THERE'S NOWHERE I'D RATHER BE!
YOU THINK ME TOO DISTRACTED TO NOTICE YOUR EFFORTS, STRAFE?
WHAT DO YOU HOPE TO ACCOMPLISH? TO CONVINCE THIS ANTEDILUVIAN BRUTE TO FOLLOW THE PATH OF PEACE?
MILLIONS OF YEARS AGO I FOUND THIS CREATURE AND MADE IT A DECEPTICON. TRYPTICON IS NO PACIFIST, STRAFE...
...AND YOU ARE NO CITYSPEAKER.

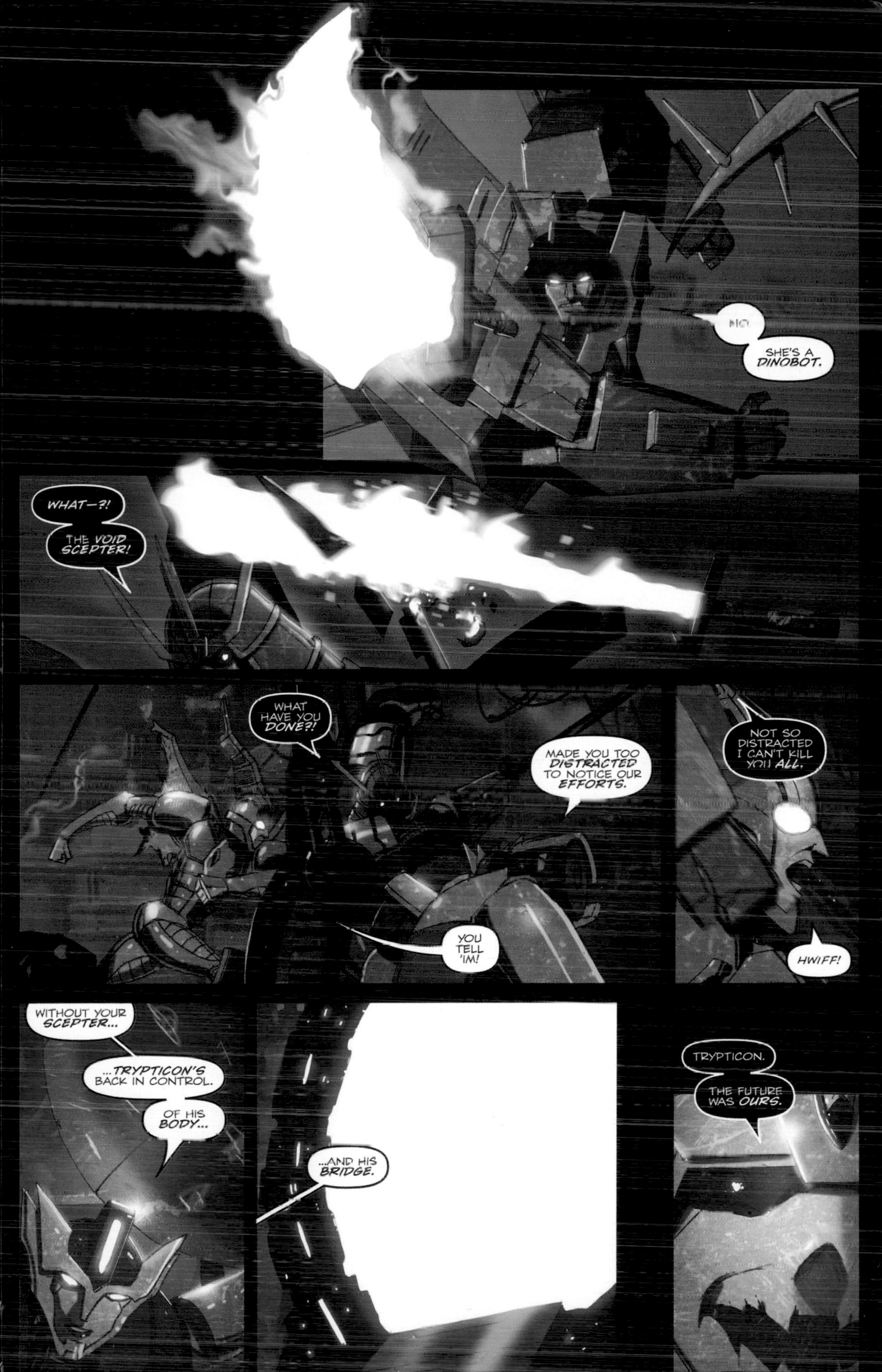
NO!
SHE'S A DINOBOT.
WHAT—?!
THE VOID SCEPTER!
WHAT HAVE YOU DONE?!
MADE YOU TOO DISTRACTED TO NOTICE OUR EFFORTS.
YOU TELL 'IM!
NOT SO DISTRACTED I CAN'T KILL YOU ALL.
HWIFF!
WITHOUT YOUR SCEPTER...
...TRYPTICON'S BACK IN CONTROL.
OF HIS BODY...
...AND HIS BRIDGE.
TRYPTICON.
THE FUTURE WAS OURS.

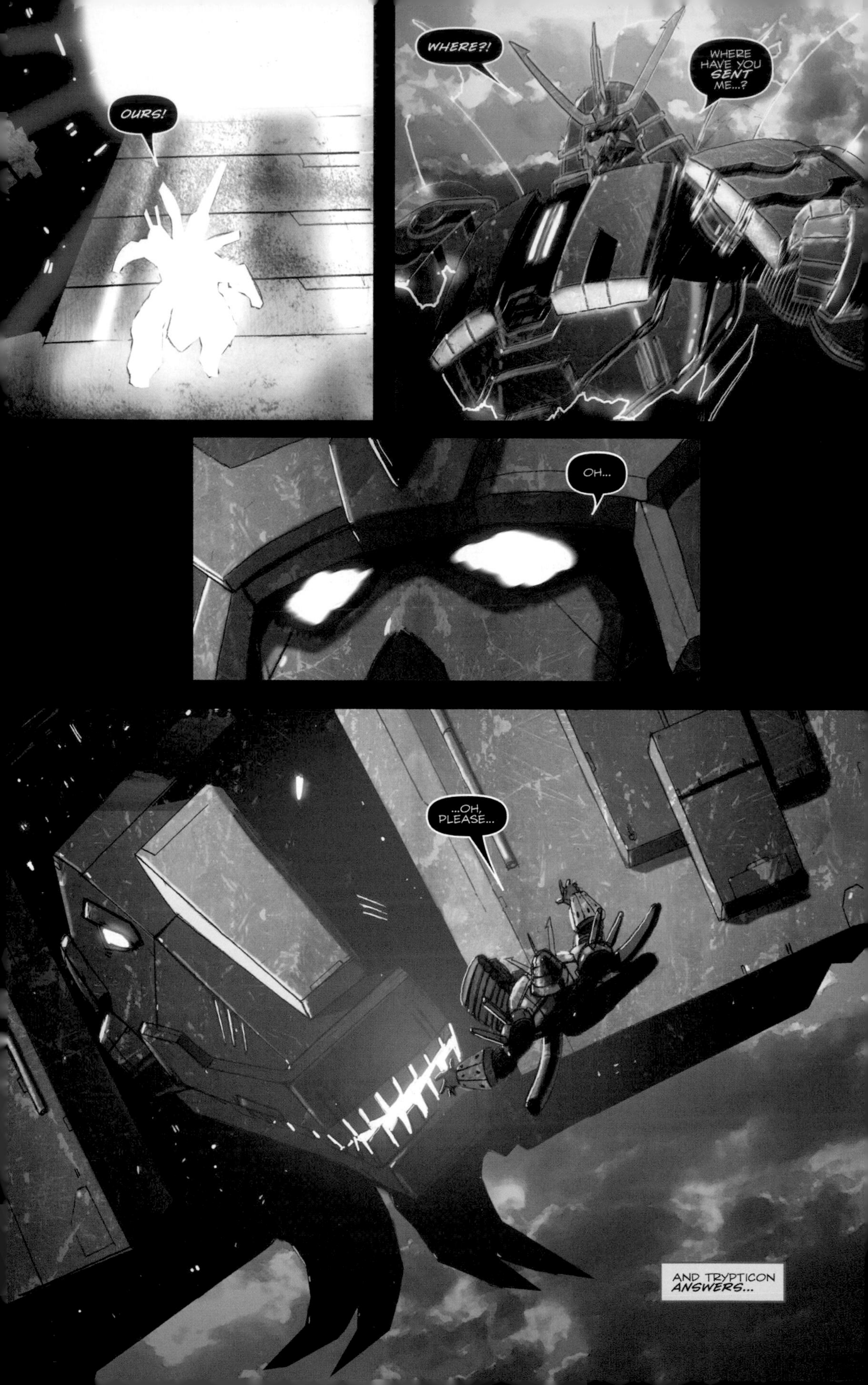
OURS!
WHERE?!
WHERE HAVE YOU SENT ME...?
OH...
...OH, PLEASE...
AND TRYPTICON ANSWERS...

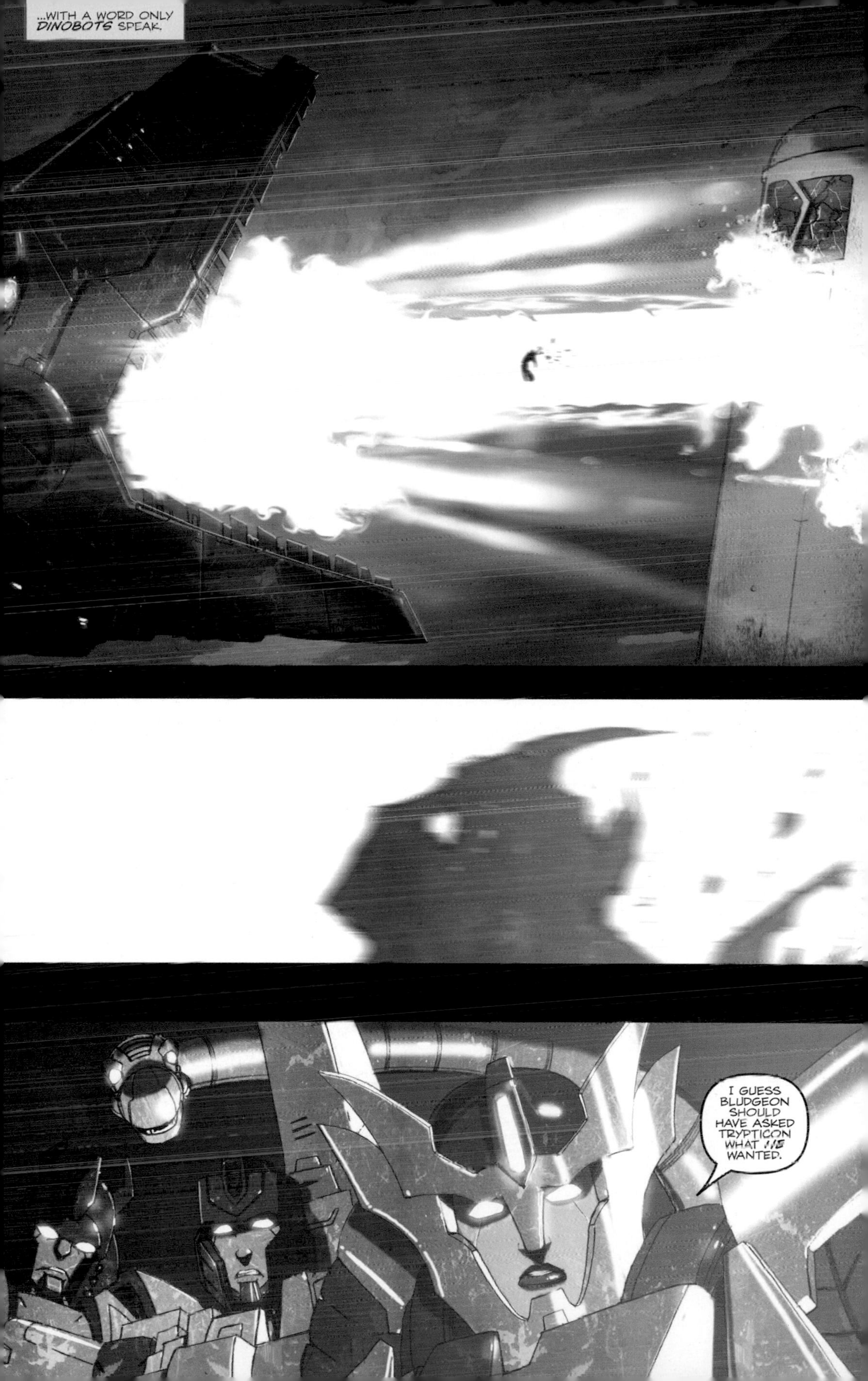
...WITH A WORD ONLY DINOBOTS SPEAK.
I GUESS BLUDGEON SHOULD HAVE ASKED TRYPTICON WHAT HE WANTED.

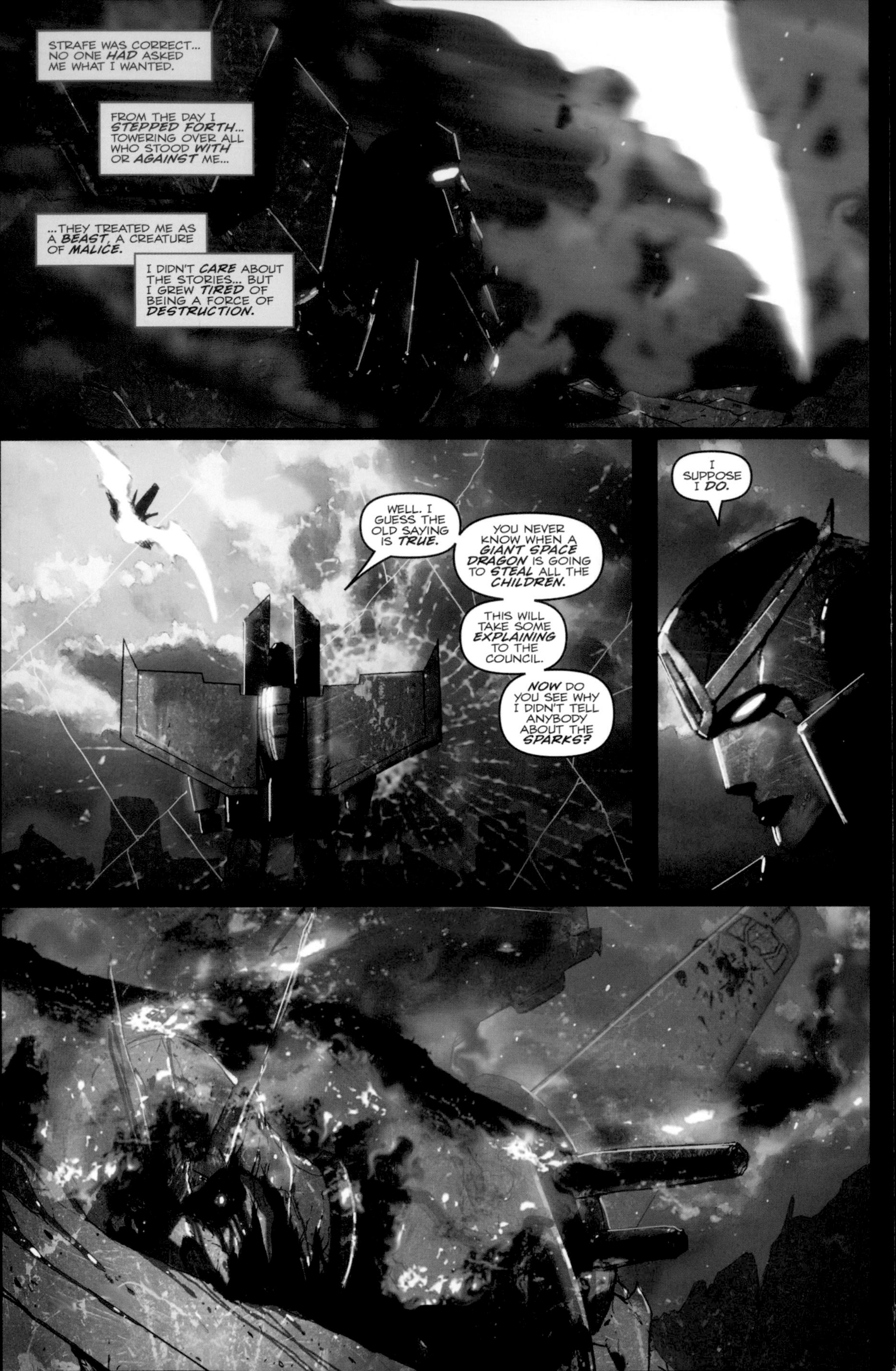
STRAFE WAS CORRECT... NO ONE HAD ASKED ME WHAT I WANTED.
FROM THE DAY I STEPPED FORTH... TOWERING OVER ALL WHO STOOD WITH OR AGAINST ME...
...THEY TREATED ME AS A BEAST, A CREATURE OF MALICE.
I DIDN'T CARE ABOUT THE STORIES... BUT I GREW TIRED OF BEING A FORCE OF DESTRUCTION.
WELL. I GUESS THE OLD SAYING IS TRUE.
YOU NEVER KNOW WHEN A GIANT SPACE DRAGON IS GOING TO STEAL ALL THE CHILDREN.
THIS WILL TAKE SOME EXPLAINING TO THE COUNCIL.
NOW DO YOU SEE WHY I DIDN'T TELL ANYBODY ABOUT THE SPARKS?
I SUPPOSE I DO.

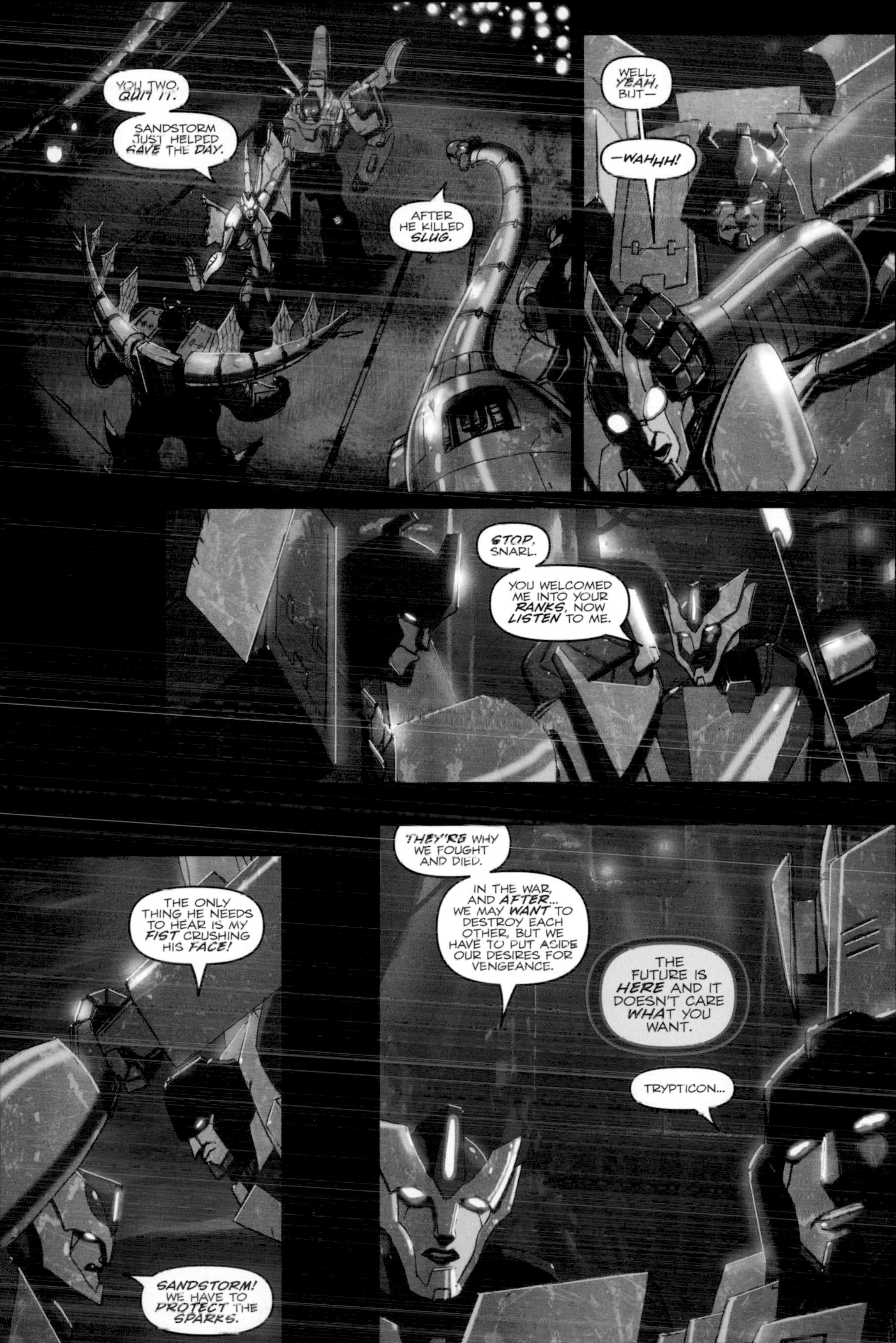
YOU TWO, QUIT IT.
SANDSTORM JUST HELPED SAVE THE DAY.
AFTER HE KILLED SLUG.
WELL, YEAH, BUT—
—WAHHH!
STOP, SNARL.
YOU WELCOMED ME INTO YOUR RANKS, NOW LISTEN TO ME.
THE ONLY THING HE NEEDS TO HEAR IS MY FIST CRUSHING HIS FACE!
SANDSTORM! WE HAVE TO PROTECT THE SPARKS.
THEY'RE WHY WE FOUGHT AND DIED.
IN THE WAR, AND AFTER... WE MAY WANT TO DESTROY EACH OTHER, BUT WE HAVE TO PUT ASIDE OUR DESIRES FOR VENGEANCE.
THE FUTURE IS HERE AND IT DOESN'T CARE WHAT YOU WANT.
TRYPTICON...

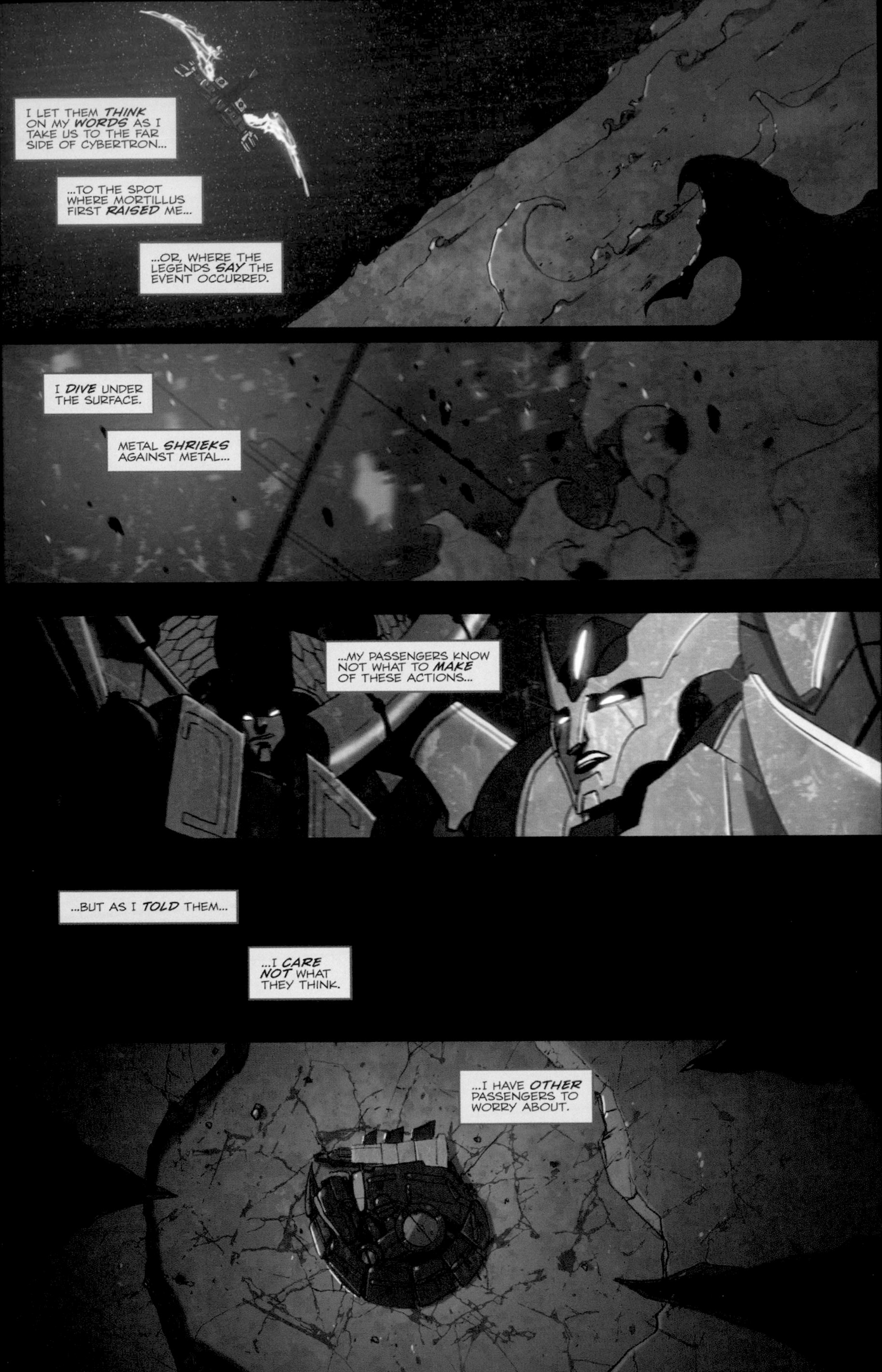
I LET THEM THINK ON MY WORDS AS I TAKE US TO THE FAR SIDE OF CYBERTRON...
...TO THE SPOT WHERE MORTILLUS FIRST RAISED ME...
...OR, WHERE THE LEGENDS SAY THE EVENT OCCURRED.
I DIVE UNDER THE SURFACE.
METAL SHRIEKS AGAINST METAL...
...MY PASSENGERS KNOW NOT WHAT TO MAKE OF THESE ACTIONS...
...BUT AS I TOLD THEM...
...I CARE NOT WHAT THEY THINK.
...I HAVE OTHER PASSENGERS TO WORRY ABOUT.

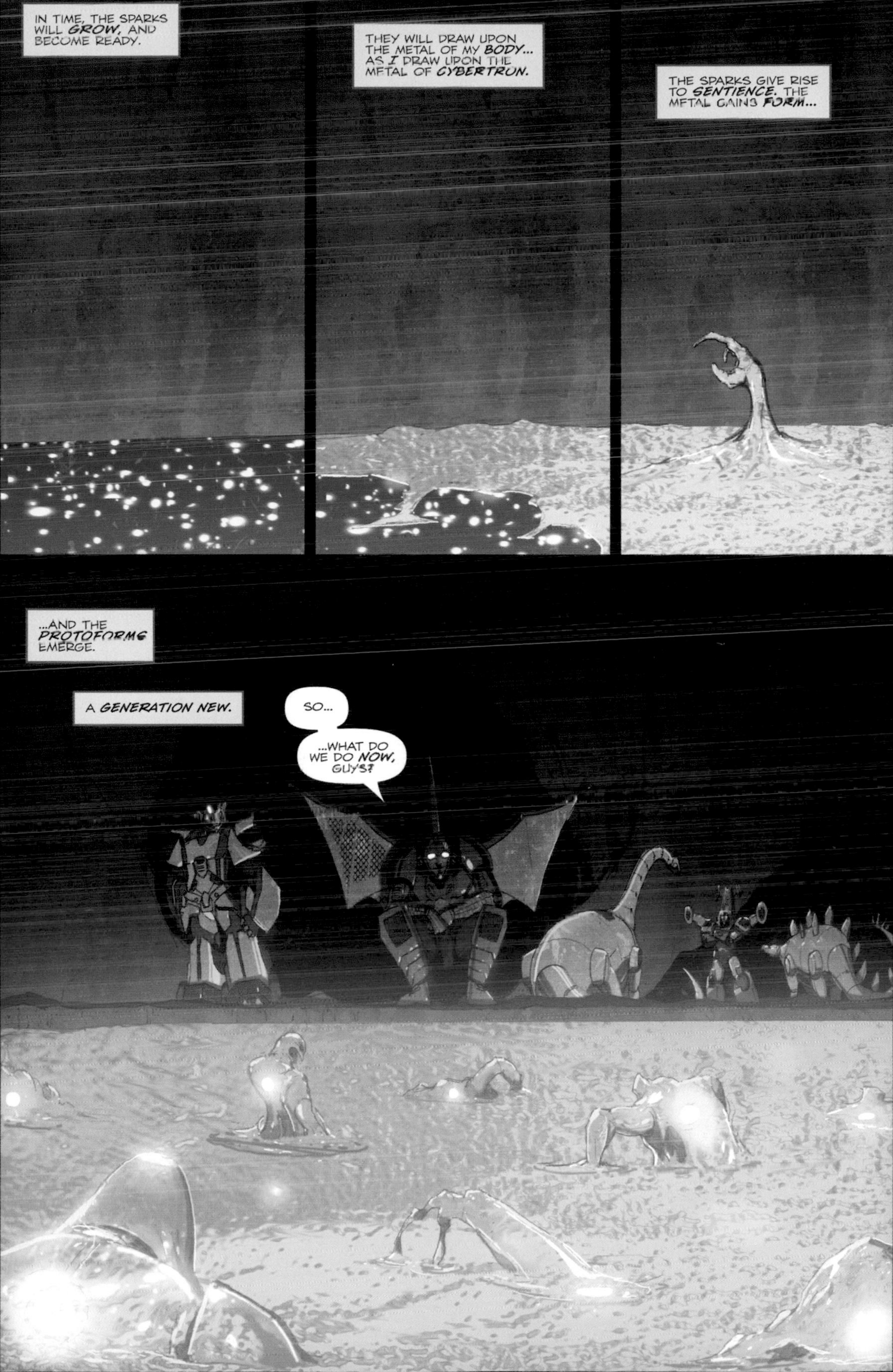
IN TIME, THE SPARKS WILL GROW, AND BECOME READY.
THEY WILL DRAW UPON THE METAL OF MY BODY... AS I DRAW UPON THE METAL OF CYBERTRON.
THE SPARKS GIVE RISE TO SENTIENCE. THE METAL GAINS FORM...
...AND THE PROTOFORMS EMERGE.
A GENERATION NEW.
SO...
...WHAT DO WE DO NOW, GUYS?

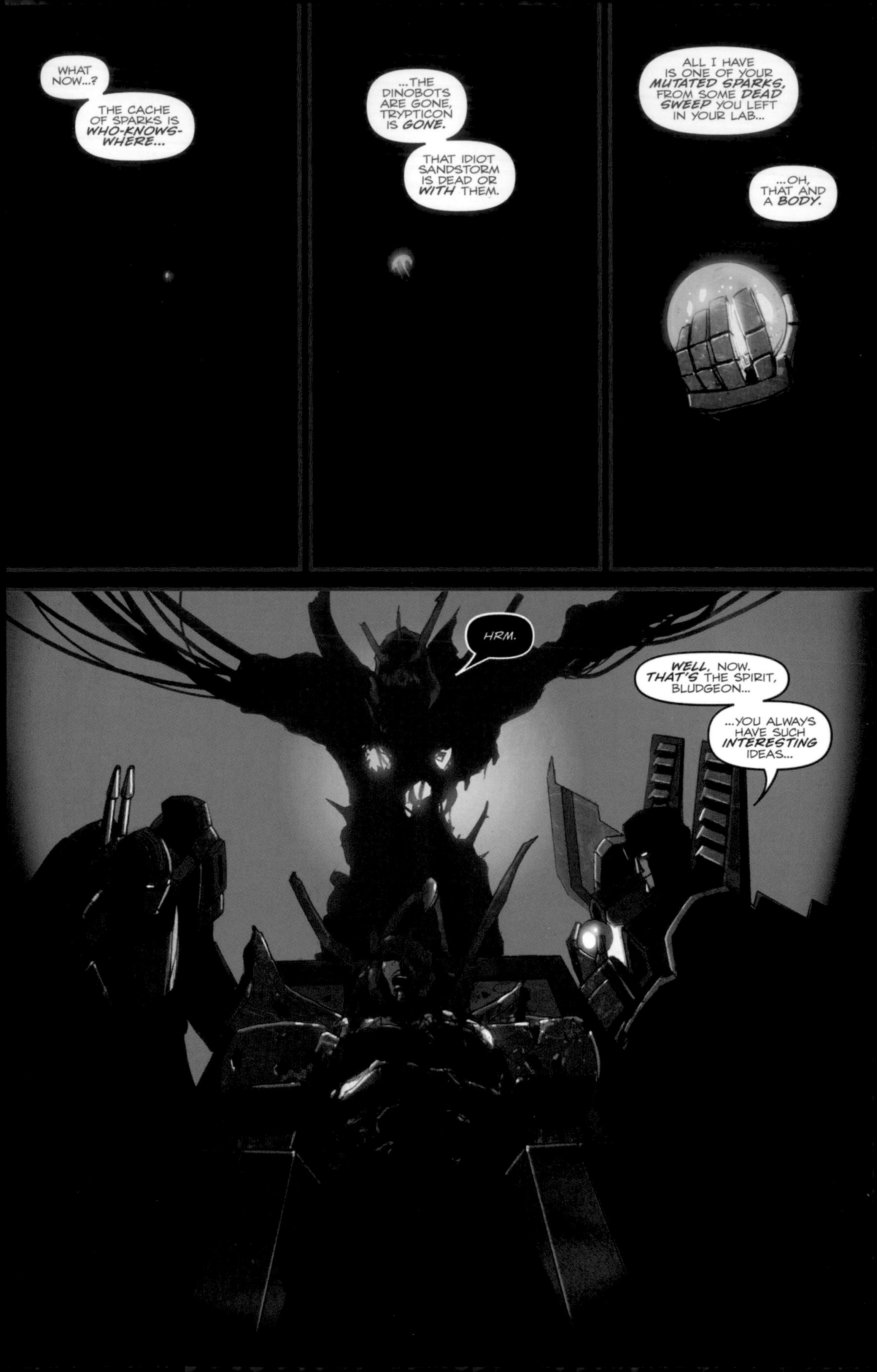
WHAT NOW...?
THE CACHE OF SPARKS IS WHO-KNOWS-WHERE...
...THE DINOBOTS ARE GONE, TRYPTICON IS GONE.
THAT IDIOT SANDSTORM IS DEAD OR WITH THEM.
ALL I HAVE IS ONE OF YOUR MUTATED SPARKS, FROM SOME DEAD SWEEP YOU LEFT IN YOUR LAB...
...OH, THAT AND A BODY.
HRM.
WELL, NOW. THAT'S THE SPIRIT, BLUDGEON...
...YOU ALWAYS HAVE SUCH INTERESTING IDEAS...

SALVATION

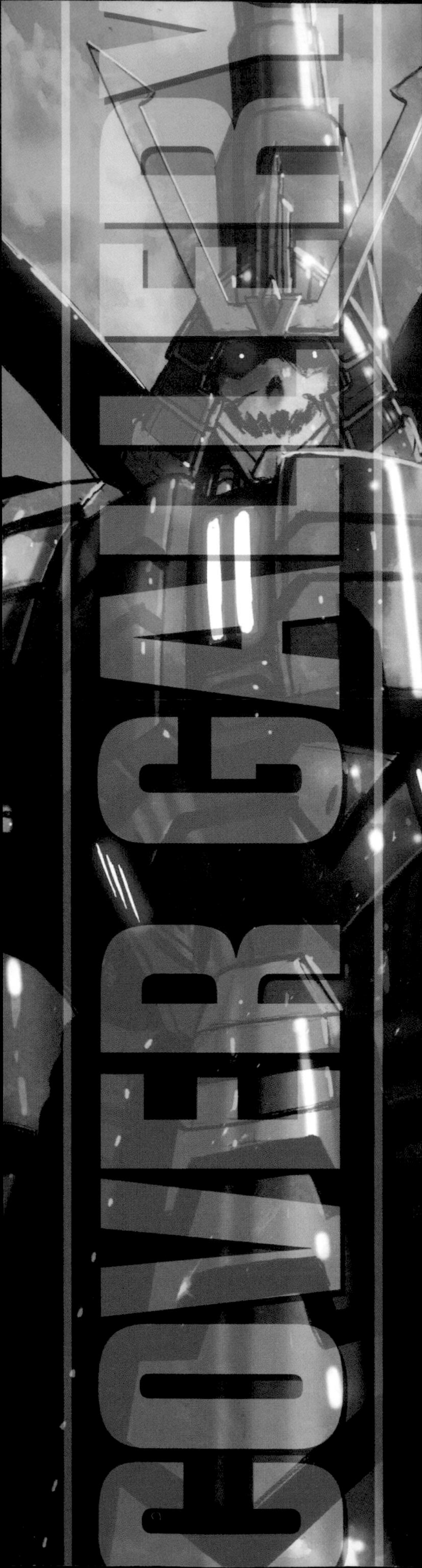
COVER GALLERY

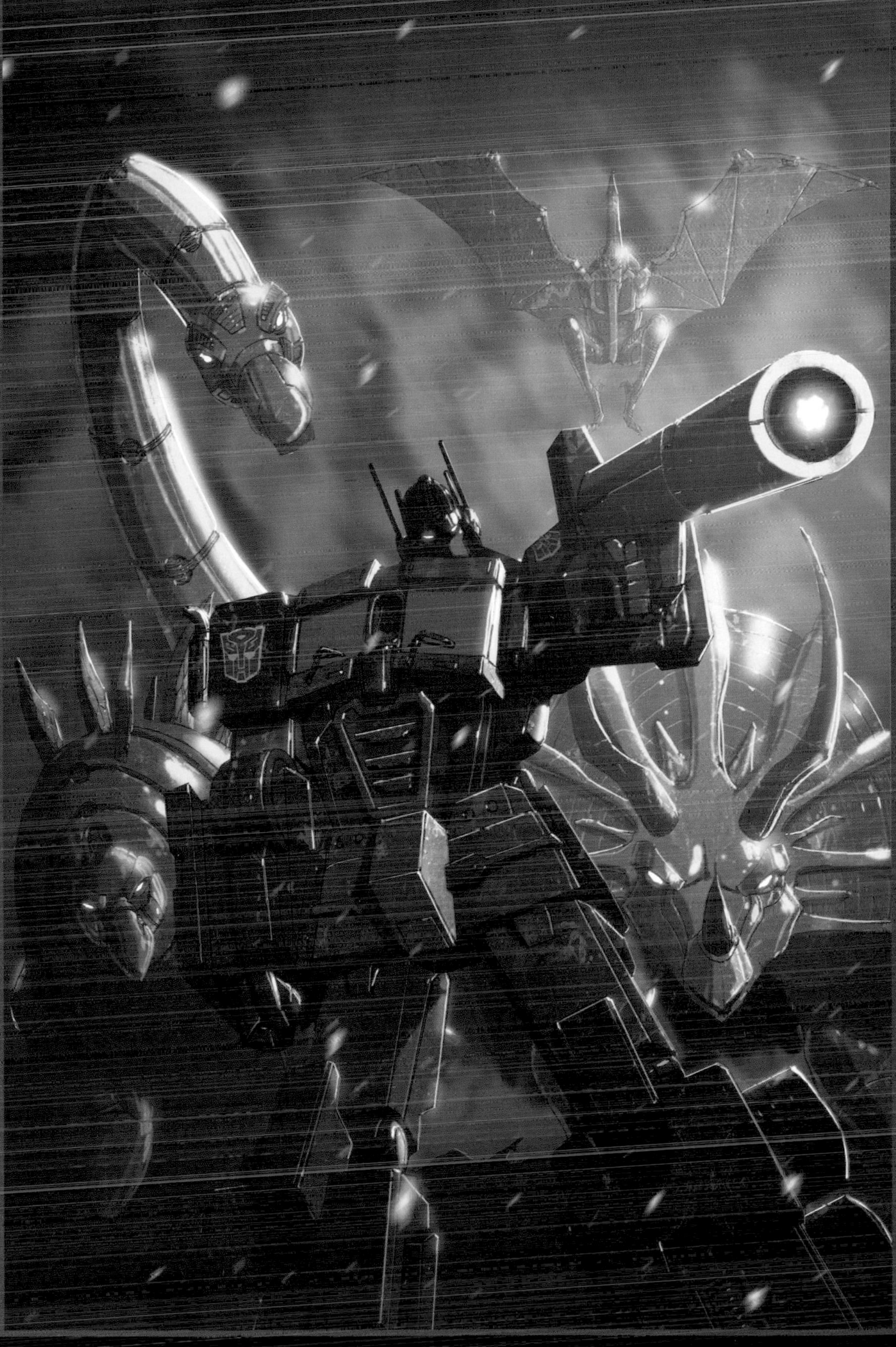

ART BY
LIVIO RAMONDELLI

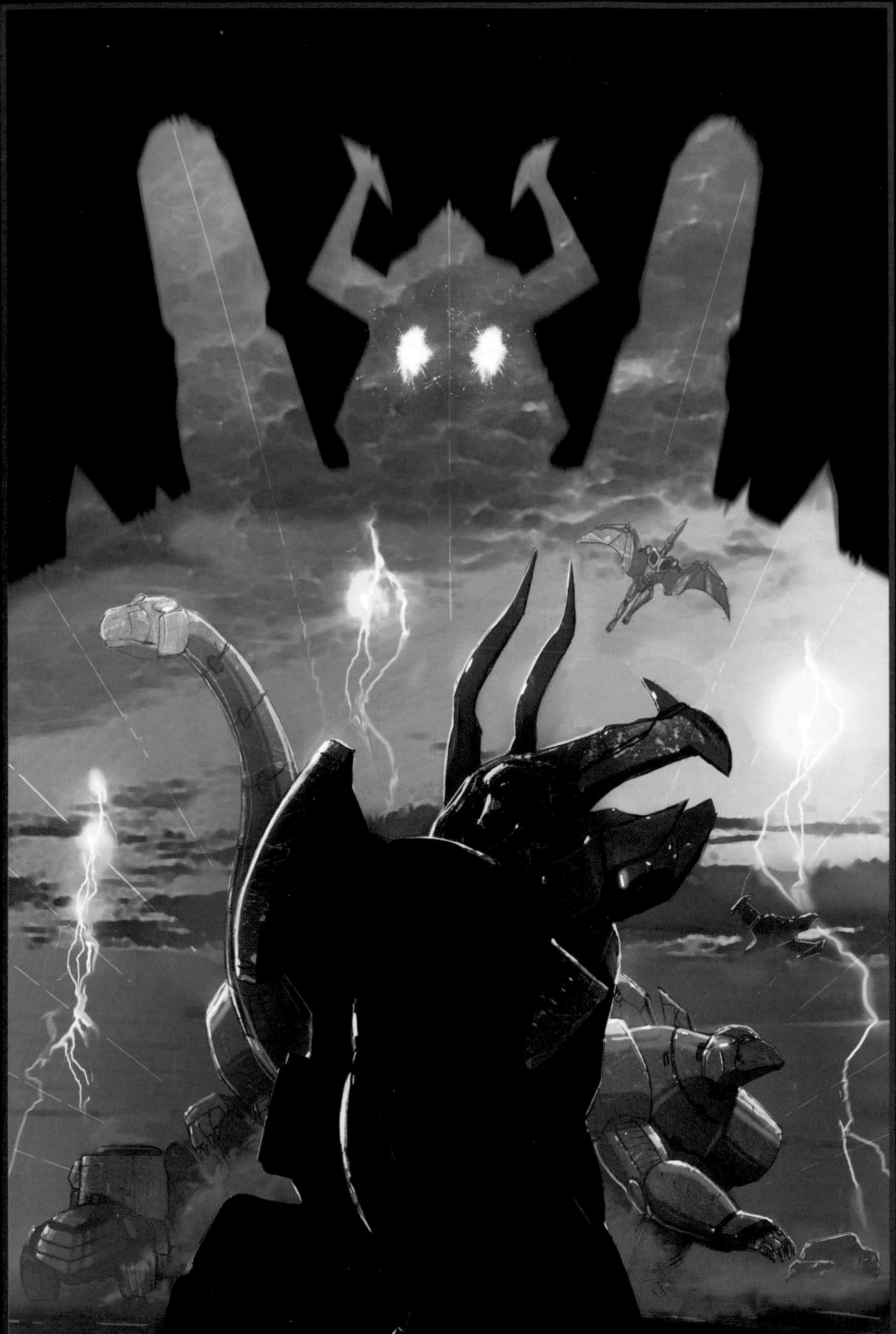

ART BY
LIVIO RAMONDELLI

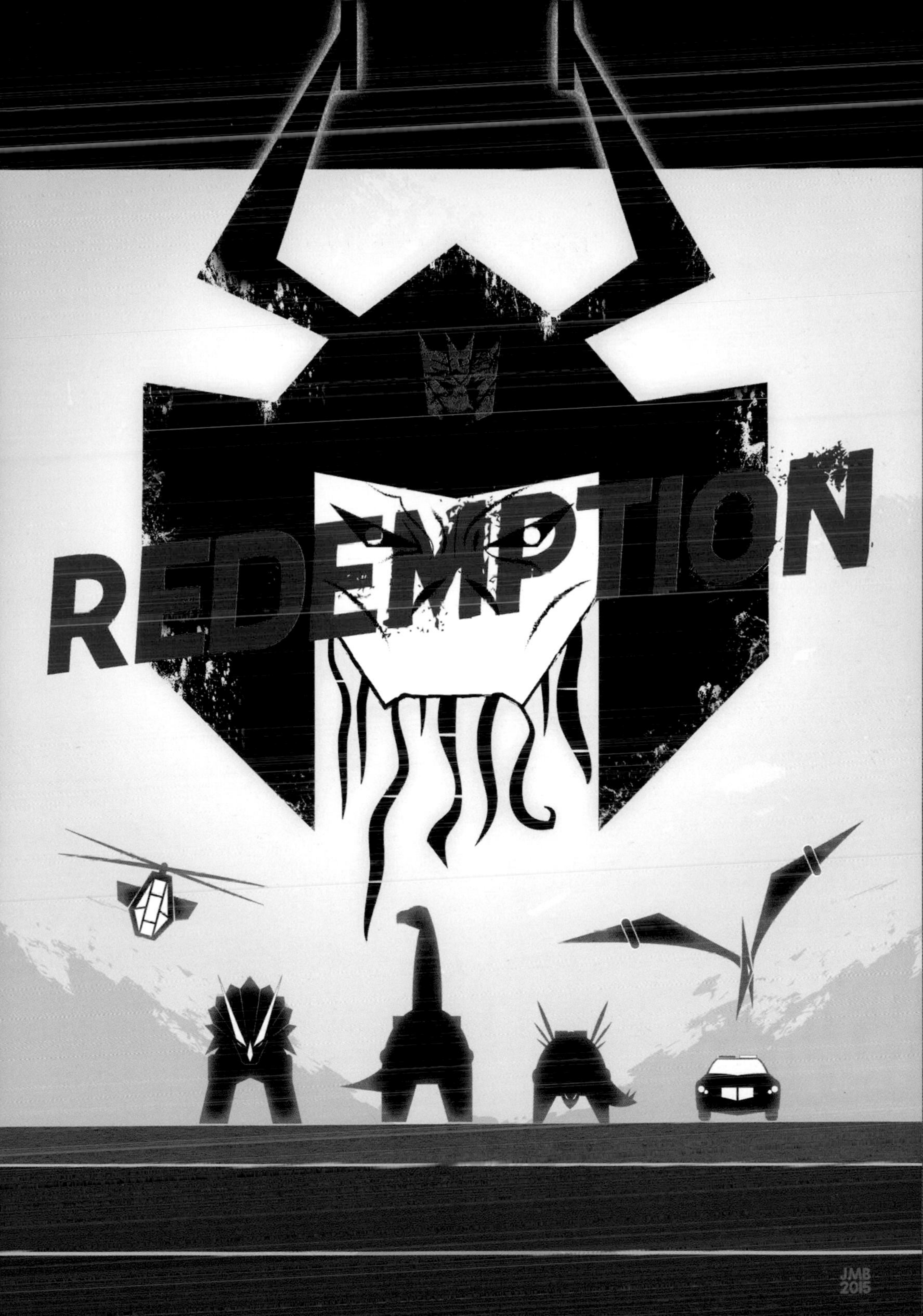
REDEMPTION
JMB
2015

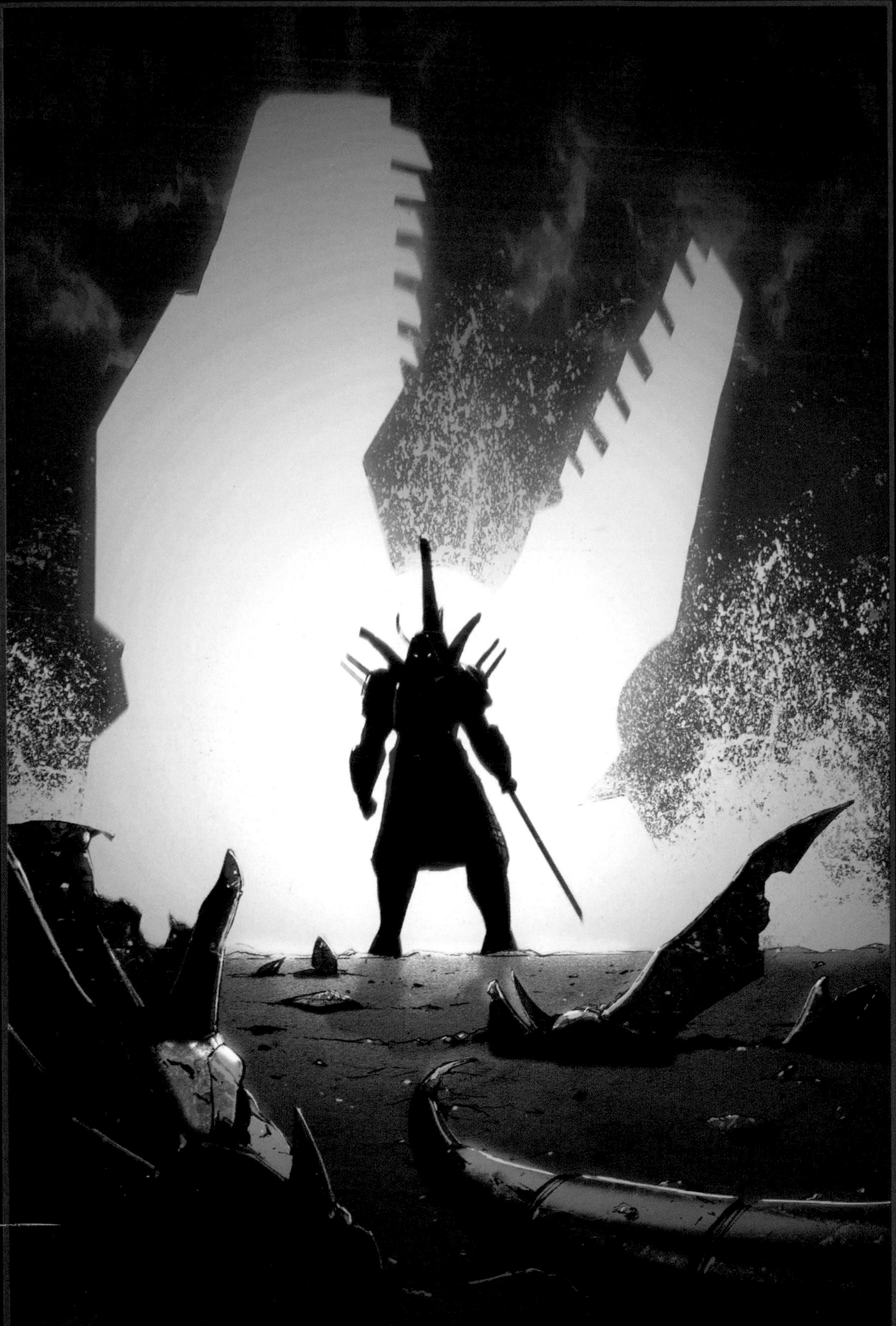

ART BY
LIVIO RAMONDELLI

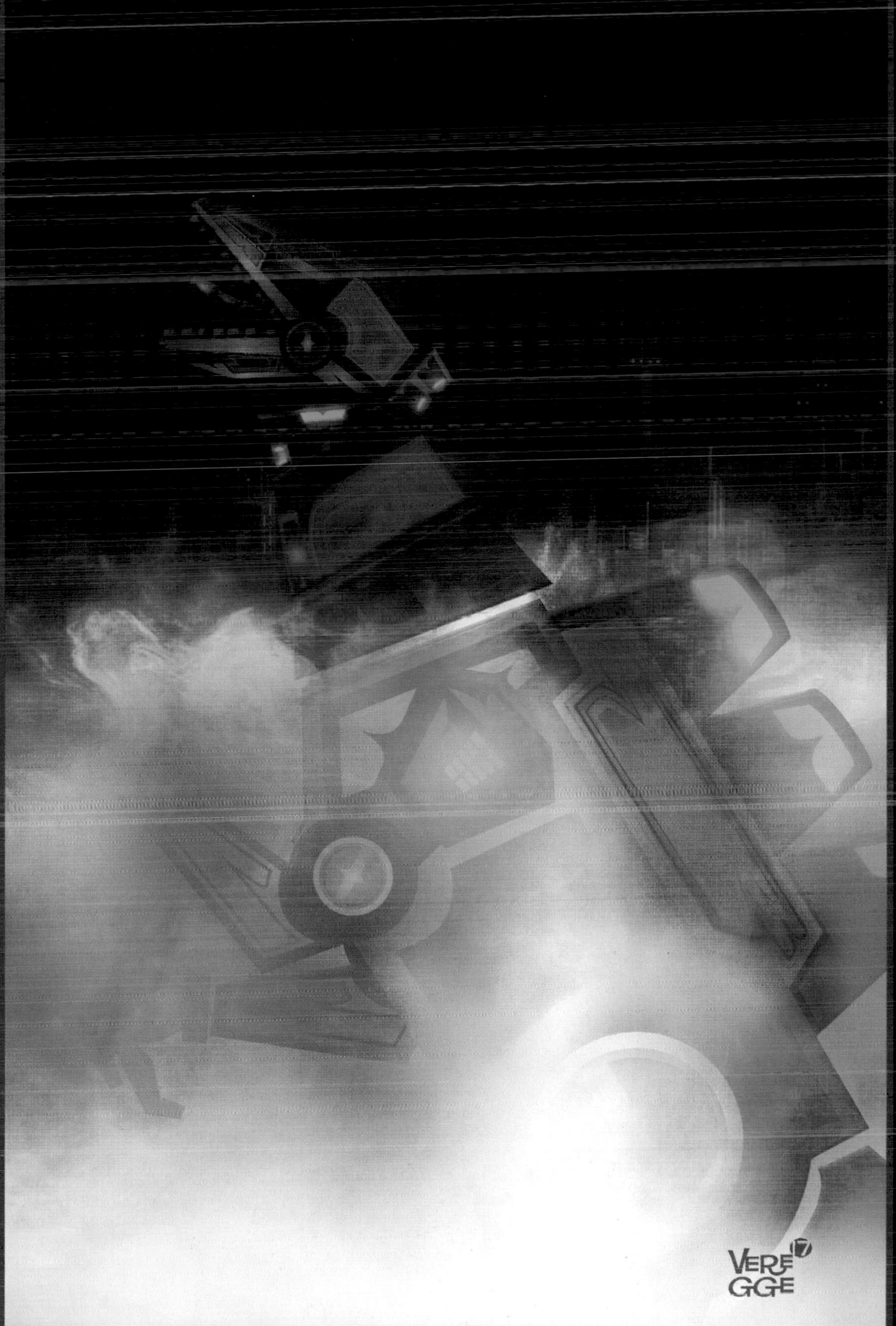
VEREGGE 17

ART BY
JEFFREY VEREGGE